How to use this book

 This symbol means that you will need to think carefully about a point. Your teacher may ask you to join in a discussion about it.

 This symbol next to a question means that you are allowed (and indeed expected) to use your calculator for this question.

 This symbol means exactly the opposite – you are not allowed to use your calculator for this question.

 This is a warning sign. It is used where a common mistake, or misunderstanding, is being described. It is also used to identify questions which are slightly more difficult or which require a little more thought. It should be read as 'caution'.

 This is the ICT symbol. It should alert your teacher to the fact that there is some additional material in the accompanying Teacher's Resource using ICT for this unit of work.

Each chapter of work in this book is divided into a series of double-page spreads – or units of work. The left-hand page is the teaching page, and the right-hand page involves an exercise and sometimes additional activities or investigations to do with that topic.

You will also come across the following features in the units of work:

 Task

The tasks give you the opportunity to work alone, in pairs or in small groups on an activity in the lesson. It gives you the chance to practise what you have just been taught, and to discuss ideas and raise questions about the topic.

Do the right thing!

These boxes give you a set of step-by-step instructions on how to carry out a particular technique in maths, usually to do with shape work.

Do you remember?

These boxes give you the chance to review work that you have covered in the previous year.

Contents

Formula One MATHS

Catherine Berry ● Margaret Bland

Dave Faulkner ● Sophie Goldie

Katie Porkess ● Julian Thomas

Leonie Turner ● Brandon Wilshaw

SERIES EDITOR: **Roger Porkess**

B1

Hodder & Stoughton

A MEMBER OF THE HODDER HEADLINE GROUP

Acknowledgements

Every effort has been made to trace and acknowledge ownership of copyright. The publishers will be glad to make suitable arrangements with any copyright holder whom it has not been possible to contact.

Illustrations were drawn by Maggie Brand, Tom Cross, Jeff Edwards and Joe McEwan.

Photos supplied by Tony Hallas/Science Photo Library (page 3); Photostore (page 30); Action Plus Photographic (pages 55, 113, 146); Ryanstock/TCL Stock Directory UK (page 148); Science Photo Library (page 156); BBC Picture Archives (page 173); Emma Lee/Life File (page 201).

Cover design and page design by Julie Martin.

Orders: please contact Bookpoint Ltd, 130 Milton Park, Abingdon, Oxon OX14 4SB. Telephone: (44) 01235 827720, Fax (44) 01235 400454. Lines are open from 9.00–6.00, Monday to Saturday, with a 24 hour message answering service. Email address orders@bookpoint.co.uk

British Library Cataloguing in Publication Data
A catalogue record for this title is available from The British Library

ISBN 0 340 779748

First published 2001
Impression number 10 9 8 7 6 5 4 3 2
Year 2007 2006 2005 2004 2003 2002

Cover photo from Jacey, Debut Art

Typeset by Tech-Set Ltd, Gateshead, Tyne & Wear.
Printed in Great Britain for Hodder & Stoughton Educational, a division of Hodder Headline Plc, 338 Euston Road, London NW1 3BH by Printer Trento, Italy.

Introduction

This book is designed for Year 8 students and is part of a series covering Key Stage 3 Mathematics. Each textbook in the series is accompanied by an extensive Teacher's Resource including additional material. This allows the series to be used with the full ability range of students.

The series builds on the National Numeracy Strategy in primary schools and its extension into Key Stage 3. It is designed to support the style of teaching and the lesson framework to which students will be accustomed.

This book is presented as a series of double-page spreads, each of which is designed to be a teaching unit. The left-hand page covers the material to be taught and the right-hand page provides examples for the students to work through. Each chapter ends with a review exercise covering all its content. Further worksheets, tests and ICT materials are provided in the Teacher's Resource.

An important feature of the left-hand pages is the Tasks, which are printed in boxes. These are intended to be carried out by the student in mid-lesson. Their aim is twofold: in the first place they give the students practice on what they have just been taught, allowing them to consolidate their understanding. However, the tasks then extend the ideas and raise questions, setting the agenda for the later part of the lesson. Further guidance on the Tasks is available in the Teacher's Resource.

Another key feature of the left-hand pages is the Discussion Points. These are designed to help teachers engage their students in whole class discussion. Teachers should see the ? as an opportunity and an invitation.

Several other symbols and instructions are used in this book. These are explained on the 'How to use this book' page for students opposite. The symbol indicates to the teacher that there is additional ICT material directly linked to that unit of work. This is referenced in the teaching notes for that unit in the Teacher's Resource.

The order of the 25 chapters in this book ensures that the subject is developed logically, at each stage building on previous knowledge. The Teacher's Resource includes a Scheme of Work based on this order. However, teachers are of course free to vary the order to meet their own circumstances and needs.

This series stems from a partnership between Hodder and Stoughton Educational and and Mathematics in Education and Industry (MEI). The authors would like to thank all those who helped in preparing this book, particularly those involved with the writing of materials for the accompanying Teacher's Resource.

Roger Porkess   2001
Series Editor

Co-ordinates in all 4 quadrants

Look at this picture. It is the
constellation of Cygnus.

 **What are the co-ordinates of
the star at A?**

 **The x co-ordinate is always
the first number.**
How can you remember this?

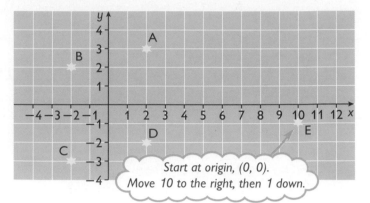

The star at E is called Vega.
The co-ordinates of Vega are $(10, -1)$

Start at origin, (0, 0).
Move 10 to the right, then 1 down.

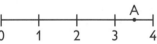 **What are the co-ordinates of the other stars B, C and D?**
Sometimes Cygnus is called the Northern Cross.
Do the stars ABCD make a perfect cross?

Task

1 On squared paper draw x and y axes. Use 2 squares per unit.
Take x from -10 to 14, y from -8 to 8.
2 Plot the following points: $(8, 0)$, $(2, 2)$, $(-2, 2)$, $(-5, 0)$, $(-6, -3)$, $(-5, -7)$,
$(-7, -5)$, $(-9, -7)$, $(-5, 2)$, $(0, 6)$, $(3, 6)$, $(8, 4)$, $(10, 2)$ and $(11, -2)$.
3 Join them up in order. Join the first and last points too. What is the picture?
4 Put in a point for the eye. What are its co-ordinates?

 Does the picture look better if you join the points with curves?

To make the dolphin look better you need more points.
Some of these may not be whole numbers.

! Be careful when working between whole numbers.

 Is the x co-ordinate of A 3.5 or 4.5?

! ? **Be extra careful when working with negative numbers.**
Is the x co-ordinate of point B -1.5 or -2.5?

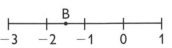

Task

1 Put these points round your dolphin to show bubbles:
$(12.5, 1)$, $(13.5, 4.5)$, $(12.5, 6.5)$ and $(13, -0.5)$.

2 Put in more bubbles of your own.
Use some decimals and some negative numbers.

3 What are the co-ordinates of your bubbles?

Exercise

1 Look at this arrowhead.

What are the co-ordinates of the points A, B, C and D?

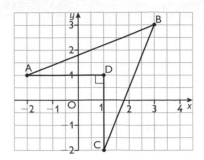

2 The four stars of this constellation are called the Square of Pegasus.

(a) Write down their co-ordinates. Is it really a square?

(b) Copy the graph with these 4 stars on it. Draw both x and y axes from -4 to $+4$.

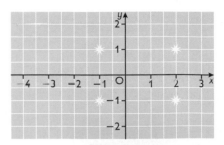

Nearby, at $(-3\frac{1}{2}, 2)$, is the Andromeda galaxy.

(c) Mark it on your graph. You can see the galaxy on a clear night. Keep your graph to help you find it.

Andromeda Galaxy, M31

3 **(a)** Draw x and y axes, both from -4 to $+4$.
(b) Plot the points W(-2, 0), X(1, 3), Y(4, 0).
These points are the three vertices of the square WXYZ.
(c) Complete the square and mark the point Z on your diagram.
(d) What are the co-ordinates of Z?
(e) Mark the centre of the square, V. What are the co-ordinates of V?

4 **(a)** Draw x and y axes, both from -5 to $+5$.
(b) Plot the points A(5, 2), B(5, -4), C(-3, -4) and D(-3, 2).
(c) What kind of quadrilateral is ABCD?
(d) Find the area of ABCD.

5 **(a)** Draw x and y axes, both from -4 to $+4$.
(b) Plot the points K(3, 2), L(1.5, -1.5), M(-1.5, -2.5) and N(-0.5, 0.5).
(c) Join the points in order. What shape have you drawn?

Activity **1** Draw a picture of your own on squared paper.
Remember to use decimals or fractions to make the picture more realistic.

2 List the co-ordinates of the points in order.

3 Ask a friend to draw your picture on squared paper.

The equation of a line

Julie and Rob are playing a game of '4 in a line'.
They take turns to plot points. They try to stop the other person getting '4 in a line'.
The winner is the first to make a straight line of 4 points.

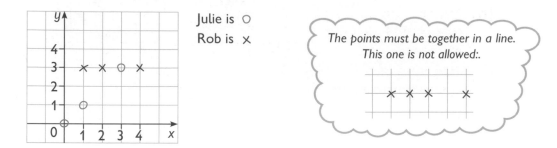

Julie is ○
Rob is ×

The points must be together in a line.
This one is not allowed:.

Here is their game. It is Julie's turn.
She can make a straight line diagonally.

? **Where must Julie go so that she gets '4 in a line'?**
What are the co-ordinates of Julie's winning line?

Julie writes down the co-ordinates of her line: $(0, 0), (1, 1), (2, 2), (3, 3)$

? **What pattern do you notice in Julie's co-ordinates?**

The equation of my line
is $y = x$

? **What are the co-ordinates of three other points on the same line?**

In another game the co-ordinates of Rob's winning line are: $(0, 3), (1, 2), (2, 1), (3, 0)$

? **What pattern do you notice in Rob's co-ordinates?**

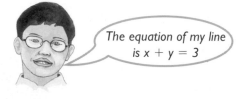

The equation of my line
is $x + y = 3$

Task
  1 With a partner play some games of '4 in a line'.
  2 Write down the co-ordinates of the winning lines.
  3 Write down an equation for each winning line.

? **Does every winning line have an equation?**
What about horizontal and vertical lines?
Is the equation of a line true for all points on it?

Exercise

1 In the diagram there are five lines.

(a) Write down the co-ordinates of the points on each line.

(b) Match each line with one of the following equations.

    (i) $y = 3$

    (ii) $x + y = 3$

    (iii) $y = x - 4$

    (iv) $y = x$

    (v) $x = -4$

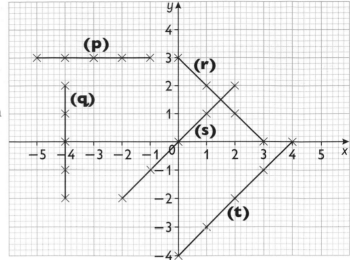

2 Complete the missing co-ordinates for the following lines. Find an equation for each line.

(a)	**(b)**	**(c)**	**(d)**
$(0, 0)$	$(6, 0)$	$(-1, 1)$	$(-2, 5)$
$(1, 1)$	$(5, 1)$	$(0, 2)$	$(-1, 5)$
$(2, 2)$	$(4, 2)$	$(1, 3)$	$(0, 5)$
$(3, ?)$	$(3, ?)$	$(2, ?)$	$(1, 5)$
$(?, 5)$	$(?, 4)$	$(?, 5)$	$(?, 5)$
$(5.5, ?)$	$(1.5, ?)$	$(3.5, ?)$	$(3, ?)$

3 Write down the co-ordinates of four points on each of the following lines.

(a) $x + y - 3$ **(b)** $y = x + 3$

(c) $y = x - 3$ **(d)** $x + y = -3$

(e) $y = 2x$ **(f)** $y = 2x + 1$

Activity Use a graphical calculator to draw the sign of Zorro, using

$$y = x + 3$$

$$y = 2x - 1$$

$$y = x - 3$$

Drawing straight line graphs

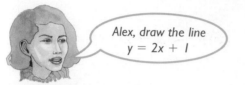

Alex, draw the line
$y = 2x + 1$

How do I do that?

Choose numbers for x.
Make a table. Use the x co-ordinate to work out y.

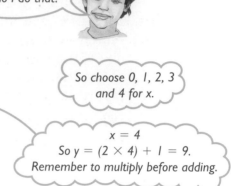

So choose 0, 1, 2, 3 and 4 for x.

$x = 4$
So $y = (2 \times 4) + 1 = 9$.
Remember to multiply before adding.

x	0	1	2	3	4
$2x$	0	2			8
$+1$	1	1	1		1
$y = 2x + 1$	1		5		9

 What are the rest of the y co-ordinates?

Draw the x and y axes. You need to choose your scales.

 How can you tell how big you need to draw your axes?

Plot all the points you have found.
Join up all your points.

 What is the scale of the x axis? What is the scale of the y axis?
Must the x and y axes have the same scales?

Task

1 Copy and complete this table.

x	0	1	2	3	4
$5x$	0				20
$+1$	1				
$y = 5x + 1$	1				

2 What scale do you use for the x axis? What for the y axis?

3 Draw the graph.

 What is the value of y when $x = 2.5$?
What is the value of x when $y = 1.5$?

Task

1 Make tables for the following equations: $y = x + 2$ $y = x - 2$ $y = 2x$
Take x from 0 to 4.

2 Draw x and y axes from -4 to 4. Use suitable scales.
Draw and label the three lines on the same graph.

 What are the co-ordinates of the meeting points of:
(a) $y = 2x$ and $y = x + 2$; **(b)** $y = 2x$ and $y = x - 2$; **(c)** $y = x + 2$ and $y = x - 2$?

Exercise

1 **(a)** Make tables for the following equations.
Take x from 0 to 4.

(i) $y = 3x$ **(ii)** $y = 3x - 1$ **(iii)** $y = 3x + 2$

(b) For each equation:

(i) Draw both axes.
Use 2 squares for each unit on the x axis.
Use 1 square for each unit on the y axis.

(ii) Draw and label the graph.

(iii) Write down the value of y when $x = 0$.

(iv) Write down the value of x when $y = 1.5$.

2 **(a)** Find the co-ordinates of five points which lie on each of the following lines. Take x from -2 to 2.

(i) $y = x + 3$ **(ii)** $y = 3 - x$

(b) Use your points to draw the graphs of both lines on the same axes.

(i) Label each line.

(ii) For each line, write down the co-ordinates of x when $y = 0$.

(iii) Write down the co-ordinates of the point where the two lines cross.

(iv) What is the angle between the two lines?

(v) Are there any other points which lie on both lines?

Investigation

Make tables for the following lines, taking x from -3 to 3.

$y = x + 1$ $y = 1 - x$ $y = x$
$y = x - 1$ $y = 1$ $x = 1$

Which of the points marked lie on the lines?

Do all the lines cross the x axis?

What are the co-ordinates of the points where each line meets the y axis?

Are there any lines which do not cross the y axis?

Are there lines which never meet?

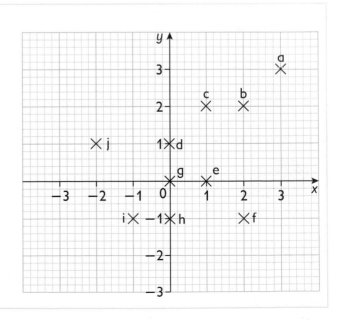

More straight line graphs

Look at this table for the line $y = 2x + 1$.
Some of the values of x are negative.

x	-2	-1	0	1	2	3	4
$2x$	-4	-2	0	2		6	
$+1$	1		1				1
$y = 2x + 1$	-3	-1			5		

Remember to multiply the x value by 2. Then add 1 to get the total.

 What are the other numbers in the table?
Draw the line. Use the same scales for both axes.
Where does the line cut the y axis?

Task

1 Make the table for the line $y = x - 1$ using
 values of x from -2 to 4.
2 Add this line to your graph of $y = 2x + 1$.
3 Now draw in the line $x + y = 7$.

 What are the co-ordinates of the points where the lines cut
the y axis?
What shape do the 3 lines make?

The point where the line crosses the y-axis is called
the **y-intercept**.

 What are the y-intercepts of the 3 lines you
have drawn?
You can tell what the y-intercept will be just by
looking at the equation of a line.
How?

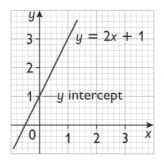

The steepness of a line is called its **gradient**.
Look at these lines.

 Which has the biggest gradient?
Which has the smallest gradient?

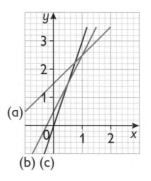

Exercise

In this exercise, you are going to draw a picture.
You will need to use the same graph for each part of the question.

(a) Draw the x axis from -12 to 12 and the y axis from -3 to 15.
Use the same scale for both.

(b) Draw

(i) $y = 2$, taking x from 1 to 8

(ii) $x = 1$, taking y from 2 to 13

(iii) the line joining $(1, 13)$ to $(8, 2)$

> *What shape have you drawn?*

(c) Draw

(i) $y = 1$, taking x from -1 to -8

(ii) $x = -1$, taking y from 1 to 15

(iii) $y = 2x + 17$, taking x
from -8 to -1

> *What is the y-intercept of the line $y = 2x + 17$?*

> *What are the co-ordinates of the meeting points of*
> *(1) $y = 1$ and $y = 2x + 17$*
> *(2) $x = -1$ and $y = 2x + 17$?*

(d) (i) Draw the line $y = -1$.
Take x from -10 to 10.

(ii) Draw the line $y = -3$.
Take x from -9 to 6.

(iii) Join the points $(-10, -1)$ and $(-9, -3)$.

(iv) Join the points $(10, -1)$ and $(6, -3)$.

> *What are the y-intercepts of these two lines?*

> *What do you notice about the lines $y = -1$ and $y = -3$?*

> *What have you drawn?*

(e) (i) Look at the two ends. Which one is steeper?
Which has a bigger gradient?

(ii) Which is the front of the boat?
How can you tell?

> *Colour your picture*

Finishing off

Now that you have finished this chapter you should be able to:

● plot co-ordinates in all four quadrants
● find the equation of a line
● draw a line using its equation
● find the *y*-intercept
● understand what is meant by the gradient of a line.

Review exercise

1 Write down the co-ordinates of the points A, B, C, D, E, F, G, H, I, J and K.

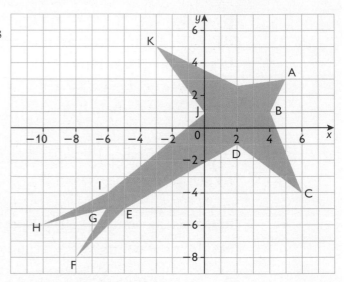

2 **(a)** Write down the co-ordinates of the points U, V, W, X, Y and Z.
(b) Find the equation of the lines ZU, VU and XY.
(c) What are the *y*-intercepts of the lines ZU and VU?
(d) Put in the 2 eyes. (It is a flat fish).
(e) What are their co-ordinates?

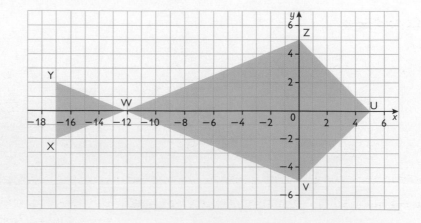

3 **(a)** Copy and complete the following tables.

(i)

x	−3	−2	−1	0	1	2	3
3x	−9	−6		0			9
−2	−2	−2	−2				
y = 3x − 2	−11						7

(ii)

x	−3	−2	−1	0	1	2	3
2x		−4			2		
+1	1			1		1	
y = 2x + 1			−1				

(b) Draw the graphs of the two lines on the same axes. Label them.
(c) Write down the y-intercepts for the lines.
(d) What are the co-ordinates of the point where the two lines meet?
(e) Which line is steeper?

4 **(a)** Make out tables for these two lines.
Take x from −1 to 4.
(i) $y = x + 2$ **(ii)** $y = 2x - 1$
(b) Draw their graphs, using the same axes.
(c) Where do the two lines cross?
(d) Write down their y-intercepts.

5 **(a)** Copy and complete this table for the lines $y = 2x + 2$ and $y = 2x - 1$.
It gives the values of x and y for the two lines.

x	−2	−1	0	1	2	3
y = 2x + 2	−2					8
y = 2x − 1		−1			3	

(b) Draw and label these two lines on the same axes.
(c) Write down the y-intercepts of the lines.
(d) What can you say about the gradients of these two lines?

Investigation

(a)   (b)   (c)

1 What do these road signs mean?   **2** Which hill is the steepest?
3 Make a list of all the hill signs near you.   **4** Put them in order of steepness with the steepest last.

Playing with numbers

In some games, like football, you score one at a time.
In other games some ways of scoring get more points than others.

 Think of some of each type of game.

Task

Danny is playing darts. She needs 67 to win.
It is her turn and she has 3 darts.
She gets 20 with her first dart.

Find 3 different ways she can win with the
other two darts.
Check whether your friends get the same 3 ways.

Task

Mel and Stanley are playing snooker.
It is Stanley's turn.
Can he win at this turn?

*If you do not know
the rules of snooker,
ask your teacher.*

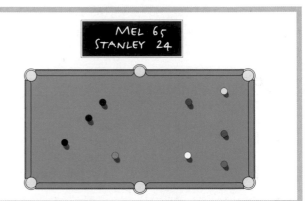

MEL 65
STANLEY 24

 **Look at the table of winnings.
Which question does not double
your winnings?**

| 12 right answers for a million £ ||
Question number	Total prize £
1	500
2	1000
3	2000
4	4000
5	8000
6	16 000
7	32 000
8	64 000
9	125 000
10	250 000
11	500 000
12	One Million

Exercise

1 (a) 279 + 120   (b) 587 + 113   (c) 312 + 156 + 676

    (d) 512 − 311   (e) 623 − 317   (f) 843 − 777

    (g) 63 × 8   (h) 68 × 5   (i) 29 × 22

2 (a) 52 × 15   (b) 28 × 25   (c) 31 × 29

    (d) 714 ÷ 7   (e) 6025 ÷ 5   (f) 2871 ÷ 11

    (g) 1239 ÷ 21   (h) 43 092 ÷ 9   (i) 4815 ÷ 15

Investigation

1 How many dominoes are there in a full set?

2 What is the total number of spots on them?

3 What is the average number of spots per domino?

Activity

ACROSS

1 Snooker. A clearance of 10 reds and blacks and then all the colours.

3 Cards. A normal pack is dealt into 4 hands.

4 Cricket. A six, ten fours and five singles.

6 Golf. Number of holes in 4 rounds of golf.

8 Athletics. How many 400 m laps are there in 4000 m?

9 High jump. 1.82 m in cm.

DOWN

1 Running. Half way in a marathon (in miles).

2 Football league. Points for 22 wins, 9 draws and 11 losses.

3 Darts. Treble 20, treble 19 and a miss.

5 Boxing. How many seconds in a 3 minute round?

7 Table tennis. Winning score.

8 Dice. Largest total on two dice.

Working with tens

This box of chocolates weighs 2.5 kilograms.

 2.5 kilograms is the same as 2500 grams. How do you know?

 180 cm is the same as 1.8 metres? How do you know?

Simon is 180 cm tall.

When you work with the metric system, you often have to multiply or divide by 10, 100 and 1000.

Task

Copy and complete this table. Stick it into your exercise book.

Length metre (m)	**Weight** gram (g)	**Capacity** litre (l)
.... mm ⎱ = 1 metre .... cm ⎰	.... mg = 1 gram	.... ml = 1 litre
.... m = 1 km	.... g = 1 kg	1000 l = 1 kl
	1000 kg = 1 tonne	

m = milli   c = centi   k = kilo

A railway carriage weighs 65.5 tonnes.

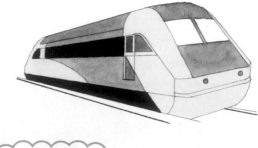

 What is this weight in (a) kilograms (b) grams?

The carriage is 26 135 millimetres long.

 What is this length in (a) centimetres (b) metres?

Sometimes 1000 is written as 10^3.
This is because $1000 = 10 \times 10 \times 10$.

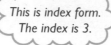
This is index form. The index is 3.

 What are the values of (a) 10^2 (b) 4×10^2? What is one million in index form?

Exercise

1 Write down

   (a) 32×10 **(b)** 32×100 **(c)** 32×1000

   (d) 6.4×10 **(e)** 6.4×100 **(f)** 6.4×1000

   (g) 0.82×10 **(h)** 0.82×100 **(i)** 0.82×1000

2 Write down

   (a) 6×0.1 **(b)** 6×0.01 **(c)** 6×0.001

   (d) 17×0.1 **(e)** 17×0.01 **(f)** 17×0.001

   (g) 415×0.1 **(h)** 415×0.01 **(l)** 415×0.001

3 Write down

   (a) $6 \div 10$ **(b)** $6 \div 100$ **(c)** $6 \div 1000$

   (d) $17 \div 10$ **(e)** $17 \div 100$ **(f)** $17 \div 1000$

4 A record lemon weighs 1130 grams.

   Write this in   **(a)** milligrams   **(b)** kilograms.

5 A cactus is 260 cm tall.

   Write this in   **(a)** millimetres   **(b)** metres.

6 Fiona and Sam are in charge of stalls at their school fete.

   (a) Fiona starts with a float of 10p coins.
      How many 10p coins are needed for a float of

> A float is money used to give change at the start.

      (i) £5   **(ii)** £10

      (iii) £12.50   **(iv)** £19.90?

   (b) At Sam's stall people throw pennies into a bowl of water.
      His float is in 1p coins.
      How many coins does he need for a float of

      (i) 50p   **(ii)** £10.00

      (iii) £12.50   **(iv)** £4.59?

7 Ali collects 10p pieces in a box for charity.
   How much money has he collected when he has

   (a) 60 coins   **(b)** 125 coins   **(c)** 205 coins?

Using scales

Task

Ruth is planning a new kitchen. It is rectangular and has one door 0.7 m wide.

These are her measurements for the width

and the length.

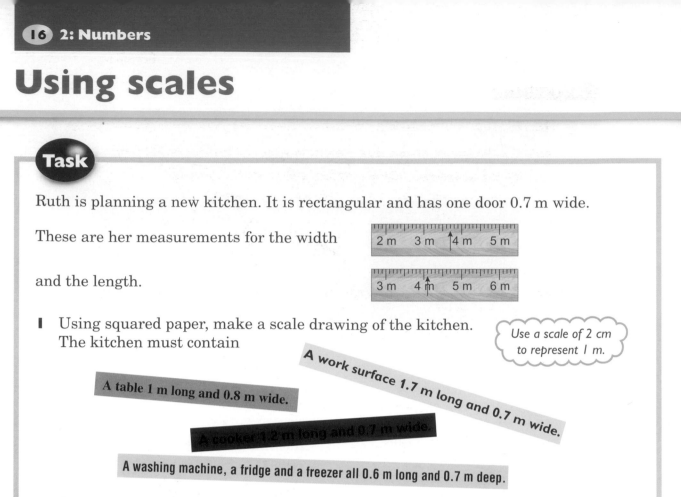

1 Using squared paper, make a scale drawing of the kitchen. The kitchen must contain

Use a scale of 2 cm to represent 1 m.

A table 1 m long and 0.8 m wide.

A work surface 1.7 m long and 0.7 m wide.

A cooker 1.2 m long and 0.7 m wide.

A washing machine, a fridge and a freezer all 0.6 m long and 0.7 m deep.

2 Cut out rectangles, drawn to scale, to represent all of the items above.

3 Now design Ruth's kitchen.

⚠ You worked with scales in the Task.
You must always be careful. Check what each division means.

A = 4.5

Each division is 0.5

B = 4.4

Each division is $\frac{1.0}{5} = 0.2$

This picture shows the dials in Ruth's car.

? **What are the readings?**

? **What do all the dials measure?**

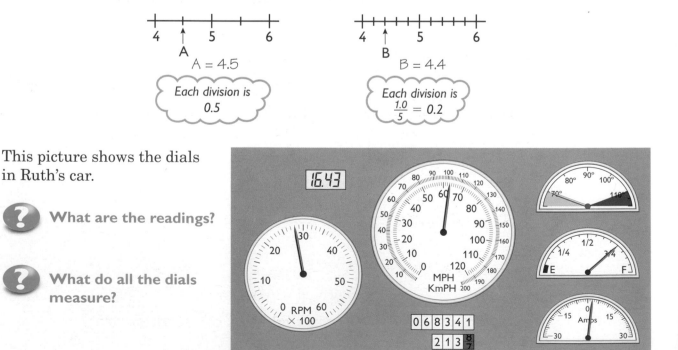

Exercise

The cockpit of an aeroplane is full of dials. The pilot must read them quickly.

1 **(a)** An *altimeter* shows the height of the aeroplane in 1000 m.
At what heights are aeroplanes A, B and C flying?

A   B   C

(b) An *air speed indicator* shows the airspeed in kilometres per hour (km h^{-1}).
At what speeds are aeroplanes D, E and F flying?

D   E   F

(c) Look at the *fuel gauge*. It is full at 3000 kg.
How much fuel is there when the pointer is at

     (i) P   **(ii)** Q   **(iii)** R?

     (iv) How much fuel is the pointer
          in the picture showing?

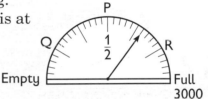

2 What numbers are shown on the number line below?

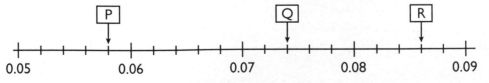

3 What numbers are shown on the number line below?

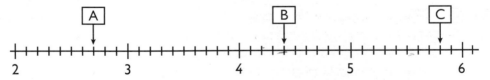

4 Copy the number line below and mark on these numbers.

     (a) 0.18   **(b)** 0.24   **(c)** 0.27

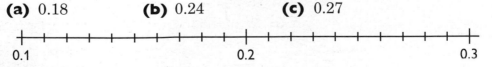

5 Copy the number line below and mark on these numbers.

     (a) 0.3   **(b)** 0.25   **(c)** 0.45

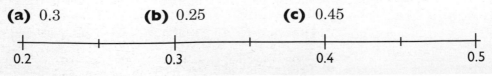

Ordering

 Look at these pairs of numbers. In each case say which is the larger and which the smaller.
(a) 99 and 101
(b) 0.09 and 0.1
(c) 10^2 and 10^3
(d) 9×11 and 10×10

Task

The planets in the solar system go round the Sun. Their orbits are nearly circles (except for Pluto).

Here are their distances from the Sun, in millions of kilometres.

Jupiter	780	Mercury	58
Earth	150	Neptune	4500
Uranus	2870	Venus	108
Mars	230	Saturn	1430

1 Put the planets in order, starting with the one nearest the Sun.

2 Which planets are between Earth and Saturn?

3 Which planet is about twice as far from the Sun as Saturn?

4 How many planets are less than one thousand million kilometres from the Sun?

5 There is a large gap between Mars and Jupiter.
How many million kilometres is the gap?
(There are a lot of small planets, called asteroids, in the gap.)

 Which planet is about 3000 million km from the Sun?

The number 3000 has been rounded to the nearest 1000.

 Round the distances of Mars and Venus from the Sun to the nearest 100 million km.

 A friend asks you for the distances of the planets from the Sun in 'round numbers'. How would you answer your friend for each planet? Which would you give to the nearest 10 million, the nearest 100 million, the nearest 1000 million km? What about Earth and Neptune?

Exercise

1 The list below shows average January noon temperatures (in °C) of 8 places. Arrange them in order starting with the coldest.

(a) Felixstowe 3.9   **(b)** Penzance   7.2   **(c)** Keswick 3.7

(d) Margate   4.6   **(e)** Greenock   3.8   **(f)** Durham 2.8

(g) Aberdeen   2.4   **(h)** Birmingham 3.5

2 Some comets pass the Earth only once, some return at regular intervals. Arrange the orbital periods of these comets in ascending order, smallest first.

Borelly	6.8 years	D'Arrest	6.2 years
Encke	3.3 years	Faye	7.4 years
Finlay	6.9 years	Pons-Winnecke	6.3 years

3 Here are the dates of some English kings.

William I	1066–1087	William II	1087–1100
Henry I	1100–1135	Stephen	1135–1154
Henry II	1154–1189	Richard I	1189–1199

Work out how long each king reigned.
Place them in order, shortest time first.

4 Write the following as decimals

(a) (i) 0.6×100 **(ii)** $\frac{1}{2}$ **(iii)** $\frac{800}{1000}$ **(iv)** 0.07×100

(b) Arrange them in order, smallest first.

5 **(a)** Work out the following

(i) 10^3 **(ii)** 10^5 **(iii)** 10^6 **(iv)** 10^2 **(v)** 10^7 **(vi)** 10^4 **(vii)** 10^1

(b) Arrange your answers in order, smallest first.

6 **(a)** Write each of these distances in metres.

(i) $50 \, \text{km}$ **(ii)** $6 \times \frac{1}{10} \, \text{m}$ **(iii)** $700 \, \text{cm}$ **(iv)** $80 \, \text{mm}$

(b) Write the distances in order, smallest first.

7 The speed of sound is 340 metres per second. This is known as *Mach One*. Write the speeds of these aeroplanes in metres per second.

(a) (i) Storm Missile   Mach 0.7

   (ii) Tornado Fighter   0.45 kilometres per second

   (iii) Jetstream aeroplane   7.12 kilometres per minute

   (iv) Nimrod   Mach 0.3

(b) Write the aircraft in order of their speeds, fastest first.

Finishing off

Now that you have finished this chapter you should be able to:

- arrange numbers in order
- understand that multiplying by 0.1 and dividing by 10 are equivalent (with similar results for 100 and 1000)
- read different scales.

Review exercise

1 Work out as decimals

  (a) $\frac{17}{100}$ **(b)** $\frac{1.7}{100}$ **(c)** $\frac{0.17}{100}$

  (d) 17×0.01 **(e)** 1.7×0.01 **(f)** 0.17×0.01

  (g) $17 \times \frac{1}{100}$ **(h)** $1.7 \times \frac{1}{100}$ **(i)** $0.17 \times \frac{1}{100}$

2 Work out as decimals

  (a) $\frac{236}{1000}$ **(b)** $\frac{9}{1000}$ **(c)** $\frac{16}{1000}$

  (d) 236×0.001 **(e)** 9×0.001 **(f)** 16×0.001

  (g) $236 \times \frac{1}{1000}$ **(h)** $9 \times \frac{1}{1000}$ **(i)** $16 \times \frac{1}{1000}$

3 Write down

  (a) 6×100 **(b)** 0.6×100 **(c)** 0.06×1000

  (d) 2×1000 **(e)** 4×1000 **(f)** 7.3×1000

4 What are the values of A, B and C on this number line?

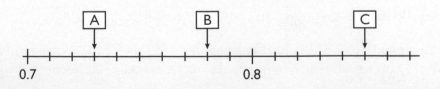

5 What are the values of X, Y and Z on this number line?

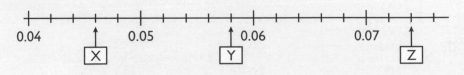

6 Read these dials

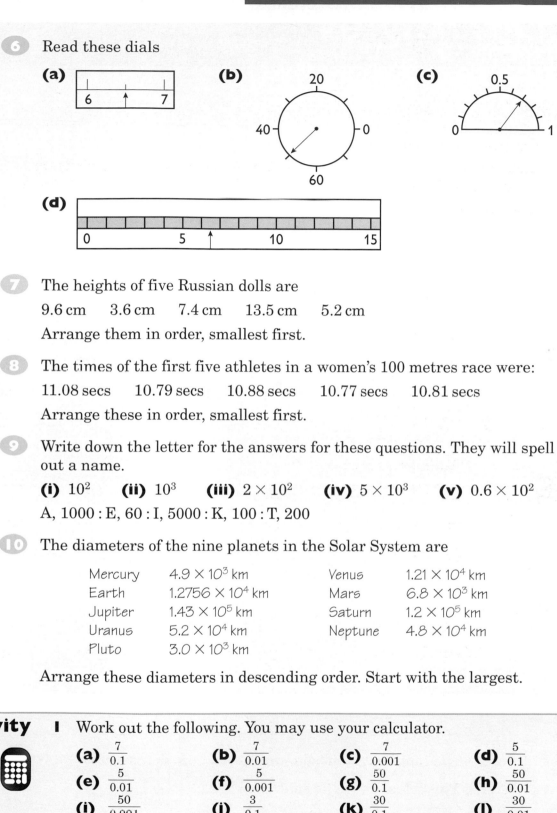

(a)

| 6 | ↑ | 7 |

(b)

20
40 ⊣   ⊢ 0
60

(c)

0.5
0   1

(d)

| 0 | | | | | 5 | ↑ | | 10 | | | 15 |

7 The heights of five Russian dolls are

9.6 cm   3.6 cm   7.4 cm   13.5 cm   5.2 cm

Arrange them in order, smallest first.

8 The times of the first five athletes in a women's 100 metres race were:

11.08 secs   10.79 secs   10.88 secs   10.77 secs   10.81 secs

Arrange these in order, smallest first.

9 Write down the letter for the answers for these questions. They will spell out a name.

(i) 10^2 **(ii)** 10^3 **(iii)** 2×10^2 **(iv)** 5×10^3 **(v)** 0.6×10^2

A, 1000 : E, 60 : I, 5000 : K, 100 : T, 200

10 The diameters of the nine planets in the Solar System are

Mercury	4.9×10^3 km	Venus	1.21×10^4 km
Earth	1.2756×10^4 km	Mars	6.8×10^3 km
Jupiter	1.43×10^5 km	Saturn	1.2×10^5 km
Uranus	5.2×10^4 km	Neptune	4.8×10^4 km
Pluto	3.0×10^3 km		

Arrange these diameters in descending order. Start with the largest.

Activity   **1** Work out the following. You may use your calculator.

(a) $\dfrac{7}{0.1}$ **(b)** $\dfrac{7}{0.01}$ **(c)** $\dfrac{7}{0.001}$ **(d)** $\dfrac{5}{0.1}$

(e) $\dfrac{5}{0.01}$ **(f)** $\dfrac{5}{0.001}$ **(g)** $\dfrac{50}{0.1}$ **(h)** $\dfrac{50}{0.01}$

(i) $\dfrac{50}{0.001}$ **(j)** $\dfrac{3}{0.1}$ **(k)** $\dfrac{30}{0.1}$ **(l)** $\dfrac{30}{0.01}$

Look carefully at your answers to find a non-calculator method.

2 Work out the following without using a calculator.

(a) $\dfrac{8}{0.1}$ **(b)** $\dfrac{8}{0.01}$ **(c)** $\dfrac{8}{0.001}$

(d) $\dfrac{6}{0.1}$ **(e)** $\dfrac{60}{0.1}$ **(f)** $\dfrac{60}{0.01}$

Types of angles

Look carefully at these angles.

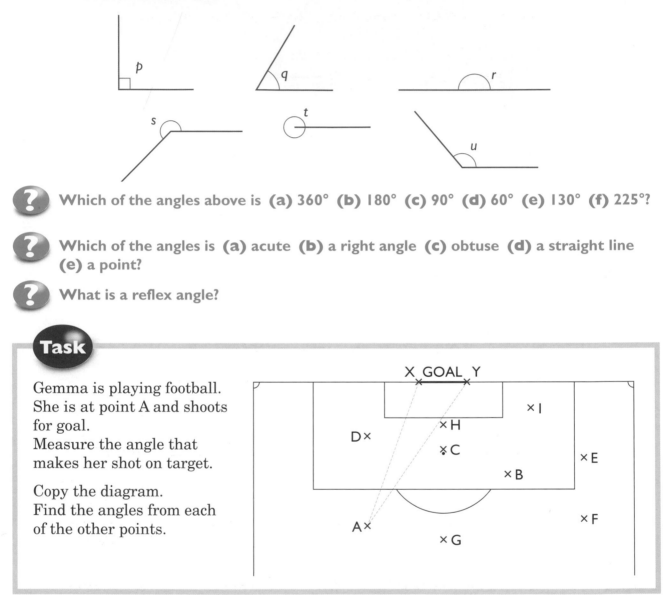

? Which of the angles above is **(a)** 360° **(b)** 180° **(c)** 90° **(d)** 60° **(e)** 130° **(f)** 225°?

? Which of the angles is **(a)** acute **(b)** a right angle **(c)** obtuse **(d)** a straight line **(e)** a point?

? What is a reflex angle?

Task

Gemma is playing football. She is at point A and shoots for goal.
Measure the angle that makes her shot on target.

Copy the diagram. Find the angles from each of the other points.

Look at the triangles outlined in the diagram above.

Triangle CXY is **isosceles**. Two of its sides are equal.

? Which two sides are equal?
Find another isosceles triangle.

Triangle HXY is **equilateral**. **?** What does this mean?

Triangle AXY is **scalene**. All its sides are different.

? Find two more scalene triangles.

Exercise

1. Write down the number of degrees in:
   (a) a whole turn **(b)** half a turn **(c)** a quarter of a turn
   (d) two turns **(e)** one tenth of a turn **(f)** three and a half turns

2. Label each of the following angles: acute, obtuse, reflex or right-angled.

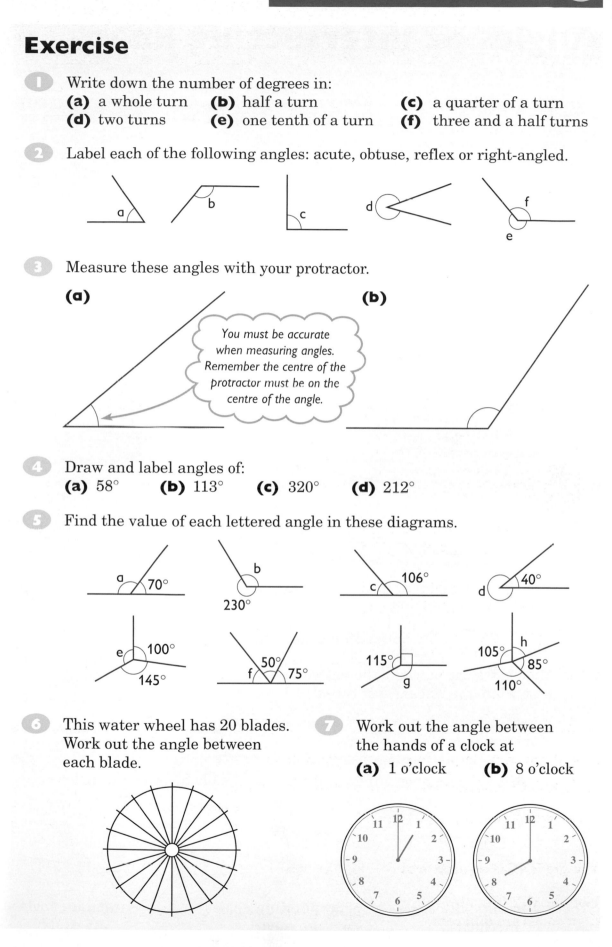

3. Measure these angles with your protractor.

   (a)
   (b)

   You must be accurate when measuring angles. Remember the centre of the protractor must be on the centre of the angle.

4. Draw and label angles of:
   (a) 58° **(b)** 113° **(c)** 320° **(d)** 212°

5. Find the value of each lettered angle in these diagrams.

6. This water wheel has 20 blades. Work out the angle between each blade.

7. Work out the angle between the hands of a clock at
   (a) 1 o'clock **(b)** 8 o'clock

Angles at intersecting lines

Do you remember?

Lines in the same direction are called **parallel**.
You show that lines are parallel by putting arrows on them.

? What can you say about the distance between two parallel lines?
Make a list of six sets of parallel lines in the classroom.

Task

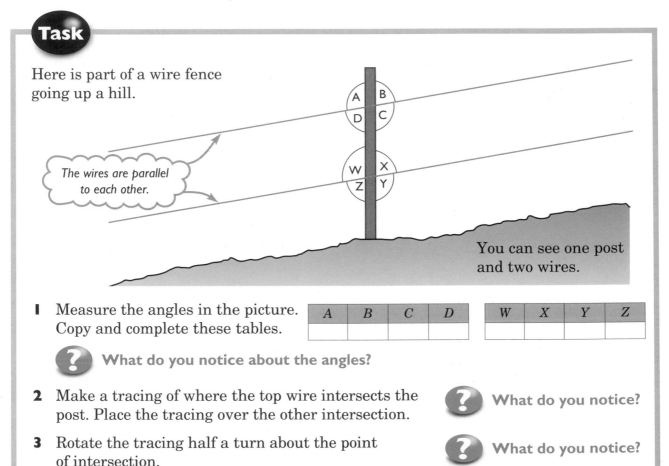

Here is part of a wire fence
going up a hill.

*The wires are parallel
to each other.*

You can see one post
and two wires.

1 Measure the angles in the picture.
Copy and complete these tables.

A	B	C	D

W	X	Y	Z

? What do you notice about the angles?

2 Make a tracing of where the top wire intersects the
post. Place the tracing over the other intersection.

? What do you notice?

3 Rotate the tracing half a turn about the point
of intersection.

? What do you notice?

The Task shows three important facts about angles made by intersecting lines.

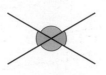

Vertically opposite angles
are equal

Corresponding angles
are equal

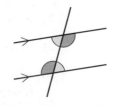

Alternate angles
are equal

Exercise

1 Find the value of each lettered angle in these diagrams.

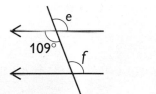

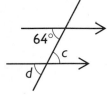

2 Find the value of each lettered angle in these diagrams.

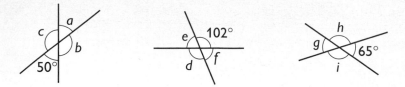

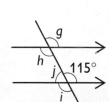

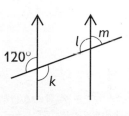

3 Ameet makes a wire fence.

The posts are vertical.
The wires are parallel.
Work out the angles
a, b, and c.

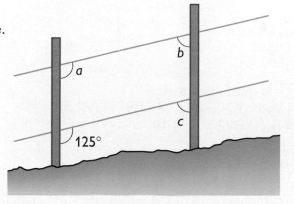

4 Here is a fence going down a hill.
The wires are parallel. The posts are vertical.

(a) What is angle A?

(b) What angle do the wires make with the horizontal?

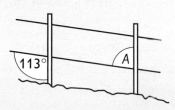

Triangles and quadrilaterals

 What kind of shapes are in these pictures?

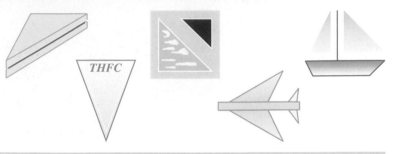

THFC

 Task

Draw a triangle.

Measure the angles *A*, *B* and *C*.
Add up the three angles, *A* + *B* + *C*.

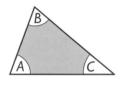

Now do the same for two more triangles.

What do you notice?

Complete this statement.
The three angles of a triangle add up to ....

Now look at this triangle.

One side has been extended.
The angle *E* is an exterior angle.

Measure the exterior angle, *E*.

Measure the two opposite interior angles *A* and *B*. Add *A* and *B* together.

What do you notice?

Repeat this for two more triangles.

Complete this statement.

For any triangle the exterior angle ...... the sum of the opposite two interior angles.

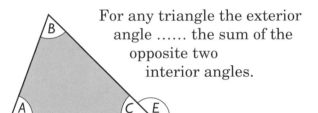

 Task

I Draw a quadrilateral.
Measure the angles *P*, *Q*, *R* and *S*.
Add up the four angles, *P* + *Q* + *R* + *S*.

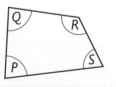

2 Now do the same for two more quadrilaterals.

What do you notice?

Complete this statement.
The four angles of a quadrilateral add up to ....

Look at this diagram.
The quadrilateral is divided into two triangles.
You know that *A* + *B* + *C* = 180° and *L* + *M* + *N* = 180°
They are the angles in the two triangles.

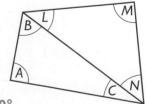

 Explain why the sum of the angles of the quadrilateral is 360°.

Exercise

1 Find the value of each lettered angle in these diagrams.

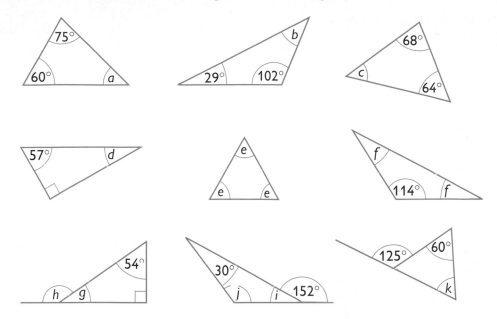

2 Find the value of each lettered angle in these diagrams.

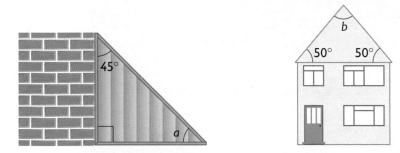

3 Find the value of each lettered angle in these diagrams.

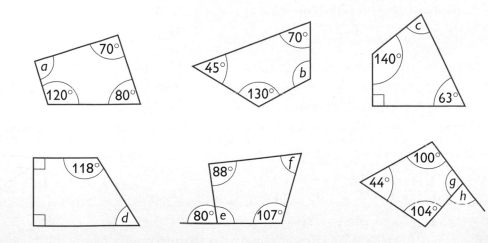

Directions

Look at this diagram.

The directions North, South, East and West are marked.

The direction halfway between North and East is called North East.

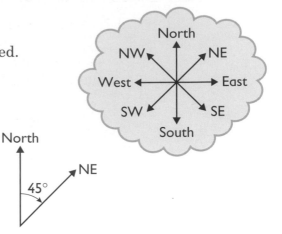

 What are the other three directions called?

You can also call North East 045°.
This is called a compass bearing.
The angle is measured clockwise from North.

 What are the bearings of East, South East, South, South West, West and North West?

Task

The map shows routes between airports.

The route Liverpool to Carlisle is due North.

1 Write down two more routes that are due North.

2 Write down three routes which are
   (a) due East,   **(b)** due South,
   (c) due West.

3 What do you notice about your results?

4 Write down two routes which are
   (a) North East,   **(b)** South East,
   (c) South West,   **(d)** North West.

5 What do you notice about your results?

Not all routes are one of the directions used so far. Some directions are in between. For example, the bearing of Southampton from Exeter is 080°.

6 Check this by measuring the angle between the North line at Exeter and the line joining Exeter to Southampton.

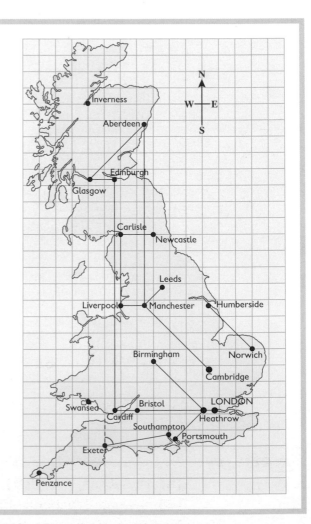

Jed says 'The bearing of Southampton from Exeter is 280°. He is wrong. What mistake is he making?

Exercise

1   Look at this diagram.

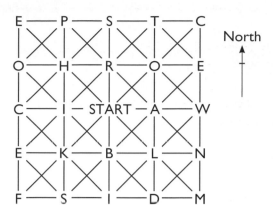

(a) Follow the directions
     to spell out a word.
     Begin at START.
     (i)   Move 2 West, then
           1 North, 3 East
           and 2 South.
     (ii) Move 2 North then
           1 East, 2 South and
           1 North West.
     (iii) Move 2 North, then
           1 West, 2 South,
           1 West and 1 South.
     (iv) Move 2 South East, then 3 North, 1 North West, 2 South, and
           1 South.

(b) Give directions to make these words.
     (i) HIT   (ii) BOP   (iii) WILD   (iv) BEAT

2   Use the map in the Task opposite for this question.
    Write down a new route whose direction is
    (a) between N and NE   (b) between NE and E
    (c) between E and SE   (d) between SE and S
    (e) between S and SW   (f) between SW and W
    (g) between W and NW   (h) between NW and N.

3   On the map opposite measure the bearings of
    (a) London from Birmingham   (b) London from Bristol
    (c) Manchester from Swansea   (d) Glasgow from Newcastle.

4   Avonford is a town with a Centre, a School, a Library, a Hospital, a Town
    Hall and a Sports Field.
    Draw a diagram showing the position of each of these buildings if
    (a) the School is North of the Centre
    (b) the Library is East of the School and NE of the Centre
    (c) the Hospital is SE of the Centre and South of the Library
    (d) the Town Hall is South of the Centre and West of the Hospital
    (e) the Sports Field is East of the Centre and SE of the Library.

Activity   At your school give directions on how to get from your classroom to
              (a) the library   (b) the dining hall   (c) the changing rooms
              (d) the headteacher's office   (e) the medical room.
              Now write down directions for three routes of your own.
              Ask a friend to check them.

Finishing off

Now that you have finished this chapter you should be able to:

- work with corresponding angles, alternate angles and vertically opposite angles
- use the result that the angles inside a triangle add up to 180°
- prove that the angles inside a quadrilateral add up to 360°
- use directions and measure bearings

Review exercise

1 Find the value of each lettered angle in these diagrams.

2 Here is a design of the London Eye.
It is the biggest observation wheel ever built.
It has 32 viewing capsules.

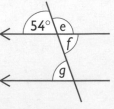

Capsules

(a) What is the angle between the centre of each capsule?

(b) The wheel takes 30 minutes to complete a turn.
One capsule is at the highest point at exactly 12 noon.
When is the next capsule at the highest point?
Answer to the nearest second.

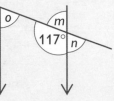

3 Find the value of each lettered angle in these diagrams.

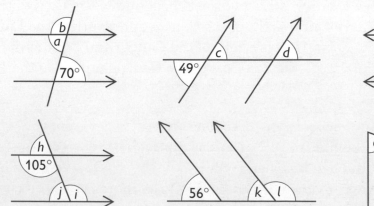

4 Find the value of each lettered angle in these diagrams.

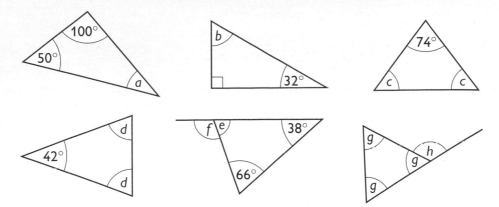

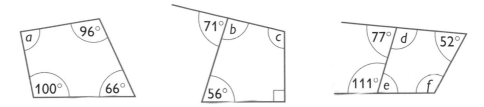

5 Find the value of each lettered angle in these diagrams.

6 Look at this map of the Isle of Wight.

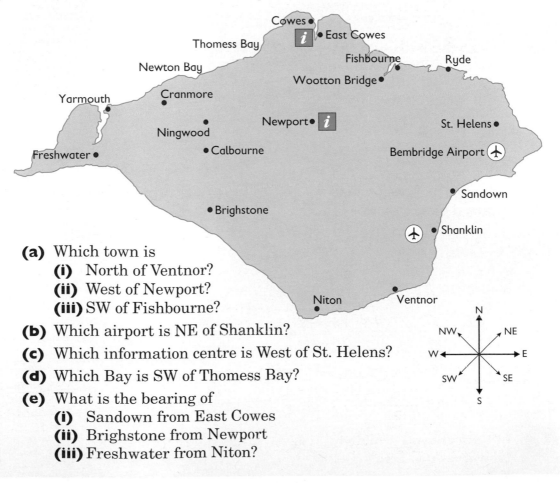

(a) Which town is
  (i) North of Ventnor?
  (ii) West of Newport?
  (iii) SW of Fishbourne?
(b) Which airport is NE of Shanklin?
(c) Which information centre is West of St. Helens?
(d) Which Bay is SW of Thomess Bay?
(e) What is the bearing of
  (i) Sandown from East Cowes
  (ii) Brighstone from Newport
  (iii) Freshwater from Niton?

4 Displaying data

Here are the results of Sarah's hockey club.

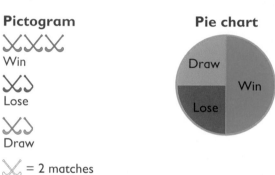

WIN LOSE WIN WIN WIN DRAW
LOSE WIN DRAW LOSE WIN DRAW

Sarah uses a **tally chart** to organise the data.

	Tally	Total
Win	⫴⫼ I	6
Draw	III	3
Lose	III	3

Then she draws these diagrams.

Pictogram

X X X
Win

X)
Lose

X)
Draw

X = 2 matches

Pie chart

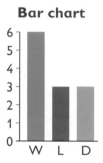

Bar chart

6
5
4
3
2
1
0
W L D

? The angles in the pie chart are 180°, 90° and 90°.
How do you work these out?

? Which of the three displays is easiest to read?

Task

Arnold plays in a Rugby team.
These are their scores this season.

0	26	25	7	8	18
28	6	21	14	26	46
26	14	3	27	9	39

(a) Copy and complete this tally chart.

Score	Tally	Total
0–9		
10–19		
20–29		
30–39		
40–49		

(b) Draw a suitable diagram to display the data.

? In this case you grouped the data.
How does this help?
When do you group data?

Exercise

1. The bar chart shows the number of days rain during September in some cities.

   (a) Which city has the most days of rain?

   (b) Draw a pictogram to illustrate these data.

   Use ⌂ to represent 2 days.

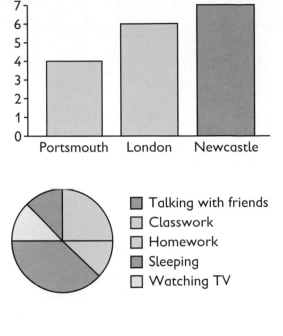

2. This pie chart shows how Sylvia spends one day.

   (a) What does she do for the longest?

   (b) One activity takes up $\frac{1}{4}$ of her day. Which is it?

   (c) She spends the same amount of time on 3 activities. Which are they?

- Talking with friends
- Classwork
- Homework
- Sleeping
- Watching TV

3. Ronny goes to the City of London. He records the number of floors of the buildings within 100 metres of Liverpool Street Station.

   Here are his results.

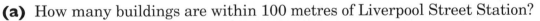

4	6	1	9	10	14	15	18
7	16	8	13	5	17	15	20
18	12	17	11	12

   (a) How many buildings are within 100 metres of Liverpool Street Station?

   (b) Make a tally chart using the groups 1–5, 6–10 and so on.

   (c) Draw a bar chart.

Activity Show this picture to your classmates.
Give them 10 seconds.
They must remember as many objects as they can.

   (a) How many objects can each person remember? Make a tally chart.

   (b) Draw a bar chart to illustrate your results.

Mean, median and mode

Three friends are discussing whether this is true.

That can't be right – my dad takes size 6.

Tom

I think it's an April Fool.

Debbie

I take size 10 already. I reckon it's true.

Rick

They ask the men who walk past their school during a 15 minute period 'What size shoes do you take?'

Here are their results.

| 6 | 8 | 10 | 13 |
| 10 | 7 | 9 | |

They each calculate an average.

Tom calculates the mean:

$$Mean = \frac{6 + 8 + 10 + 13 + 10 + 7 + 9}{7} = 9$$

Rick finds the mode

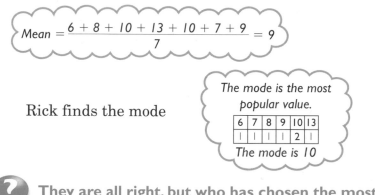

The mode is the most popular value.

6	7	8	9	10	13
1	1	1	1	2	1

The mode is 10

Debbie finds the median:

Arrange all the data in order. The median is the middle value.

6 7 8 ⑨ 10 10 13

Median

? They are all right, but who has chosen the most suitable average?

? Another man arrives. His shoes are size 7.
What are **(a)** the mean **(b)** the mode now?

? How do you find the new median?

Task

Find the shoe size of everyone in your class.
(a) Draw a bar chart of the data. **(b)** Calculate the mean, median and mode.

? The bar chart tells you the mode. How?

Exercise

1 For the following numbers find **(i)** the mean **(ii)** the median **(iii)** the mode.

> *To find the median first arrange the numbers in order of size.*

(a) 3, 4, 5, 8, 10

(b) 6, 2, 4, 10, 24, 18, 6

(c) 6, 3, 6, 10, 8, 6, 15, 10

2 Think about these situations. Each one involves an average. Say which average each should be: mean, median or mode.

(a) A cricketer works out his average score.

(b) A school cricket team buys a helmet to share.

(c) Monika works for a small company. She finds the average pay (including the owner).

3 Jack and Delroy are comparing their end of term results.

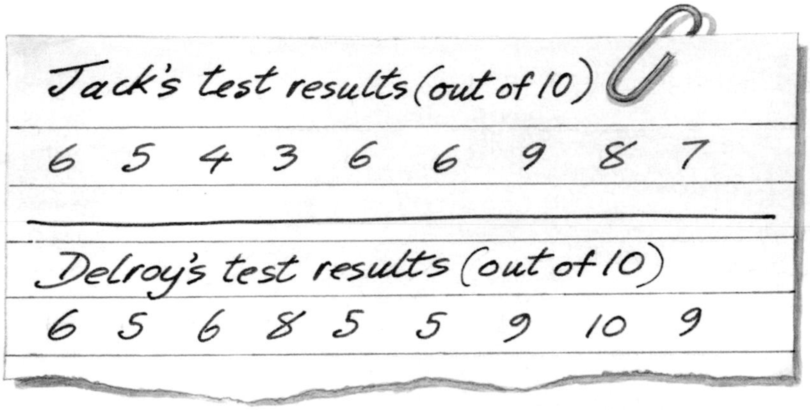

Jack's test results (out of 10)

6 5 4 3 6 6 9 8 7

Delroy's test results (out of 10)

6 5 6 8 5 5 9 10 9

(a) Find the median score for each boy.

(b) Find the mean score for each boy.

(c) Who has performed better? Explain.

Activity

1 Fill a jam jar with sweets.

2 Ask everyone in your class to estimate the number of sweets.

3 Find the mean, median and mode of your results.

Which is nearest to the correct answer?

4 Are the boys or the girls in your class better at estimating?

Measuring the spread of data: range

Lucy and her friends now ask 11 women about their shoe sizes. Here are their results.

They find out the spread of the data.

They calculate the **range**.

> *Range = highest data value − lowest data value*
> *= 9 − 3 = 6*

Task

Calculate the mean, median and mode for the women's shoe sizes.
Compare the data for men and women.
Which has the greater mean?
Which has the greater range?

Outliers

Peter finds the age of all the competitors in two local BMX competitions.

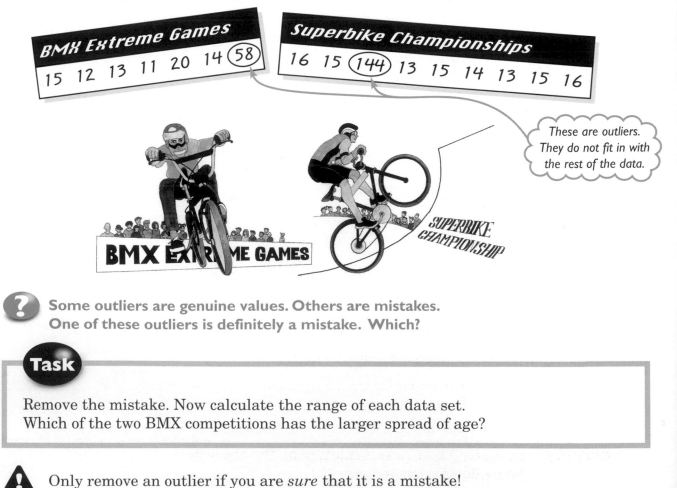

BMX Extreme Games
15 12 13 11 20 14 (58)

Superbike Championships
16 15 (144) 13 15 14 13 15 16

> These are outliers. They do not fit in with the rest of the data.

? Some outliers are genuine values. Others are mistakes.
One of these outliers is definitely a mistake. Which?

Task

Remove the mistake. Now calculate the range of each data set.
Which of the two BMX competitions has the larger spread of age?

! Only remove an outlier if you are *sure* that it is a mistake!

Exercise

1 All these data sets include outliers.

(i)	Jenny's examination marks (%)	55	25	70	30	152	40
(ii)	Age of competitors at a skateboard contest	18	13	54	17	12	
(iii)	Total rolled on two dice	5	6	16	7	9	12
(iv)	Number of miles run by Phil on each day of a week	3	5	3	4	2	1	26

In each case

(a) State the value of the outlier.

(b) Decide whether you should remove it. Explain why.

(c) Calculate the range.

2 Caroline is taking a typing test. She types for 1 minute and the number of correct words is recorded. She does this 6 times.

Here are her results.

46 49 44 43 45 49

In order to pass she must have
- a mean of greater than 45.
- a range of less than 7.

Does she pass?

3 Here are the lap times for two racing drivers during a 5 lap race.

Roy Stephens				
64 s	66 s	63 s	63 s	64 s

Mark Henderson				
66 s	67 s	61 s	66 s	60 s

(a) Calculate the mean and range for both drivers.

(b) Who drives the fastest lap?

(c) Who drives the slowest lap?

(d) Who is the more consistent driver?

(e) Who wins the race?

Activity Imagine you are commentating on the above race.
Write down what you say.

Discrete and continuous data

Claire and Adam are collecting data.

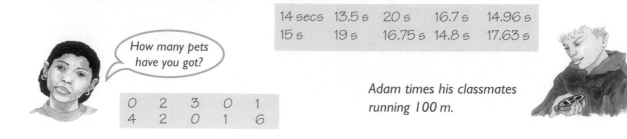

| 14 secs | 13.5 s | 20 s | 16.7 s | 14.96 s |
| 15 s | 19 s | 16.75 s | 14.8 s | 17.63 s |

How many pets have you got?

| 0 | 2 | 3 | 0 | 1 |
| 4 | 2 | 0 | 1 | 6 |

Adam times his classmates running 100 m.

? **Look at the two sets of data.**

For Claire's data each value is a whole number. You cannot own 4.2 pets!
This type of data is called **discrete** data.

Adam's data can take any value. The time for 100 metres can be 14 seconds, 15.2 seconds, 13.98 seconds etc.

This type of data is called **continuous** data.

Task

With a friend, write down
(a) 5 examples of discrete data and **(b)** 5 examples of continuous data.
Now, as a whole class, make a poster with two long lists of discrete and continuous data.

Adam groups his data.
He makes this table.

! You must be careful how you describe the groups.

 What are the meanings of the words 'at least' and 'below'?

 What is wrong with 12–14, 14–16, 16–18 etc?

 What is wrong with 12–13, 14–15, 16–17 etc?

Time (secs)		
At least	**Below**	**Frequency**
12	14	
14	16	
16	18	
18	20	
20	22	

Another way to describe the groups is $12 \leqslant t < 14,$ $14 \leqslant t < 16,$ $16 \leqslant t < 18$ etc.

 Explain what this means.

 Complete the table.

Exercise

1 Are the following data discrete or continuous?
(a) The number of people in cars passing your school.
(b) The wing-spans of golden eagles.
(c) The scores on a die.
(d) The weights of new-born dolphins.

2 The maximum temperature (to the nearest degree) is recorded in Auckland for 2 weeks.

16 12 17 13 16 15 14 17 14 16
15 14 15 14

(a) Copy and complete this tally chart and frequency table.

Tempereature (°C)		Tally	Frequency
At least	**Below**		
12	14		
14	16		
16	18		
18	20		

On how many days is the temperature
(b) at least 16°C but less than 18°C?
(c) less than 16°C?
(d) at least 12°C?

3 The time, in seconds, for 15 fireworks to burn out is recorded.

7	21	21	27	20
16	27	31	16	18
29	15	32	34	33

Copy and complete the tally chart and frequency table.

Time, t (secs)	Tally	Frequency
$5 \leqslant t < 10$		
$10 \leqslant t < 15$		
$15 \leqslant t < 20$		
$20 \leqslant t < 25$		
$25 \leqslant t < 30$		
$30 \leqslant t < 35$		

Activity

1 Write out the numbers 1–10 randomly as shown opposite.

2 Make a number of copies.

3 Time how long your classmates take to join up the numbers in order, 1, 2, 3, …, 10. Use a stopwatch.

4 Make a tally chart and frequency table showing your results.

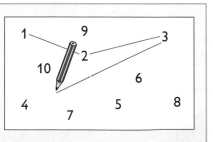

Scatter diagrams

John and Cath are having an argument.

I think that people with long legs can jump further than people with short legs.

Rubbish! The length of a person's legs does not affect how far they can jump.

They decide to collect data from their friends to find out who is right.

	Alan	Barry	Claire	Dipak	Ernie	Flora
Inside leg measurement (cm)	60	70	50	65	65	70
Standing jump distance (cm)	85	90	65	90	80	100

Task

Plot the points (60, 85), (70, 90), (50, 65) and so on, on graph paper.

Copy and complete this scatter diagram.

? **Does the scatter diagram support John or Cath?**

Have they got enough data to be certain?

Standing Jump Distance (cm)

(60, 85) (70, 90)

(50, 65)

50 55 60 65 70 75
Inside Leg Measurement (cm)

This is called a *scatter diagram*.

A scatter diagram tells you about **correlation** between the values of the two quantities.

Positive correlation

When one quantity increases, so does the other.

Negative correlation

When one quantity increases, the other decreases.

No correlation

There is no connection between the two quantities.

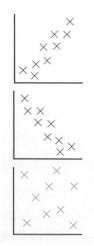

? **Describe the correlation in the scatter diagram for John and Cath's data.**

? **Think of everyday examples of**
  (a) positive correlation   **(b)** negative correlation   **(c)** no correlation.

Exercise

1 Here are some scatter diagrams.

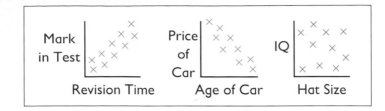

What type of correlation exists between

(a) revision time and marks in test?

(b) age and price of car?

(c) hat size and IQ?

2 This table shows the marks (out of 10) given by judges at a local dog control competition.

Contestant	Mrs. Giles	Mr. Hands	Mr. Smith	Mr. Taylor	Mr. Thomas	Ms. Barrett
Judge 1	1	6	3	5	7	2
Judge 2	2	8	3	5	8	3

(a) Draw a scatter diagram showing the marks of the two judges.

(b) Is there any correlation between the marks of the two judges? If so, what kind?

3 This scatter diagram shows the relationship between the price of some 1-bedroomed flats and their distance from the centre of London.

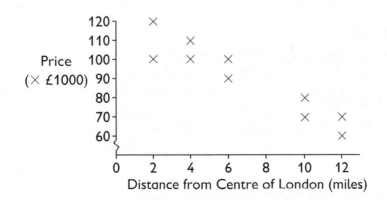

Use the scatter diagram to *estimate* roughly

(a) the price of a flat 8 miles from the centre of London.

(b) the distance from the centre of London of a flat costing £105 000.

Finishing off

Now that you have finished this chapter you should be able to:

- represent data using a pictogram, bar chart or pie chart
- find the mean, median and mode, and know when to use them
- find the range and understand that it is a measure of how spread out the data is
- understand the difference between discrete and continuous data, and be able to group both types using a frequency table
- know when to use a scatter diagram and understand the meaning of correlation.

Review exercise

1. Rachana asks her friends to record the number of minutes they spend playing computer games during the Christmas holiday.

25	150	60	30	140	0	55	180	70	60
65	140	40	170	74	120	45	125	90	90

(a) Copy and complete this tally chart

(b) Draw a bar chart to illustrate these data.

Time spent playing computer games (min)	Tally	Frequency
0–50		
51–100		

2. The members of a Computer Games Club are asked to mark a new game, out of 10.

Boys	6	7	3	4	3	6	3	8
Girls	3	5	77	2	7	8	5	

CRYPT STORMER

(a) Which value is an outlier?
Do you include it?

(b) Calculate the median and mean for
(i) the boys and (ii) the girls.
Who rate the game higher, the boys or the girls?

(c) Calculate the range for the boys and girls.
Whose marks are more spread out?

3. Are the following data discrete or continuous
(a) numbers of pupils in each class at school
(b) weights of moon rock specimens
(c) distances travelled by snails in a day
(d) numbers of letters arriving each day at your house?

4 Natalie asks her friends to 'Sing a musical note for as long as possible without taking a breath'.

Here are the results.

Time (secs)		Frequency
At least	**Below**	
10	15	3
15	20	6
20	25	4
25	30	3
30	35	2

(a) How many people take part in the experiment?

Don arrives late. He is not included in the original table. He sings a note for 35 seconds exactly.

(b) Don's result cannot be recorded in the table. Explain why.

(c) Rewrite the table so that Don's result is included.

5 A group of friends take part in a sponsored swim.

Name	Abdul	Sonia	Lizzy	Geoff	Angey	Carrie	Cherry
Age	20	38	60	51	28	33	26
No of lengths	30	19	14	11	26	34	42

(a) Copy these axes and draw a scatter diagram.

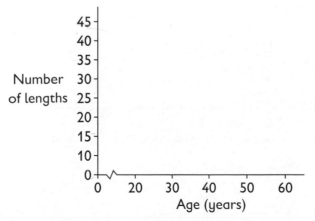

(b) Describe the correlation between the ages of these swimmers and the number of lengths they swim.

(c) Terry is 46 and Clara is 31. They also swim.
   (i) Who do you expect to swim further?
   (ii) Can you be sure?

5 Decimals

Rounding

The numbers on this line go up by 100 each time.

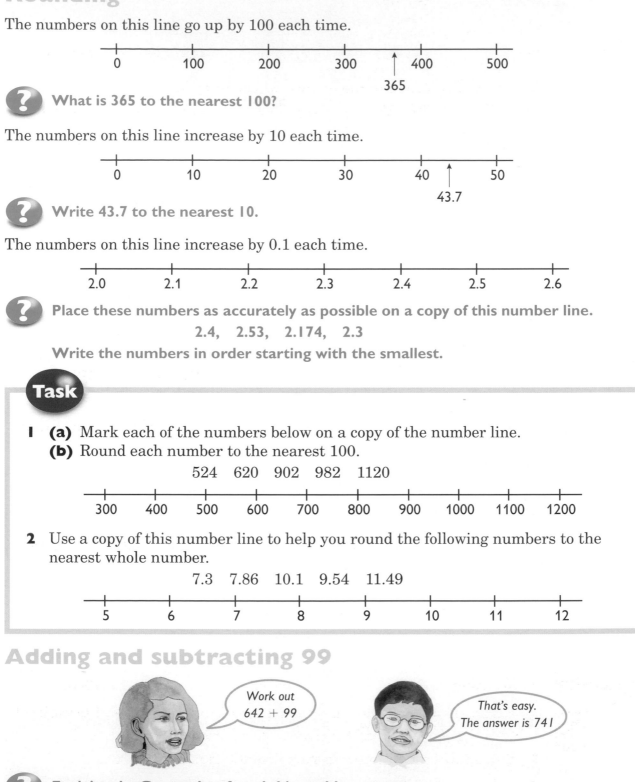

? What is 365 to the nearest 100?

The numbers on this line increase by 10 each time.

? Write 43.7 to the nearest 10.

The numbers on this line increase by 0.1 each time.

? Place these numbers as accurately as possible on a copy of this number line.

2.4, 2.53, 2.174, 2.3

Write the numbers in order starting with the smallest.

Task

1 **(a)** Mark each of the numbers below on a copy of the number line.
   (b) Round each number to the nearest 100.

524   620   902   982   1120

2 Use a copy of this number line to help you round the following numbers to the nearest whole number.

7.3   7.86   10.1   9.54   11.49

Adding and subtracting 99

Work out 642 + 99

That's easy.
The answer is 741

? Explain why George has found this problem so easy.
Work out 1206 + 99. Now try 432 − 99.
Suggest an easy way to add and subtract 999.

Exercise

1 Round these numbers to the nearest 10.

(a) 342   **(b)** 2341   **(c)** 889   **(d)** 796   **(e)** 999

2 Round these numbers to the nearest 100.

(a) 642   **(b)** 491   **(c)** 889   **(d)** 4890   **(e)** 999

3 Round these numbers to the nearest whole number.

(a) 2.4   **(b)** 3.7   **(c)** 2.41   **(d)** 3.784   **(e)** 9.9

4 Write these numbers in order starting with the largest:

4.5,   4.13,   4.82,   4.098,   4.14

5 Write down the next three numbers in each of these sequences.

(a) 80, 90, 100, 110, ..., ..., ...

(b) 600, 700, 800, ..., ..., ...

(c) 3.2, 3.3, 3.4, ..., ..., ...

(d) 224, 234, 244, ..., ..., ...

(e) 4682, 4782, 4882, ..., ..., ...

6 Add 10 to each of these numbers.

(a) 35   **(b)** 162   **(c)** 4567   **(d)** 94   **(e)** 999

7 Subtract 100 from these numbers.

(a) 654   **(b)** 7894   **(c)** 1023   **(d)** 67 345   **(e)** 10 001

8 Work out

(a) $22 + 99$ **(b)** $135 - 99$ **(c)** $945 + 99$ **(d)** $4005 - 99$

(e) $10\,000 - 999$

9 Brian buys two pencils at 19p each, a ruler costing 39p and a pencil case costing 99p. He was charged £1.77 for these items.

(a) How do you know that this is wrong?

(b) What is the correct total for the bill?

(c) How can you work this out in your head?

Activity   **1** Work out   **(a)** 35×10 **(b)** 45×100 **(c)** 27×1000

2 Explain how to use the answers you have found in question 1 to work out

(a) 35×9 **(b)** 45×99 **(c)** 27×999

3 Write down the answers to the calculations in question 2.

4 Work out **(a)** 56×9 **(b)** 142×9 **(c)** 12×99 **(d)** 26×99

         (e) 112×99 **(f)** 99×9 **(g)** 99×99 **(h)** 999×99

Rounding and decimal places

Tim is placing the number 35.654 on a number line.
First he looks at the whole numbers.

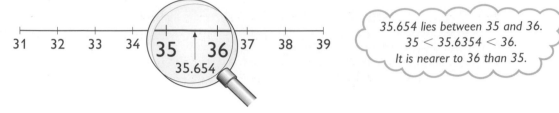

35.654 lies between 35 and 36.
35 < 35.6354 < 36.
It is nearer to 36 than 35.

 What is 35.654 to the nearest whole number?
Which of the numbers after the decimal point helps you decide this?

Next he looks at the first decimal place.

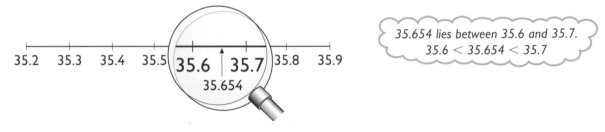

35.654 lies between 35.6 and 35.7.
35.6 < 35.654 < 35.7

 Tim has marked the number on the line. Do you agree with him?
What is 35.654 to 1 decimal place?
Explain why you had to look at both the 2nd and 3rd decimal places to help you decide this.

35.654 lies between 35.65 and 35.66.

 Use this to place the number in the correct place on a copy of the number line above?
What is 35.654 to 2 decimal places?

Task

 1 Place the number 8.156 on an accurate number line.
2 Round 8.156 **(a)** to the nearest whole number **(b)** to one decimal place
(c) to two decimal places

 Tim must write 5.364 to 1 decimal place.
He chooses between 5.3 and 5.4. Which should he choose? Explain why.

 11.49 < 11.498 < 11.50 Write 11.498 to 2 decimal places.

Exercise

1 **(a)** Add 0.1 to
  (i) 4   **(ii)** 7.6   **(iii)** 10   **(iv)** 2.9   **(v)** 9.9

(b) Subtract 0.1 from
  (i) 8.4   **(ii)** 0.6   **(iii)** 0.12   **(iv)** 10   **(v)** 100

(c) Write down the number that is 0.01 more than
  (i) 6.48   **(ii)** 12.33   **(iii)** 0.02   **(iv)** 0.09   **(v)** 9.99

(d) Write down the number that is 0.01 less than:
  (i) 7.56   **(ii)** 0.04   **(iii)** 3.452   **(iv)** 0.1   **(v)** 1

2

$$72.35 < 72.3586 < 72.36$$

These are the numbers with 2 decimal places that are nearest to 72.3586.

$72.3586 = 72.36$ correct to 2 decimal places.

For each of the numbers below, complete the inequalities.
Then write each correct to 2 decimal places.

(a) ☐ $< 13.24379 <$ ☐   **(b)** ☐ $< 0.19632 <$ ☐

(c) ☐ $< 0.0614 <$ ☐   **(d)** ☐ $< 6.3257 <$ ☐

(e) ☐ $< 0.092 <$ ☐   **(f)** ☐ $< 0.0962 <$ ☐

3 Write each of the following numbers   **(i)** to 1 decimal place
                                              (ii) to 2 decimal places.

(a) 12.6723   **(b)** 1.438   **(c)** 0.6951   **(d)** 0.076
(e) 1.0359   **(f)** 4.0032   **(g)** 9.951   **(h)** 0.9999

4 Write the following sets of numbers in ascending order, smallest first.
(a) 1.345, 1.4, 1.38, 1.045
(b) 0.2956, 0.3, 0.29, 0.29513
(c) 0.0657, 0.06612, 0.06571

5 Find a number that lies between
(a) 2.95 and 2.96
(b) 3.99 and 4.01
(c) 0.23 and 0.37

6 Find the number that is exactly half way between each pair of numbers in Question 5.

7 Do the following calculations on your calculator.
Give your answers to 2 decimal places.
(a) $7 \div 3$ **(b)** $12 \div 7$ **(c)** $17 \div 11$ **(d)** $23 \div 6$

Interpreting decimal answers

 How long does it take to walk 14 km at a speed of 5 km per hour?

 Five T-shirts cost £14. How much is this each?

Special offer
T-SHIRTS £3·50 each
OR   5 for £14

 14 kg of sand is used to fill 5 sacks. What weight of sand is in each sack?

The problems above all involve the calculation $14 \div 5 = 2.8$
For each the decimal part (0.8) must be changed into an appropriate unit.

0.8 hours $= 0.8 \times 60$ minutes   *60 minutes = 1 hour.*

$£0.8 = 0.8 \times 100$ pence   *100 pence = £1.*

0.8 kilograms $= 0.8 \times 1000$ grams   *1000 grams = 1 kilogram.*

Work out the calculations above to obtain an appropriate answer to each problem.

 How many inches is 0.8 feet? Give your answer to the nearest inch.

Task

George has worked out $123 \div 20$ on his calculator.

This is what his calculator shows: **6.15**

1 The calculation involved time. Write the answer in hours and minutes.
2 The answer is in kilometres. Write it in km and metres.
3 The answer is in £. Write it in £ and pence.
4 Write the answer in feet and inches to the nearest inch.

You may wish to display mixed units as a decimal on your calculator.
The following sequence will change 3 hours 24 minutes into 3.4 hours.

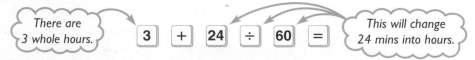
There are 3 whole hours.   **3** **+** **24** **÷** **60** **=**   *This will change 24 mins into hours.*

 How would you change 5 feet 9 inches into feet?

Exercise

1 Give an appropriate answer to the following problems:

(a) Rashide cycles 45 km at an average speed of 11 km per hour.
How long does this take?

(b) Vera is paid £35 for working 9 hours.
How much is this per hour?

(c) Weldon takes 20 strides to walk 18 metres.
How long is each stride?

(d) Alex collected £115 after doing a 35-mile sponsored walk.
How much money is this per mile?

(e) A lift can carry a maximum of 8 people or 650 kilograms.
What does this give as the average weight of a person?

(f) A garden bench 5 feet long seats 3 people.
How much room does each person have?

2 Write

(a) £6.7 in £ and pence. **(b)** 21.47 km in km and metres.

(c) 7.5 feet in feet and inches. **(d)** 8.2 hours in hours and minutes.

3 Write

(a) £34 and 20p in £. **(b)** 4 feet 3 inches in feet.

(c) 24 km and 45 m in km. **(d)** 5 hours 12 minutes in hours.

(e) 2 days 18 hours in days. **(f)** 8 pounds 4 ounces in pounds.

4 Find the cost of the following telephone calls:

(a) 5 minutes 12 seconds at the weekend.

(b) 3 minutes 25 seconds at peak rate.

(c) 10 minutes 17 seconds off peak.

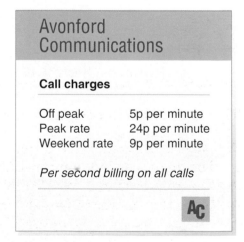

Avonford
Communications

Call charges

Off peak	5p per minute
Peak rate	24p per minute
Weekend rate	9p per minute

Per second billing on all calls

AC

5 Work out Jane's earnings for the week.

HOURS WORKED	12th July to 18th July
NORMAL PAY	25 hours 30 mins at £3.60 per hour
OVER TIME	5 hours 20 mins at £5.40 per hour
SUNDAY	2 hours 40 mins at £7.20 per hour

Rough calculations

Stuart and his sister Mary are arguing about the volume of this box.

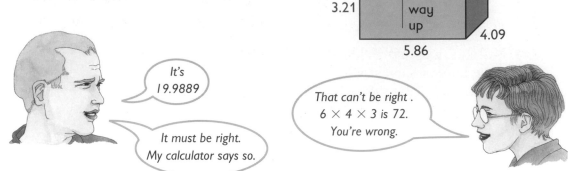

3.21

This way up

5.86

4.09

It's 19.9889

It must be right. My calculator says so.

That can't be right . 6 × 4 × 3 is 72. You're wrong.

 How does Mary get 6 × 4 × 3?
Who is right, Stuart or his sister?

It is easy to press the wrong button on your calculator.

So you need a rough check.

You round the numbers in your calculation.

Example $\dfrac{28 \times 0.43}{4.9}$

Number	Rounded
28	30
0.43	0.4
4.9	5

Roughly $\dfrac{30 \times 0.4}{5} = 2.4$

The accurate answer is 2.457 … .

This is near the rough check, 2.4.   O.K. ✔

The … mean there are more numbers on your calculator.

Task

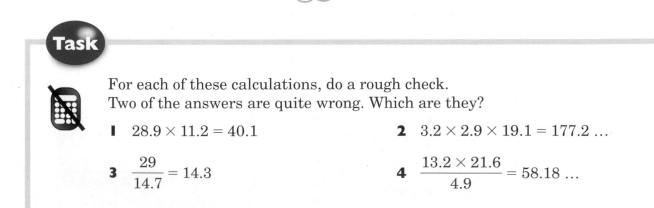

For each of these calculations, do a rough check.
Two of the answers are quite wrong. Which are they?

1 $28.9 \times 11.2 = 40.1$

2 $3.2 \times 2.9 \times 19.1 = 177.2 \ldots$

3 $\dfrac{29}{14.7} = 14.3$

4 $\dfrac{13.2 \times 21.6}{4.9} = 58.18 \ldots$

 Each wrong answer in the Task comes from pressing a wrong calculator button.
Find the wrong button used in each case.

Exercise

1 These numbers appear in calculations. Round them for a rough check.

(a) $9.012 \to 9$ **(b)** 212.4   **(c)** 62.9   **(d)** 3.141

(e) 1.006   **(f)** 419   **(g)** 6730   **(h)** 2 146 309

(i) 52.40   **(j)** 0.102   **(k)** 0.0081   **(l)** 0.000 406

(m) 0.079   **(n)** 0.987   **(o)** 9.86

2 Des does some rough checks for his calculator sums.
For each one, answer either 'Near enough' or 'Too far away'.

(a) Rough 6   Calculator 7.162 ...

(b) Rough 0.1   Calculator 10.29 ...

(c) Rough 450   Calculator 489.2 ...

(d) Rough 24   Calculator 2.414 ...

(e) Rough 0.048   Calculator 0.0511 ...

(f) Rough 17.5   Calculator 84.23 ...

3 For each of the following

(a) Do the calculation on your calculator

(b) Do a rough check

(c) Give the right answer

(i) $8.623 + 10.001 - 5.8324$ **(ii)** 23.4×18

(iii) $79 \times 11.4 \times 103$ **(iv)** $\dfrac{42.1}{2.03}$

(v) $\dfrac{3.92}{8.02}$ **(vi)** $\dfrac{29 \times 2.1}{43}$

(vii) 0.029×389 **(viii)** 276×0.0019

4 Next week a new girl, Miggy, is joining your class.
No one has seen her yet. Here are some statements about Miggy.
For each one say *Possible* or *Impossible*.

(a) Miggy is 300 cm tall

(b) Miggy is 150 months old

(c) Miggy weighs 40 kg

(d) Miggy's waist is 15 cm.

Finishing off

Now that you have finished this chapter you should be able to:

- write numbers to the nearest 10 and 100
- work out quick calculations involving 9 and 99
- write numbers to one and 2 decimal places
- express a decimal answer in an appropriate form
- change mixed units to decimals when using your calculator
- do rough calculations.

Review exercise

Use the questions in this exercise to check that you have understood everything.

1 **(a)** Write the following correct to the nearest 10.
    (i) 123   **(ii)** 465   **(iii)** 12.6   **(iv)** 6599

    (b) Write these numbers to the nearest 100.
    (i) 3265   **(ii)** 1599   **(iii)** 2999   **(iv)** 195

2 Write down the answers to the following:
    (a) $23 + 9$ **(b)** $147 + 99$ **(c)** $1362 + 999$ **(d)** 14×9
    (e) 14×99 **(f)** 45×9 **(g)** 237×99 **(h)** 72×999

3 Choose the smallest from the following sets of numbers.
    (a) 1.3 and 1.29   **(b)** 15.89 and 15.98   **(c)** 0.123 and 0.231
    (d) 4.8, 4.75 and 4.745   **(e)** 0.12, 0.012, 0.021 and 0.21

4 Add 0.1 to each of the numbers below.
    (a) 4.2   **(b)** 23.5   **(c)** 4   **(d)** 0.25   **(e)** 0.9

5 Add 0.01 to each of the numbers below.
    (a) 5   **(b)** 6.4   **(c)** 3.45   **(d)** 1.39   **(e)** 9.99

6 Write the following correct to the number of decimal places in the brackets.
    (a) 34.34 (1)   **(b)** 14.45 (1)   **(c)** 1.646 (1)   **(d)** 1.646 (2)
    (e) 0.137 (2)   **(f)** 0.95 (1)   **(g)** 0.4962 (2)   **(h)** 0.998 (2)

7 Find the number that is exactly halfway between
    (a) 11 and 12   **(b)** 1.6 and 1.7   **(c)** 0.35 and 0.36   **(d)** 0.4 and 0.6
    (e) 1.82 and 1.86   **(f)** 4.1 and 4.6   **(g)** 0.9 and 1.1   **(h)** 6.99 and 7.01

8 Write
    (a) 7 litres 20 millilitres in litres   **(b)** 16 hours 36 minutes in hours
    (c) 12 minutes 15 seconds in minutes   **(d)** £5 and 4 pence in £
    (e) 8.3 hours in hours and minutes   **(f)** 2.9 km in km and metres

9 For each of the following
(a) do the calculation on your calculator
(b) do a rough check
(c) give the right answer

(i) $8.89 + 2.99 - 3.01$ (ii) 591×30.7

(iii) $\dfrac{25\,039}{49}$ (iv) $\dfrac{63.2 \times 0.029}{11.6}$

10 Give an appropriate answer to each of the following:

(a) What is the price of 1 video?   (b) How much washing powder is used for 1 wash?

(c) A bicycle wheel makes 15 revolutions in a distance of 100 feet. How far does it travel in one revolution?

(d) Paulo takes 3 hours and 20 minutes to walk a distance of 16 km. How far does he walk in 1 hour?

Investigation   Many fractions cannot be written as exact decimals. The decimals are called **recurring decimals**.

Example

$\dfrac{1}{3} = 0.33333$ The 3 repeats or **recurs**   *Place a dot above the number that recurs.*
This is written as $0.\dot{3}$

$\dfrac{2}{7} = 0.285714285714$ The 2 85 714 all **recur**   *Place dots above the numbers at the start and end of the recurring pattern*
This is written as $0.\dot{2}8571\dot{4}$

I Write the following fractions as decimals correct to
(i) 1 decimal place   (ii) 2 decimal places   (iii) 15 decimal places

(a) $\dfrac{2}{3}$ (b) $\dfrac{3}{7}$ (c) $\dfrac{5}{11}$ (d) $\dfrac{4}{13}$ (e) $\dfrac{2}{9}$

2 Try some more fractions of your own.

3 Describe any patterns that you discover.

6 Using variables

Writing expressions

Tim buys 5 MDs on the Internet.
His brother, Lou, buys 3 more.
Their mother is angry.

She writes

> How much have you boys spent?

> 5m means 5 × m.
> You write 5m not m5.

> 5m + 3m is an **expression**.

5m + 3m = 8m
What is m?
Tim? Lou?

> Making 5m + 3m into 8m is called **simplifying**. 8m is simpler.

 What does *m* stand for?

Tim thinks the MDs are £4 each.
Lou thinks they are £15 each.

 What is the total cost if (a) Tim is right (b) Lou is right?

Task

Kofi buys 2 T-shirts at £*a* each. He also buys 3 more at £*b* each.
1 Write down an expression for the total cost.

The total cost of the T-shirts is £30.
2 Show that this works when $a = 3$ and $b = 8$.
3 Does this work if $a = 12$ and $b = 2$?

 There are two more pairs of possible whole number values of *a* and *b*. What are they?

Sometimes expressions have letters and numbers, like $10 + 2p$.

BOAT TRIPS
Hire a Boat for £10
plus £2 per person

> 10 is called a **constant**.
> *p* can take different values.
> It is called a **variable**.

 What is the cost of hiring a boat for:
(a) 2 people   (b) 5 people   (c) *p* people?

Exercise

1 Letty buys 10 transfers at x pence each and Kelly buys 12 at y pence each.
(a) Write down an expression for the cost in pence.
The total cost of the transfers is £1.20.
(b) Show that this works when $x = 6$ and $y = 5$.

2 Penny goes into a souvenir shop and buys 2 pencils at x pence and 4 postcards at y pence.
(a) Write an expression for the cost in pence.
The total cost of the shopping is £2.50.
(b) Show that this works when $x = 25$ and $y = 50$.
(c) Does this work if $x = 21$ and $y = 52$?

3 A mobile phone company is advertising its phones.
(a) A call lasts m minutes. Write an expression for the cost of the call in pence.

What is the cost of making a call for:
(b) 4 minutes **(c)** 12 minutes
(d) 16 minutes **(e)** 20 minutes?

> ## Sunny Mobiles
> Calls cost
> 10p connection fee
> plus 3p per minute

4 While on holiday Manik buys 4 T-shirts and 3 baseball caps. The T-shirts cost £t and the caps cost £c.
(a) Write down an expression for the cost in £.
Manik's bill comes to £41.
(b) Show that $t = 5$ and $c = 7$ are possible values.
(c) Can $t = 11$?
Sam buys 2 T-shirts and 5 baseball caps.
(d) Write down an expression for the cost.
(e) Write an expression for the cost of both Manik's and Sam's shopping.

Investigation

THE AVONFORD STAR

End of Season Under 14 Cricket Results

Teams	Win (x points)	Draw (y points)	Lose (z points)
Avonford	5	2	3
Broomhill	1	3	6
Newchurch	2	8	0
Plystar	3	2	5
Shellbury	6	0	4
Swynton	4	3	3

The organisers try to decide on the best scoring system.
Put the teams in order when
(a) $x = 2, y = 1, z = 0$ **(b)** $x = 3, y = 1, z = 0$ **(c)** $x = 4, y = 2, z = 1$
(d) $x = 6, y = 4, z = 0$ **(e)** $x = 10, y = 7, z = 0$
Which of the scoring systems do you think is best?

Simplifying expressions

Erico buys 2 bars of toffee and Amaria buys 3 bars. Erico also buys 4 packets of sweets and Amaria buys 5 packets.

They want to work out the total cost.

 How many bars of toffee do they buy together? How many packets of sweets?

Erico writes $2t + 4s$ Amaria writes $3t + 5s$

Erico puts the sum together: $2t + 4s + 3t + 5s$

Amaria **simplifies** this by **collecting like terms**: $2t + 3t + 4s + 5s$
$$= 5t + 9s$$

 What does 5t + 9s mean?
Is it possible to simplify this any further?

 A bar of toffee costs 60p and a packet of sweets costs 80p.
What is the total cost of the shopping?

 How would you simplify $6m - 2m + 7 + 8n - 3n + 4m - 6m - 2n - 3$ **?**

Task

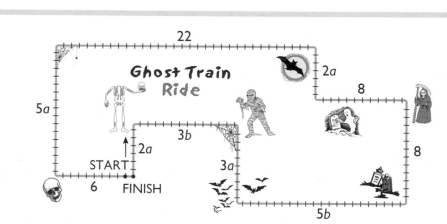

The diagram shows the route of the ghost train at a fair.

Find

1   the total distance travelled in terms of a, b and numbers

2   the values of a and b

3   the length of the journey in metres.

 How would you simplify 5b − 4b?
How should you write 1b?
How would you simplify 6a − 4a − 2a?
How should you write 0a?

Exercise

1 Simplify the following expressions:

(a) $b + b + b + b$ **(b)** $6q + 5q + 15q$

(c) $3x + 6 + 7x + 8$ **(d)** $5g + 7g - 2g - 4g$

(e) $7t - 2t + 19 - 7$ **(f)** $7y - 3y + 3$

(g) $15w - 9w + 12w$ **(h)** $25f - 10 - 12f + 12$

(i) $25s - 19 + 20 - 20s$ **(j)** $10 - 5 + 7z + 8z$

2 Simplify the following expressions:

(a) $a + a + a + a + a$ **(b)** $5m + 6m + 12m + 8m$

(c) $3b + 6 + 2b + 5$ **(d)** $7g + 5g - 3g - 2g$

(e) $5t - 4t + 9 - 7$ **(f)** $5y - 3y - 2 + 3$

(g) $10x - 9x + 2x$ **(h)** $15f + 12 - 10f - 9$

(i) $75s - 21 + 30 + 50s$ **(j)** $100 - 100z - 50 + 70z + 80z$

3 Nigel and Janet are simplifying the expression $4r - 6s + 5t - 2r - t.$

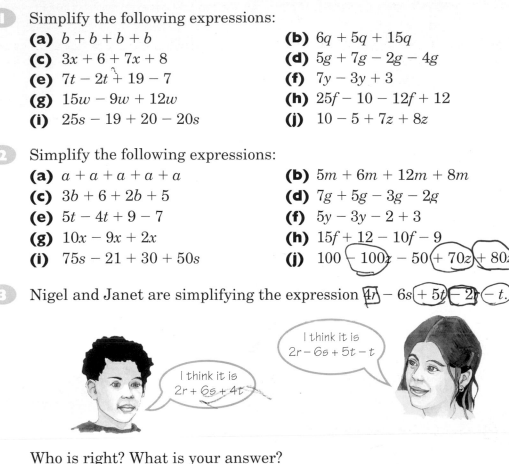

I think it is
$2r + 6s + 4t$

I think it is
$2r - 6s + 5t - t$

Who is right? What is your answer?

4 Simplify the following expressions:

(a) $5y - 3x + 4y - 2x + 3y$ **(b)** $3m + 2n - n + n$

(c) $a - 2b + 3c - a + 3b - 2c$ **(d)** $5r - 6t + 3t - 2r - 3r + s$

(e) $3d - 4e + 5e - f + 2f - 2d$ **(f)** $21g - 13h + 10g + 20h + 45$

(g) $29p + 31p + 11q + 23r + 89q - 23r$ **(h)** $35k - 29l - 29k + 35l$

(i) $10x + 9y + 8z + 7 - 6x - 5y - 4z - 3$ **(j)** $3x + 7x - 4 - 6x + 1$

5 **(a)** Write down the lengths of the sides of this triangle when $x = 2$. Add them together to find the perimeter.

(b) Now find a formula for the perimeter in terms of x. Substitute $x = 2$ in your formula. Do you get the same answer?

In parts (a) and (b) you found the perimeter by different ways. In (a) you found the sides first and added them. In (b) you used your formula.

(c) Do you get the same answer working both ways when

     (i) $x = 3$ **(ii)** $x = 20$ **(iii)** $x = 100$?

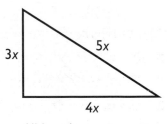

$3x$ $5x$

$4x$

All lengths are in metres.

Using brackets

Look at this rectangle.

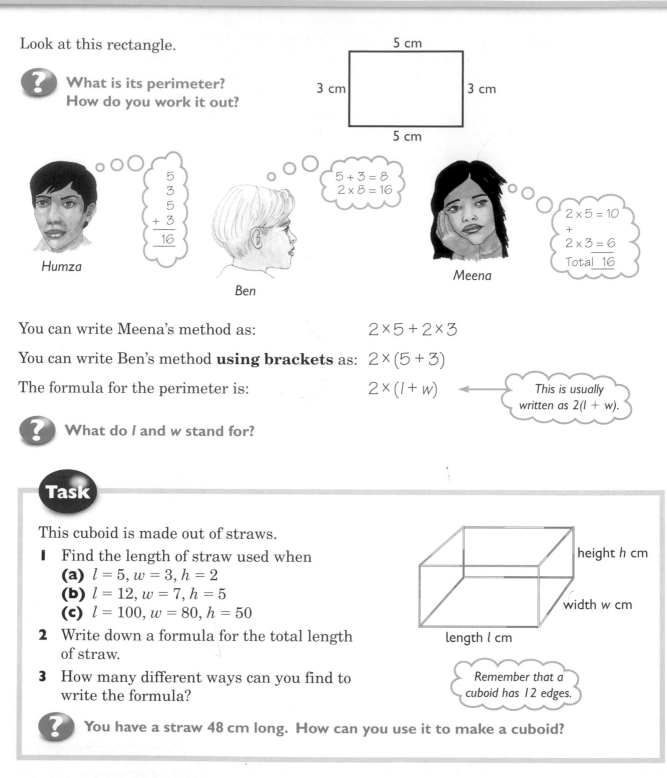

? **What is its perimeter?
How do you work it out?**

Humza

Ben

Meena

You can write Meena's method as: $2 \times 5 + 2 \times 3$

You can write Ben's method **using brackets** as: $2 \times (5 + 3)$

The formula for the perimeter is: $2 \times (l + w)$ *This is usually written as $2(l + w)$.*

? **What do l and w stand for?**

Task

This cuboid is made out of straws.

1 Find the length of straw used when
   (a) $l = 5, w = 3, h = 2$
   (b) $l = 12, w = 7, h = 5$
   (c) $l = 100, w = 80, h = 50$

2 Write down a formula for the total length of straw.

3 How many different ways can you find to write the formula?

Remember that a cuboid has 12 edges.

height *h* cm

width *w* cm

length *l* cm

? **You have a straw 48 cm long. How can you use it to make a cuboid?**

Another way of writing the formula $2(l + w)$ is $2l + 2w$.
This is called **expanding the bracket**.

? **How do you expand the following brackets?**
   (a) $6(p + q)$ (b) $12(a + b)$

Exercise

1 Work out:

(a) $(2 \times 3) + (2 \times 7)$
(b) $2 \times (3 + 7)$
(c) $(5 \times 2) + (5 \times 3)$
(d) $5 \times (2 + 3)$
(e) $(6 \times 10) + (6 \times 1)$
(f) $6 \times (10 + 1)$
(g) $7 \times (5 + 2)$
(h) $(7 \times 5) + (7 \times 2)$
(i) $10 \times (8 + 2)$
(j) $(10 \times 8) + (10 \times 2)$
(k) $12 \times (3 + 8)$
(l) $(12 \times 3) + (12 \times 8)$

2 Find the value of $2(l + w)$ when:

(a) $l = 3$ and $w = 7$
(b) $l = 5$ and $w = 5$
(c) $l = 10$ and $w = 2$
(d) $l = 4$ and $w = 0$
(e) $l = 2$ and $w = 2$
(f) $l = 10$ and $w = 12$
(g) $l = 5$ and $w = 9$
(h) $l = 8$ and $w = 5$
(i) $l = 18$ and $w = 20$
(j) $l = 25$ and $w = 50$

3 Expand the following brackets:

(a) $5(w + 2)$
(b) $4(m + n)$
(c) $3(x + 2y)$
(d) $6(2 - 3r)$
(e) $2(6 - 9r)$
(f) $3(4 - 6r)$
(g) $2(p - 2q + 5)$
(h) $7(a + 3b - c + 4)$
(i) $12(10a - 8b - 6c - 4)$
(j) $20(l - 2s + 3t - 4u)$

Investigation

This picture shows a model of a garden swing seat.
The frame is made out of thin wire. Lengths are in cm.
Each end is in the shape of a right-angled triangle.

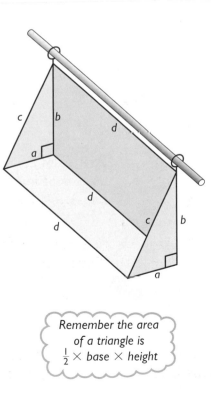

1 Write down a formula for the perimeter of the triangle.

2 What is the perimeter when

(a) $a = 3$ $b = 4$ $c = 5$
(b) $a = 6$ $b = 8$ $c = 10$
(c) $a = 15$ $b = 20$ $c = 25$

3 **(a)** Write down a formula for the total length of wire.
(b) Simplify this expression.

4 What is the total length of wire when

(a) $a = 9$ $b = 12$ $c = 15$ $d = 25$
(b) $a = 12$ $b = 16$ $c = 20$ $d = 30$
(c) $a = 18$ $b = 24$ $c = 30$ $d = 50$

5 The back, sides and seat are made out of cardboard.
(a) What is the total area of the cardboard when
    $a = 12$, $b = 16$, $c = 20$ and $d = 30$?
(b) Write down a formula for the area of cardboard.
(c) Use your formula to check the answer to 5(a).

Remember the area of a triangle is $\frac{1}{2} \times base \times height$

Finishing off

Now that you have finished this chapter you should:

- know the meaning of the terms **expression**, **simplify** and **expand**
- be able to simplify an expression
- be able to expand a bracket

Review exercise

1 Simplify the following expressions:
  (a) $4x + 5y + 3x + 7y$ **(b)** $3k + 5 + 2k + 4$
  (c) $5a - 2a + 3b - b$ **(d)** $5f + 6 - 5f - 7$
  (e) $5s - 3s + 5t + 4s + 6t$ **(f)** $6g + 6h - 7g - 7h + 2g$

2 Expand the following brackets:
  (a) $5(2 + c)$ **(b)** $3(x - 6)$ **(c)** $7(p + q)$
  (d) $4(2d + 3)$ **(e)** $4(b + 8)$ **(f)** $8(2r - 1)$
  (g) $3(1 - k)$ **(h)** $3(1 + 2m - 3n)$ **(i)** $5(2a - 3b)$
  (j) $12(2 + 2d + 2e)$ **(k)** $2(6u - 8v - 4w - 10x)$ **(l)** $6(2l - x - z)$

3 Each coloured expression has a matching white expression. Find the matching pairs.

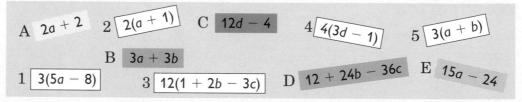

A $2a + 2$ 2 $2(a + 1)$ C $12d - 4$ 4 $4(3d - 1)$ 5 $3(a + b)$

B $3a + 3b$

1 $3(5a - 8)$ 3 $12(1 + 2b - 3c)$ D $12 + 24b - 36c$ E $15a - 24$

4 Sue is having a party.
She wants to buy some food and drink.
Bottles of cola cost c pence and
bottles of lemonade cost l pence.
  (a) Look at the picture.
    Write down an expression for
    the cost of the drinks.

Sue spends £16.00 on the drinks, and $c = 150$.
  (b) What is the cost of a bottle of lemonade?

5 Sue's brother, Alex, helps her with
the party. Here is his shopping list.
  (a) Write an expression for the total
    cost of his shopping.
  (b) He goes to a shop where $x = 30$,
    $y = 80$ and $z = 90$.
    What is the cost of his shopping?

	No of pkts	cost (P)
CRISPS	20	x
CHEESE STRAWS	5	y
CHOCOLATE BUTTONS	10	z

6 Hannah buys make-up for Sue's party. She buys 2 lipsticks at £s each and hair mascara in 4 different glitters at £g each.
  (a) Write down an expression for the cost of the make-up.
  (b) Hannah spends £20. Both s and g are whole numbers.
   Is it possible to have:
   (i) $s = 2$ and $g = 4$ **(ii)** $s = 4$ and $g = 3$
   (iii) $s = 6$ and $g = 2$ **(iv)** $s = 8$ and $g = 1$?

7 Sue's party is by a swimming pool. It is a rectangle l metres long and w metres wide.
  (a) Write down an expression for the perimeter of the pool.
  (b) The perimeter is 26 m. Find possible whole number values for l and w.
  (c) Write an expression for the area of the surface of the pool, in terms of l and w.
  (d) Find the area of the surface when:
   (i) $l = 11$ and $w = 2$ **(ii)** $l = 9$ and $w = 4$ **(iii)** $l = 7$ and $w = 6$.

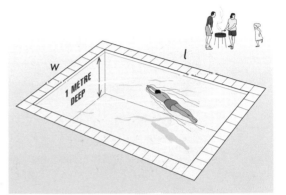

8 Sue and her friends are not allowed in the pool while eating.
  (a) What is the depth of the pool? (Look at the picture.)
  (b) Write down an expression for the volume of the pool.
  (c) What is the volume of the pool when
   (i) $l = 10$ and $w = 3$ **(ii)** $l = 8$ and $w = 5$?

> *Volume is length × width × depth*

Activity   Nina and Ali are playing a game of Algebra Snap.
They both have a set of cards with expressions on them.
They take turns in laying down cards.
They can say 'Snap!' when the expressions on the cards mean the same.

1 Here is Nina's first card: $4 + 4a$ Here is Ali's first card: $4(a + 1)$

  (a) Nina calls SNAP! Is she right?

  (b) Is this card the same as Nina's? $2(2 + a)$

2 Nina lays another card: $12a + 24$ Ali lays another card: $30 - 60a$

  (a) Ali calls SNAP! Is he right?
  (b) Make three other cards that SNAP with Nina's card.

7 Construction

Constructing triangles

Bernie and Flo want to make rabbit hutches in Design and Technology.
They must draw their plans. Here are their sketches.

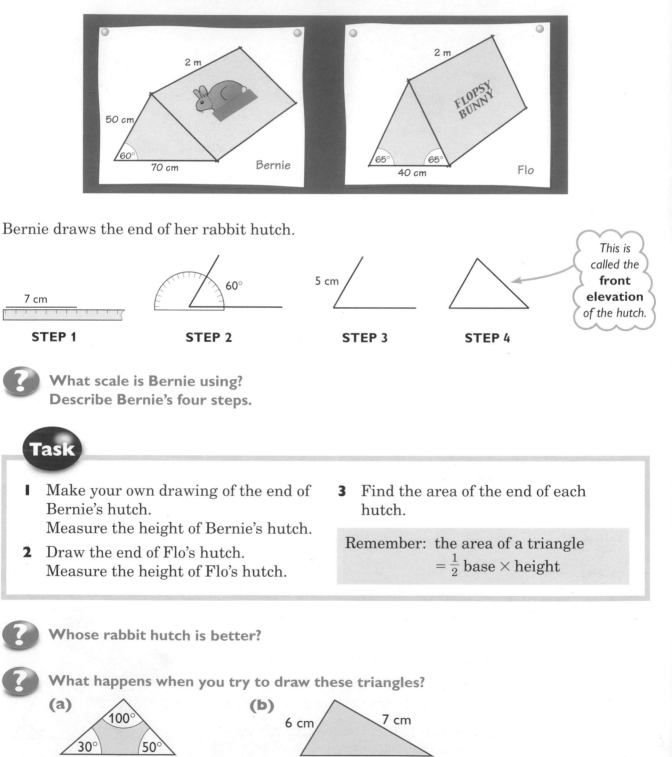

Bernie draws the end of her rabbit hutch.

STEP 1   7 cm

STEP 2   60°

STEP 3   5 cm

STEP 4

> This is called the **front elevation** of the hutch.

?   **What scale is Bernie using?**
Describe Bernie's four steps.

Task

1   Make your own drawing of the end of Bernie's hutch.
    Measure the height of Bernie's hutch.

2   Draw the end of Flo's hutch.
    Measure the height of Flo's hutch.

3   Find the area of the end of each hutch.

> Remember: the area of a triangle
> $= \frac{1}{2}$ base $\times$ height

?   **Whose rabbit hutch is better?**

?   **What happens when you try to draw these triangles?**

(a)   100°   30°   50°

(b)   6 cm   7 cm   8 cm

Exercise

In this exercise you are expected to use a ruler and a protractor.

1 For each triangle

    (i)   make an accurate drawing
    (ii) measure the third side
    (iii) measure the two other angles.

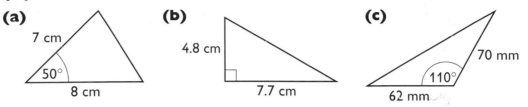

(a)   7 cm   50°   8 cm

(b)   4.8 cm   7.7 cm

(c)   70 mm   110°   62 mm

2 In triangle ABC, AB = 4.8 cm, BC = 6.6 cm and angle $B = 57°$.

    (a) Make an accurate drawing of the triangle.

    (b) Measure the length AC.

3 For each triangle

    (i)   make an accurate drawing
    (ii) measure the third angle
    (iii) measure the two other sides.

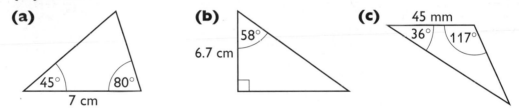

(a)   45°   80°   7 cm

(b)   58°   6.7 cm

(c)   45 mm   36°   117°

4 In triangle XYZ, angle $X = 38°$, angle $Y = 71°$ and XY = 7.3 cm.

    (a) Make an accurate drawing of the triangle.

    (b) Measure the lengths XZ and YZ.

5 Bradley makes this sail for his boat.

    (a) Make an accurate scale drawing of the sail.
          Use a scale of one centimetre to represent one metre.

    (b) By measuring find the length of the other edge.

    4.9 m   2.8 m

6 The diagram shows the cross-section of a roof.

    (a) Make a scale drawing of the roof.
          Use a scale of one centimetre to represent one metre.

    (b) By measuring find the lengths of the
          two sloping parts of the roof.

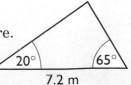

    20°   65°   7.2 m

More triangles

You will need a sheet of plain paper, a ruler, a pair of compasses and red, blue and green pens for this task.

Task

1 Your teacher marks a point P near the centre of the sheet of plain paper.

2 You have to estimate a distance of 6 cm from P. It can be in any direction.
Make a small cross and write your name (or initials) by it.
Pass the paper on to the next student.

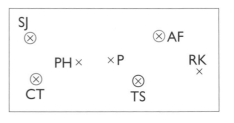

3 Next, measure how far your point is from P. Draw a small coloured circle round your point.

red if it is less than 6 cm from P
blue if it is exactly 6 cm from P
green if it is more than 6 cm from P.

4 How many blue circles are there?

5 How would you describe all the points which are 6 cm from P?

 What is the best way to draw all the points which are 6 cm from P?

Now you can construct a triangle given its three sides.

 How would you construct triangle ABC?

You can also construct an angle of 60°.

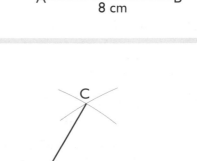

Do the right thing!

STEP 1 Draw a line AB. It can be any length. In the diagram it is 5 cm.

STEP 2 Open the compasses to the same length as AB.
Put the point on A and draw an arc.
Put the point on B and draw an arc.

STEP 3 Where the two arcs cross is C. Join C to A. Angle *A* is 60°.

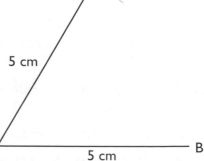

 Why is angle *A* equal to 60°?

Exercise

In this exercise you are expected to use a ruler and a pair of compasses.

1 For each triangle
   (i) make an accurate drawing
   (ii) measure the angles.

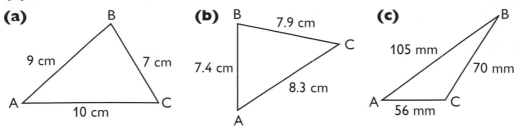

(a) **(b)** **(c)**

2 Construct these isosceles triangles.
   Measure the angles in each triangle. What do you notice?
   (a) Triangle ABC with AB = 7 cm, AC = 7 cm and BC = 5 cm.
   (b) Triangle DEF with DE = 43 mm, DF = 43 mm and EF = 52 mm.

3 Waterford village green is a triangle ABC.
   AB is 60 m, BC is 50 m and AC is 45 m.

   (a) Make a scale drawing of the village green.

   Jo stands at C and throws a ball across the green.
   Jo can throw a ball 35 m at best.

   (b) Show the area which the ball may reach.

4 Avebury is 8 km west of Barby.
   Connor is 6 km from Avebury and 10 km from Barby.

   (a) Make a scale drawing showing Connor's two possible positions.

   (b) For each of Connor's positions write down the direction of Avebury.

Activity   Set the compass ends 5 cm apart throughout this Activity.

1 Mark O near the centre of your page and
   construct equilateral triangle OAB of side 5 cm.

2 Using OB as a side construct a new equilateral
   triangle OBC. What shape is OABC?

3 Using OC as a side construct a new equilateral
   triangle OCD. The diagram on the right shows
   the start of the step. What shape is ABCD?

4 Continue constructing equilateral triangles around O.
   Label these ODE, OEF and the last one will be OFA.

5 Describe carefully the shape ABCDEF.

6 Explain how you could add more equilateral triangles to produce
   (a) a rhombus   **(b)** an equilateral triangle   **(c)** a trapezium   **(d)** another hexagon.

Constructing 90° and bisecting a line

A dog is tied up at A.
Another dog is tied at B.

A cat wants to run across between them.
The cat's safest path is always the
same distance from A as from B.

Copy the diagram onto a piece of paper.

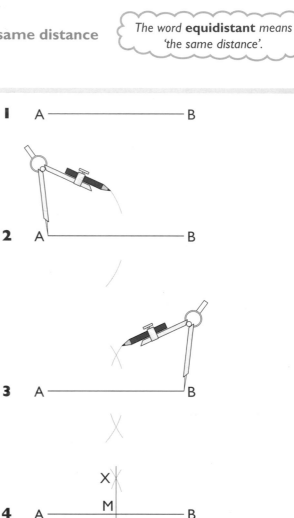

cat

A   B

dog   dog

 Find one point on the path.
Find two more points on the path.

 Describe the set of points which are the same distance
from A and B.

> The word **equidistant** *means*
> *'the same distance'.*

❝ Do the right thing!

Follow these steps to bisect a line.

STEP 1   Draw a line AB near the
centre of a sheet of paper.

STEP 2   Open your compasses.
Put the point on A.
Draw arcs above and below
the line.

STEP 3   Do not adjust the
compasses.
Put the point on B.
Draw two more arcs.
They cut the first two.

STEP 4   The arcs meet at X and Y.
Draw the line XY.
It meets AB at M.
M is the midpoint of AB.

1   A ———————— B

2   A ———————— B

3   A ———————— B

4   A ——— M ——— B
     X
     Y

 Measure the angles **AMX** and **BMX**. What do you find?
XY is called the **perpendicular bisector** of **AB**. Explain this name.

You can construct an angle of 90° in this way.

Exercise

1 **(a)** Draw a straight line PQ of length 10 cm.

(b) Construct the perpendicular bisector of PQ.

Point M is the midpoint of PQ.

(c) Use a protractor to check that the angles at M are right angles.

2 A and B are the positions of two harbour lights. A boat enters harbour so that it is always the same distance from each light.

(a) Draw two crosses to represent the lights.

(b) Construct a line to represent the boat's path.

(c) What is the name of this line?

3 Two teams are having a snowball fight.

They each have a base. These are marked X and Y.

(a) Copy the diagram.

The line halfway from X and Y gives each team's territory.

(b) Construct this line.

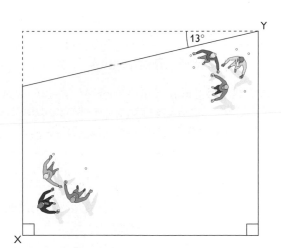

Investigation

1 Draw any triangle.

2 Construct the perpendicular bisectors of each side of your triangle. What do you notice about these three lines?

3 Repeat Parts 1 and 2 with a different triangle.

4 Compare your diagrams with other members of your class.

5 What can you say about the perpendicular bisectors of each side of a triangle?

Activity Use LOGO to construct a path with 90° turns.
The path starts and finishes at the same place.

What is the smallest number of legs that your path can have?

Bisecting an angle

Look at this plan of a new street.

The rectangles are building plots for houses.

The extra land between plots 91 and 93 is shared equally between the two houses.

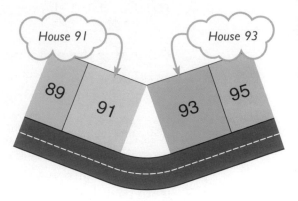

 Where does the dividing wall go between the two plots of land?

 How do you draw it on the plan?

You need to **bisect** the angle between the two plots.
Use a pair of compasses to do this accurately.

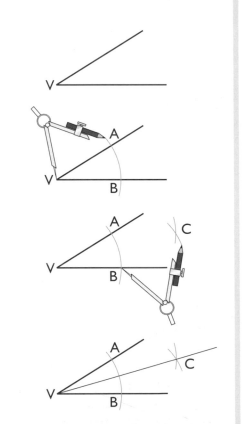

" Do the right thing!

You will need a pencil, a pair of compasses and a ruler.

STEP 1 Draw an angle on the left side of a piece of paper.

STEP 2 Put the point of the compasses on V.
Draw an arc cutting both lines.

STEP 3 Put the point of the compasses at A.
Draw an arc.

Do not adjust the compasses.
Put the point of the compasses at B.
Draw an arc.

These two arcs meet at C.

STEP 4 Join V to C.
VC is the **angle bisector**.

Measure the angles to check that the line VC divides angle at V into two equal parts.

 **Now set the ends of the compasses further apart.
Repeat STEPS 3 and 4.
What do you find?**

 Do the arcs in STEP 3 have to be the same radius as in STEP 2?

Exercise

1 **(a)** Use a protractor to draw and label the angles below.

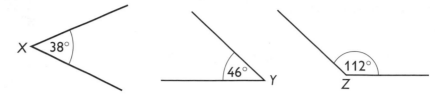

X 38°

46° Y

112° Z

(b) Follow the steps on the opposite page to bisect each of the angles.

(c) Check the accuracy of your constructions with a protractor.

2 **(a)** Draw this right-angled triangle accurately.

(b) Construct the bisector of the angle at C.

(c) The bisector cuts AB at D. Label D.
Measure AD and DB.

(d) Is D the midpoint of AB?

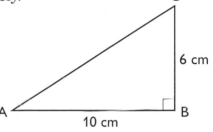

C

6 cm

A

10 cm

B

Investigation

1 Draw any triangle.

2 Construct the bisectors of each of the angles of your triangle.

3 What do you notice about the three bisectors?

4 Do this again with a different triangle.

5 Compare your diagrams with other members of your class.

6 What can you say about the bisectors of the angles of a triangle?

Activity

Construct a compass rose.

Before the 20th century navigators used a compass rose to describe direction.

Use a pair of compasses and a ruler to construct one like this.

Use a whole page.

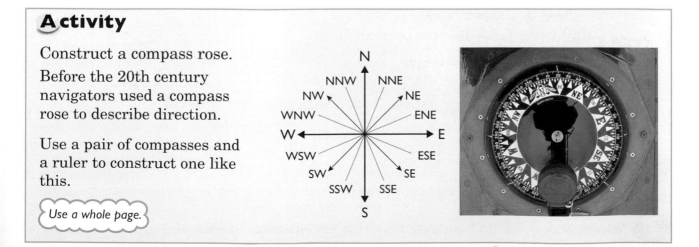

Constructing nets

Naveen is drawing a rectangle.

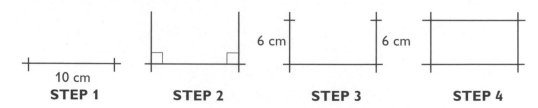

STEP 1   **STEP 2**   **STEP 3**   **STEP 4**

 Describe the four steps.
What instruments does she use?

Now you are going to draw the nets for a cuboid and a pyramid.
These contain rectangles and triangles.

Task

You are making a model of a clock tower.
You need a cuboid and a pyramid.

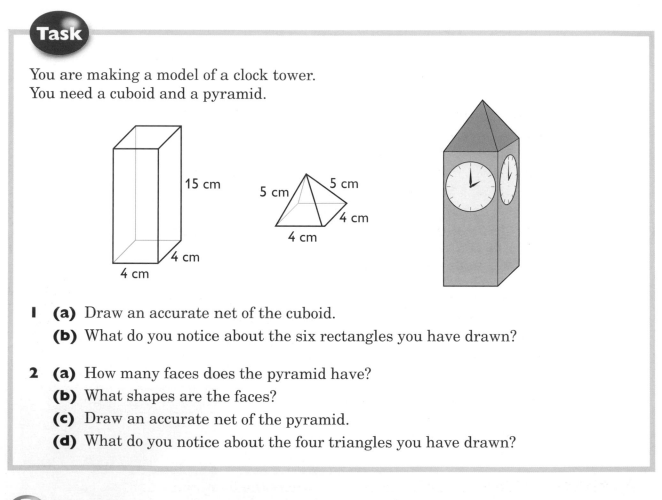

1 **(a)** Draw an accurate net of the cuboid.

   (b) What do you notice about the six rectangles you have drawn?

2 **(a)** How many faces does the pyramid have?

   (b) What shapes are the faces?

   (c) Draw an accurate net of the pyramid.

   (d) What do you notice about the four triangles you have drawn?

 You also have to make a clock face for your model.
What is the greatest radius that your clock face can have?

 How can you mark 12 o'clock, 1 o'clock, 2 o'clock, etc. without using a protractor?

Exercise

1 A cuboid has length 6 cm, width 4 cm and height 3 cm.
  (a) Draw an accurate net of this cuboid.
  (b) Work out the surface area of the cuboid.

2 A pyramid has a rectangular base 7 cm by 4 cm.
  The slant edges are 6 cm.
  (a) Draw an accurate net of this pyramid.
  (b) Does your net fit on a piece of paper 20 cm
     by 15 cm? Explain your answer.

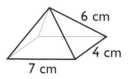

3 Amy and Jordan are making hats for a fancy dress party.
  Here are their designs.

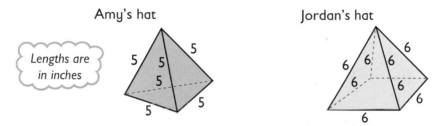

  Amy's hat   Jordan's hat

  Lengths are in inches

  Neither design has a base (otherwise the head doesn't fit in!)
  (a) Draw a net for Amy's hat.
     Use a scale of 1 cm to represent 1 inch.
  (b) Does this net tessellate? Explain your answer.
  (c) Draw a net for Jordan's hat.
     Use a scale of 1 cm to represent 1 inch.
  (d) Does the net of the real hat fit on a sheet of cardboard
     11 inches by 10 inches?
     Explain your answer.

4 **(a)** How many rectangular faces does this prism have?
  (b) How many triangular faces does it have?
  (c) Construct an accurate net of this prism.
  (d) Explain why the two triangles
     are congruent.
  (e) The cross-section of the prism
     is a triangle.
     What type of triangle is it?

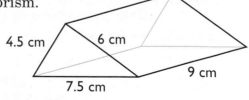

Activity Make a square based pyramid where the four triangular faces are
equilateral of side 5 cm. Your friend makes another pyramid like this.
Now carefully stick the bases of your pyramids together.
How many faces does the new solid have?
What can you say about each of these faces?

Finishing off

Review exercise

1 For each triangle

(i) make an accurate drawing.

(ii) measure the other sides and angles.

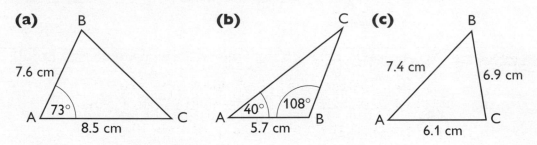

(a) B   **(b)**   C   **(c)**   B

7.6 cm   40°   108°   7.4 cm   6.9 cm

A   73°   A   5.7 cm   B   A   C

8.5 cm   C   6.1 cm

2 Jake is finding the height of a tree. He stands 32 m away. From this position the **angle of elevation** of the top of the tree is 28°.

Make a scale drawing to find the height of the tree to the nearest metre.

Use a scale of 1 cm to represent 4 m.

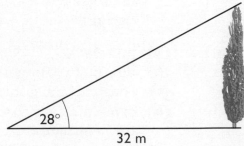

28°   32 m

3 Mark two points, A and B, which are 6 cm apart.

(a) Mark all points which are 5 cm from A. What shape do you get?

(b) Mark all points which are 5 cm from B. What shape do you get?

(c) How many points are both 5 cm from A and 5 cm from B?

4 Look at this diagram.

Jack is being chased by wild animals. He has to swim across the river to reach safety.

He sees two man-eating crocodiles at A and B.

(a) Copy the diagram.

(b) Construct the line showing the safest path across the river.

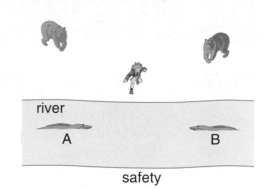

5 **(a)** Draw a straight line. Mark a point A on it. The angle at A is 180°.

(b) Construct an angle of 90° by bisecting the angle at A.

(c) Check the accuracy of your construction with a protractor.

6 Draw accurate diagrams of these nets.

(a) A cuboid with length 77 mm, width 52 mm and height 38 mm.

(b) A square based pyramid with a square base of edge 4 cm and slant edges of length 6 cm.

(c) A prism 8.3 cm long whose cross-section is an equilateral triangle of side 6.2 cm.

Activity Look at this map of an island.

It gives instructions to find hidden treasure.
The island is drawn on a centimetre square grid.

The scale of the map is 1 cm represents 10 m.

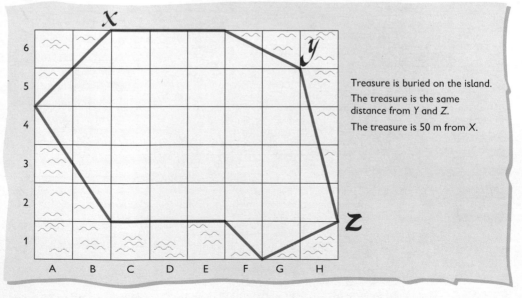

Treasure is buried on the island.

The treasure is the same distance from Y and Z.

The treasure is 50 m from X.

1 Make a copy of the map.

2 Use your construction skills to find the position of the treasure.

3 Which square contains the treasure?

4 How far is the treasure from Y?

8 Using graphs

One cat year is the same as 7 human years, Katie.

But Mum Tiger is 20.

The information that Katie's mother has given can be used to produce this conversion graph between cat years and human years.

 Look at this graph.
Does it agree with Katie's mother?

 According to this graph, what is Tiger's human age?

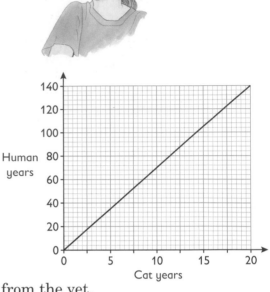

Human years (y-axis: 0, 20, 40, 60, 80, 100, 120, 140)
Cat years (x-axis: 0, 5, 10, 15, 20)

Katie does not believe her mother. She gets this graph from the vet.

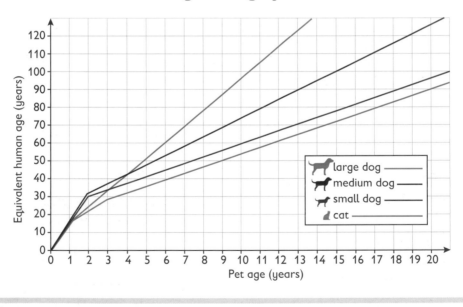

Equivalent human age (years) (y-axis: 0, 10, 20, 30, 40, 50, 60, 70, 80, 90, 100, 110, 120)
Pet age (years) (x-axis: 0 to 20)

large dog
medium dog
small dog
cat

Task

1 What is Tiger's age in human years?
2 Which is older, in human years, a 10-year-old large dog or a 19-year-old cat?
3 **(a)** Is it ever true that a dog's human age is 7 times its real age?
   (b) What about a cat?

 Look at the gradients of the lines on this graph.
What do they tell you?

Exercise

1 This graph shows the temperature throughout one day, starting at midnight.

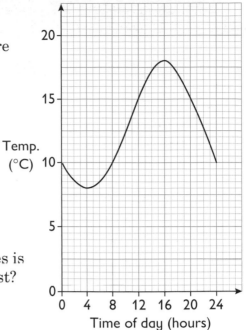

(a) What is the highest temperature?

(b) When is it hottest?

(c) What is the lowest temperature?

(d) When is it coldest?

(e) Roughly between which times is the temperature rising fastest?

2 The graph shows the height of a tree over its lifetime.

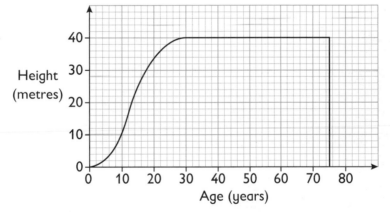

(a) When is the tree fully grown?   **(b)** What is the tree's greatest height?

(c) How long does it live?   **(d)** Roughly between which ages is it growing fastest?

3 This graph shows the volume of water in a bath. For each part of this story, state the times.

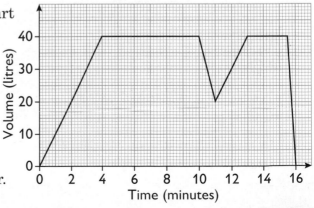

(a) The taps are turned on. The bath fills.

(b) Sergio is lying in the bath.

(c) Sergio lets out some of the water.

(d) He puts in more hot water.

(e) He has a final soak.

(f) He gets out and lets out all the water.

Travel graphs

Look at this graph showing the height of a hot air balloon.

It is called a **travel graph** or **distance–time graph**.

 How high does the balloon go?
What is shown by the line BC and DE?

 For how long is the balloon at a height of 300 m?
How long does the balloon take to land?
When is the balloon at a height of 500 m?

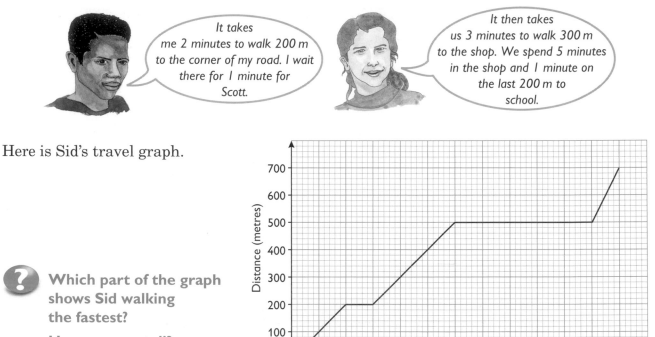

Sid draws a travel graph of his journey to school.

It takes me 2 minutes to walk 200 m to the corner of my road. I wait there for 1 minute for Scott.

It then takes us 3 minutes to walk 300 m to the shop. We spend 5 minutes in the shop and 1 minute on the last 200 m to school.

Here is Sid's travel graph.

 Which part of the graph shows Sid walking the fastest?

How can you tell?

 Task

1 Describe your journey to school.
2 Draw a travel graph of your journey.
3 Make a poster of your graph and describe it.
4 Make up two questions for a friend to answer about your travel graph.

Exercise

1. Kylie leaves home at 10.00 am
to cycle to Avonford town centre.
Here is a travel graph of
her journey.

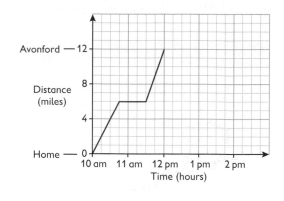

(a) How far away is Avonford
town centre from Kylie's home?

(b) How long does Kylie take
to get to Avonford town centre?

On the way Kylie gets a puncture.

(c) How long does it take for Kylie to mend her puncture?

Kylie spends 1 hour in town. It takes her 30 minutes to cycle home.

(d) Copy the travel graph and complete it.
Show Kylie's stay in town and her journey home.

2. Neil cycles to June's house.
At the same time, June leaves her house and runs to Neil's house.
They do not see each other.
Here is a travel graph of their journeys.

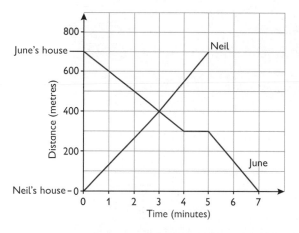

(a) When do the two friends pass each other?
(b) How far has Neil travelled when he passes June?
(c) How far has June travelled when she passes Neil?
(d) Who travels the faster? How can you tell?

3. The table shows Rachel's journey to work by car.

Time	8.00	8.10	8.20	8.25	8.30	8.40
Distance from home (miles)	0	6	10	10	14	20

(a) Draw a travel graph to show Rachel's journey.
(b) How far is Rachel from home at
   (i) 8.05   **(ii)** 8.15   **(iii)** 8.22?

Finishing off

Now that you have finished this chapter you should be able to:

- draw and interpret graphs representing real situations
- draw and interpret a travel (or distance–time) graph.

Review exercise

1. Water from a tap runs steadily into this 3 litre container.
It flows at 1 litre every 20 seconds.
Draw a graph to show the volume of water in the container against time.

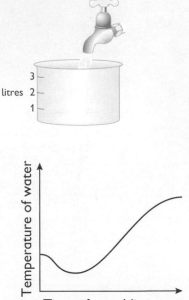

2. Topol cooks some frozen peas.
He records the temperature of the water after adding the peas.
He displays his data on a graph.

   Explain the shape of Topol's graph.

3. Abdul hires a canoe at a boating pond.

   Boat hire charges

Type of boat	Fixed charge	Rate per hour
Canoe	£4	£2
Motor boat	£2	£6
Rowing boat	£1	£3

   Part hours allowed
   You only pay for the time you use
   Maximum time 4 hours

   (a) Draw a graph of cost against time (up to 4 hours) for a canoe.
   (b) On the same graph add in lines for a motor boat and a rowing boat.
   (c) Which is more expensive, a canoe or a rowing boat?

4 This is a conversion graph between stones and kilograms.

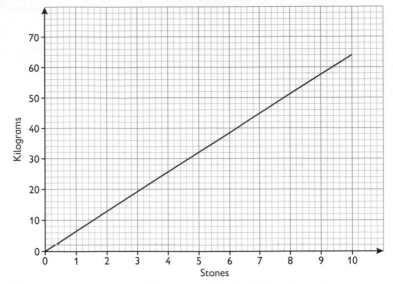

(a) A child weighs 5 stones. What is this in kilograms?
(b) Mary weighs 64 kilograms. What is her weight in stones?
(c) How many kilograms are there in 1 stone?

5 Becky cycles from Bridgetown to Avonford and then back again.
Here is a travel graph showing her journey.

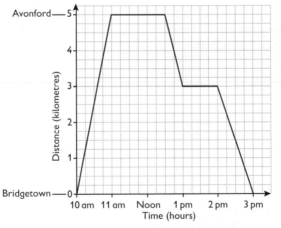

(a) When does Becky leave Bridgetown?
(b) How long does she spend in Avonford?

On the way back Becky sees a friend. She stops to talk.

(c) How far is Becky from Bridgetown when she stops?
(d) How long does she stop for?

Dorje is a long distance runner. He runs from Bridgetown to Avonford.
He leaves at 1 pm and arrives at 1.30 pm.

(e) How far does he run?
(f) Copy Becky's graph on to graph paper.
Add a line to your graph representing Dorje's journey.
(g) At what time does Dorje pass Becky?
What is Becky doing at that time?
(h) How far is Dorje from Avonford when he passes Becky?

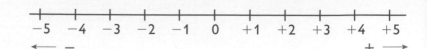 Negative numbers

Negative and positive numbers can be shown on a number line.

$$-5 \quad -4 \quad -3 \quad -2 \quad -1 \quad 0 \quad +1 \quad +2 \quad +3 \quad +4 \quad +5$$

$\longleftarrow\ -$ $+\ \longrightarrow$

? **Put these numbers in order of size, starting with the smallest.**
$$2, -1, -5, 4, -1.5, 1$$
What numbers are between −2 and +1?
Find the number that is halfway between −2 and +4.

Adding and subtracting negative numbers

Jane and John are playing Ladder of Fortune. The counter starts at 0 on the number line.

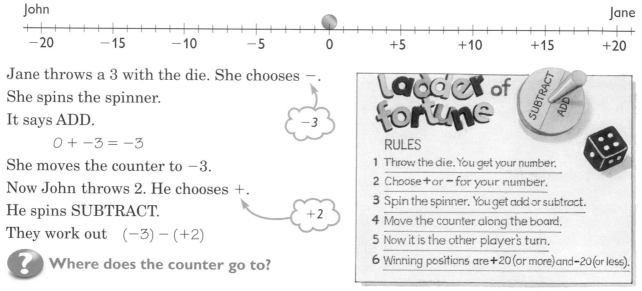

John   Jane

$$-20 \qquad -15 \qquad -10 \qquad -5 \qquad 0 \qquad +5 \qquad +10 \qquad +15 \qquad +20$$

Jane throws a 3 with the die. She chooses −.
She spins the spinner.
It says ADD.
$$0 + -3 = -3$$
She moves the counter to −3.
Now John throws 2. He chooses +.
He spins SUBTRACT.
They work out $(-3) - (+2)$

−3

+2

RULES
1 Throw the die. You get your number.
2 Choose + or − for your number.
3 Spin the spinner. You get add or subtract.
4 Move the counter along the board.
5 Now it is the other player's turn.
6 Winning positions are +20 (or more) and −20 (or less).

? **Where does the counter go to?**

On Jane's next turn, she throws 4. She chooses +. The spinner says SUBTRACT.

? **Write down the sum Jane must work out. Where is the counter moved to on the 3rd go?**

If the counter reaches −20, John wins. At +20, Jane wins.
The counter is on +18. It is Jane's turn. She throws 2.

? **What are the two ways that Jane can win?**

Task

Play the Ladder of Fortune game with a partner. You can use a coin for a spinner.
Heads is Add, Tails is Subtract.

? **When do you move the counter in the positive direction?**
When do you move it in the negative direction?

? **Do these calculations without a number line.**
$$(-4) + (-3), \quad (+5) + (-7), \quad (-4) - (-8), \quad (+0.6) + (-0.2), \quad (-0.4) - (-0.1)$$

Exercise

1 Write the following in order, starting with the smallest.

$$-2, -1.25, -1.5, -2.1, -1, -2.3$$

2 Write down a number that lies between:

(a) -1 and $+4$ **(b)** -2 and $+1$ **(c)** -5 and -4 **(d)** -2 and -3

3 Find the number that is exactly halfway between:

(a) -3 and $+1$ **(b)** -2 and $+4$ **(c)** -2 and -1 **(d)** -1 and 0

4 Work out the following.

(a) $(-7) + (-10)$ **(b)** $(+8) - (-3)$ **(c)** $(-4) + (-9)$

(d) $(+10) - (-15)$ **(e)** $(+100) + (-20)$ **(f)** $(-70) - (-30)$

(g) $(+0.5) + (-0.5)$ **(h)** $(+1.5) - (-0.5)$

5 The following problems can be worked out as an addition.
For each problem, write down the addition and then solve it.

Example: The temperature is $-5°C$. What will it be after a rise of $8°C$?
This can be solved by working out $(-5) + (+8) = +3$.

(a) I have £25 in my savings bank. I pay a bill for £34.
How much money do I have?

(b) A lift starts in the basement (-1) and goes up 4 floors.
What floor is it on?

(c) A seagull dives 20 ft from a height of 15 ft above the water.
How far below the surface does it dive?

(d) The temperature inside my house is $10°C$ more than outside.
The outside temperature is $-4°C$. What is the inside temperature?

Activity

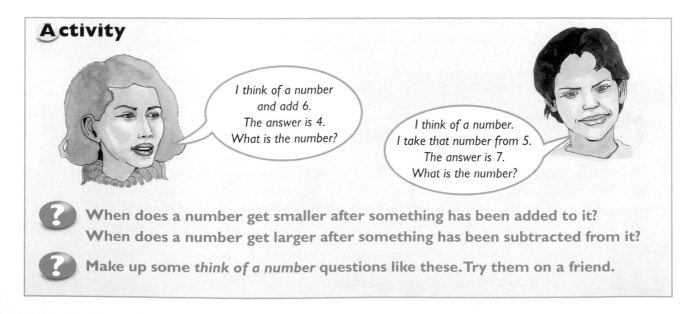

I think of a number
and add 6.
The answer is 4.
What is the number?

I think of a number.
I take that number from 5.
The answer is 7.
What is the number?

? When does a number get smaller after something has been added to it?

When does a number get larger after something has been subtracted from it?

? Make up some *think of a number* questions like these. Try them on a friend.

Multiplying and dividing negative numbers

? Work out $(-2) + (-2) + (-2) + (-2)$.
Why does this give the same answer as $(-2) \times 4$?

? Work out $(-3) \times 5$ and $5 \times (-3)$.

Task

Jason is drawing a graph of $y = 3x$.
He has worked out the following table of values and plotted them on a graph.

x	1	2	3
$y = 3x$	3	6	9

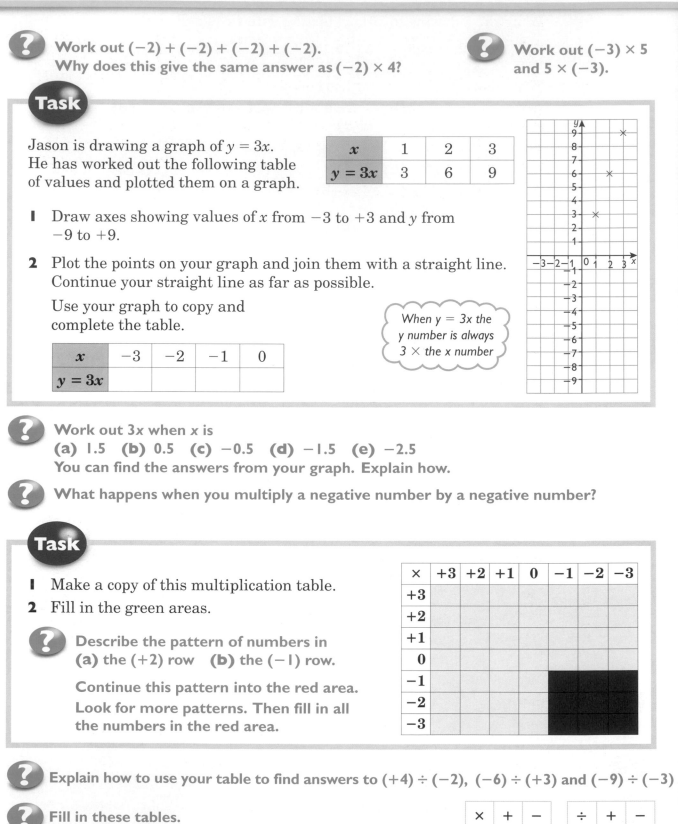

1 Draw axes showing values of x from -3 to $+3$ and y from -9 to $+9$.

2 Plot the points on your graph and join them with a straight line. Continue your straight line as far as possible.

Use your graph to copy and complete the table.

When $y = 3x$ the y number is always $3 \times$ the x number

x	-3	-2	-1	0
$y = 3x$				

? Work out $3x$ when x is
(a) 1.5 **(b)** 0.5 **(c)** -0.5 **(d)** -1.5 **(e)** -2.5
You can find the answers from your graph. Explain how.

? What happens when you multiply a negative number by a negative number?

Task

1 Make a copy of this multiplication table.
2 Fill in the green areas.

? Describe the pattern of numbers in
(a) the $(+2)$ row **(b)** the (-1) row.

Continue this pattern into the red area.
Look for more patterns. Then fill in all the numbers in the red area.

×	+3	+2	+1	0	−1	−2	−3
+3							
+2							
+1							
0							
−1							
−2							
−3							

? Explain how to use your table to find answers to $(+4) \div (-2)$, $(-6) \div (+3)$ and $(-9) \div (-3)$

? Fill in these tables.
They help you work out when an answer is negative or positive when you multiply or divide directed numbers.

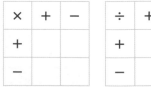

×	+	−
+		
−		

÷	+	−
+		
−		

Exercise

1. Evaluate:
   (a) $4 \times (-5)$
   (b) $(-10) \times (+3)$
   (c) $(-14) \times (-2)$
   (d) $(-5) \times (-5)$
   (e) $(+20) \times (-40)$
   (f) $(-50) \times (-30)$
   (g) $(-0.4) \times (+7)$
   (h) $(-3) \times (-0.3)$
   (i) $(-0.2) \times (+0.1)$

2. Work out the following:
   (a) $(+6) \div (-2)$
   (b) $(-15) \div (+3)$
   (c) $(-12) \div (-4)$
   (d) $(-16) \div (-2)$
   (e) $(+40) \div (-20)$
   (f) $(-120) \div (-30)$
   (g) $(+0.6) \div (-2)$
   (h) $(-18) \div (+0.6)$
   (i) $(-0.6) \div (-0.2)$

3. Copy and complete the following multiplication table.

$\times$			6		12
5					
4	-16				
-2					
-3		9			
-10				70	

4. Complete the following table of values for $y = 4x$.

x	-3	-2	-1	0	1	2	3
$y = 4x$							

   Use the table to draw the graph of $y = 4x$.

5. George multiplies two numbers together. He gets the answer -18. What other whole numbers can he use? Find three more pairs.

$18 \times (-1) = -18$

6. George multiplies two more numbers together. He gets 24. What whole numbers can he use? Find all the different pairs.

Investigation $(-4)^2 = (-4) \times (-4) = +16$

Work out (a) $(-2)^2$ (b) $(-6)^2$ (c) $(-10)^2$

? **What can you say about the square of a negative number?**

? **Write down the square roots of the following numbers. Each of them has two answers.**
   36 49 81 144 256

Finishing off

Now that you have finished this chapter you should be able to:

- place negative and positive numbers in order
- add, subtract, multiply and divide negative and positive numbers
- solve problems using negative and positive numbers.

Review exercise

1   Write the following in order, smallest first.

$$-2, -3, -1.5, -1.4, 1, -2.3$$

2   Write down three numbers between -7 and 2.

3   **(a)** Find the number that is exactly halfway between:

     (i) -1 and -2 **(ii)** -4 and -10 **(iii)** -7 and 3

     (iv) -12 and 5   **(v)** -3.5 and -4.5 **(vi)** -6.3 and -6.4

     The formula $\frac{A+B}{2}$ gives the number that is exactly halfway between A and B.

    (b) Copy and complete the following table.
Compare your answers with question 3(a).

A	B	$A+B$	$\frac{A+B}{2}$
-1	-2		
-4	-10		
-7	3		
-12	5		
-3.5	-4.5		
-6.3	-6.4		

4   Work out:

    (a) $(+7) + (-3)$ **(b)** $(-2) + (-4)$ **(c)** $(-5) + (+6)$

    (d) $7 - 10$ **(e)** $(-2) - (+5)$ **(f)** $(+10) - (-12)$

    (g) $(+20) - (+30)$ **(h)** $(-2) + (-3) - (+4)$ **(i)** $(-1.6) + (-0.2)$

    (j) $(+4.9) - (-1.3)$ **(k)** $(-8) \times (+6)$ **(l)** $(-20) \times (-30)$

    (m) $18 \div (-3)$ **(n)** $(-27) \div (-9)$ **(o)** $(-200) \div (+10)$

5 Jane is doing an exam paper.
She gets 5 marks for each correct answer (C) and (-2) marks for each wrong answer (W).
She uses the formula $M = 5 \times C + (-2) \times W$

> *M is the final mark for the exam.*

(a) What do C and W stand for?
(b) Explain the formula.
(c) Copy and complete this table

	C	W	$5C$	$-2W$	$5C - 2W$
Jane	10	10			
Edward	12	8			
Jessica	9	11			
Davinda	5	15			

6 Work out the following problems.
Each question is a subtraction.

(a) A diver is 30 ft below the surface.
He dives a further 20 ft.
What depth is he below the surface?

> *This can be written as $(-30) - (+20)$.*

(b) John arrives at the bus stop
20 minutes early ($+20$).
The bus is 10 minutes late (-10).
How long does he wait?

(c) The temperature drops
from $+3°C$ to $-4°C$.
How many degrees does it drop?

depth (feet)

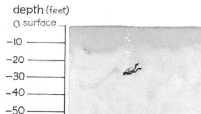

0 surface
−10
−20
−30
−40
−50

Activity

The manager of a bank opens his safe by turning
a numbered dial.
The number 0 is at the top.
The turns needed to open the safe are written as:

$(+2) + (-4) + (+6) + (-2) + (-3)$

> *Turn 2 to the left, then 4 to the right.*

Which number is at the top after the first
turn of the dial?

> *Work out $0 + (+2)$.*

......after the second turn?
Which number is at the top when the
manager opens the safe?

> *Work out $+2 + (-4)$.*

The code for a different safe is written:

$+2, -1, +5, +1, -3, -5$

These are the numbers that must appear at
the top after each turn.

> *What turn is needed to go from $+2$ to -1? ... from -1 to $+5$?*

Write this code in words.
Write down a sequence of numbers for your own code.
Ask a friend to crack your code by describing the turns needed.

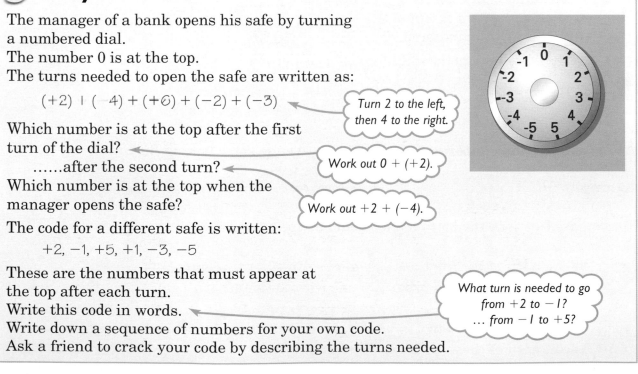

10 Fractions

Equivalent fractions

Here are Jane's last three maths marks.

Jane writes **15 out of 25** or $\frac{15}{25}$

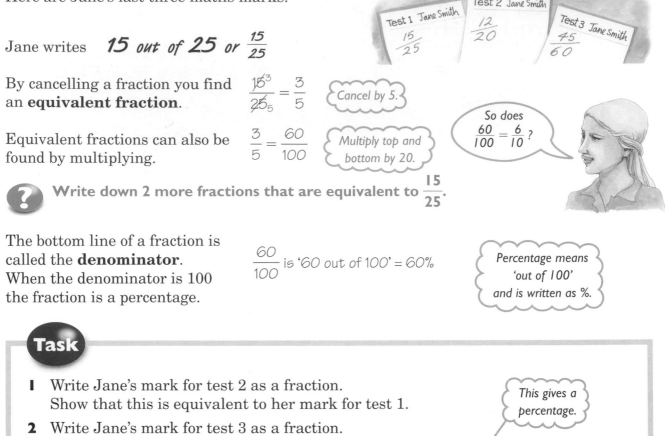

By cancelling a fraction you find an **equivalent fraction**.

$$\frac{\cancel{15}^3}{\cancel{25}_5} = \frac{3}{5}$$

Cancel by 5.

Equivalent fractions can also be found by multiplying.

$$\frac{3}{5} = \frac{60}{100}$$

Multiply top and bottom by 20.

So does $\frac{60}{100} = \frac{6}{10}$?

? **Write down 2 more fractions that are equivalent to $\frac{15}{25}$.**

The bottom line of a fraction is called the **denominator**. When the denominator is 100 the fraction is a percentage.

$\frac{60}{100}$ is '60 out of 100' = 60%

Percentage means 'out of 100' and is written as %.

Task

1 Write Jane's mark for test 2 as a fraction.
   Show that this is equivalent to her mark for test 1.

2 Write Jane's mark for test 3 as a fraction.
   Find an equivalent fraction:
   (a) with a denominator of 20   **(b)** with a denominator of 100.

   This gives a percentage.

3 What was Jane's percentage for test 3. Is her maths getting better?

Common denominators

A **common denominator** is when fractions have the same bottom line.

Example $\frac{6}{10}, \frac{4}{10}, \frac{8}{10}$ *The common denominator is 10.*

To compare fractions the bottom line should be the same.

? **Write each of the fractions $\frac{3}{4}, \frac{2}{5}$ and $\frac{5}{8}$ with a bottom line of 40.**
Write the fractions in order starting with the smallest.

? **Compare the fractions $\frac{1}{2}, \frac{3}{5}$ and $\frac{7}{10}$. Find a common denominator.**
Write each of these fractions as percentages.

Exercise

1 Which of these fractions are equivalent to $\frac{4}{5}$?

(a) $\frac{8}{10}$ **(b)** $\frac{5}{6}$ **(c)** $\frac{12}{15}$ **(d)** $\frac{8}{9}$ **(e)** $\frac{40}{50}$ **(f)** $\frac{80}{100}$

(g) $\frac{16}{25}$ **(h)** $\frac{44}{55}$ **(i)** $\frac{14}{15}$ **(j)** $\frac{34}{35}$ **(k)** $\frac{404}{505}$ **(l)** $\frac{5}{4}$

2 Which of these fractions are equivalent to $\frac{9}{12}$?

(a) $\frac{18}{24}$ **(b)** $\frac{6}{9}$ **(c)** $\frac{12}{15}$ **(d)** $\frac{12}{16}$ **(e)** $\frac{15}{20}$ **(f)** $\frac{30}{40}$

3 Choose pairs of equivalent fractions from the list below.

(a) $\frac{3}{4}$ **(b)** $\frac{4}{7}$ **(c)** $\frac{3}{8}$ **(d)** $\frac{6}{10}$ **(e)** $\frac{3}{9}$ **(f)** $\frac{2}{8}$

(g) $\frac{3}{5}$ **(h)** $\frac{6}{16}$ **(i)** $\frac{3}{12}$ **(j)** $\frac{9}{12}$ **(k)** $\frac{8}{14}$ **(l)** $\frac{4}{12}$

4 **(a)** Find a common denominator for the following fractions.

$$\frac{1}{2}, \frac{2}{3}, \frac{7}{12}, \frac{3}{4}, \frac{11}{24}$$

(b) Write the fractions in order starting with the smallest.

5 Write the following fractions as percentages. Place them in order starting with the largest.

$$\frac{1}{2}, \frac{2}{5}, \frac{3}{10}, \frac{7}{20}, \frac{8}{25}$$

6 What is Jane's best test mark from the previous page?
Her next test is out of 50. She wants to get a higher score.
How many marks must she get?

7

Write this as:
(a) a fraction
(b) a percentage.
Jane's granny has 30 cats. How many prefer Kati-kins?

Activity   Collect newspaper headlines and
advertisements similar to the
advertisement in Question 7.
Display these on a poster.
Use equivalent fractions and
percentages to explain each statement.

Adding fractions

Victor's mother has two partly used jars of coffee.

She puts all of the coffee into one jar.

Victor works this out for his mother. He changes both fractions into $\frac{1}{12}$ ths.

$\frac{2}{3} + \frac{1}{4} = \frac{8}{12} + \frac{3}{12} = \frac{11}{12}$

*The answer can be found by adding the top numbers (**numerators**).*

$\frac{1}{4} = \frac{3}{12}$

Multiply top and bottom by 3.

It is now easy to see that the jar is $\frac{11}{12}$ ths full.

$\frac{2}{3} = \frac{8}{12}$

Multiply top and bottom by 4.

? 8, 16 and 32 are all common denominators for $\frac{1}{4}$ and $\frac{3}{8}$.

8 is called the **Lowest Common Denominator**.

It is the lowest common multiple (LCM) for 4 and 8

Why is it easier to work with the Lowest Common Denominator?

Change $\frac{1}{4}$ into $\frac{1}{8}$ ths. Work out $\frac{1}{4} + \frac{3}{8}$.

Task

1 Look at the following pairs of fractions.
   (a) Find the lowest common denominator for each pair.
   (b) Add up each pair.

   (i) $\frac{2}{5}$ and $\frac{1}{5}$ **(ii)** $\frac{3}{4}$ and $\frac{1}{8}$ **(iii)** $\frac{1}{3}$ and $\frac{1}{5}$ **(iv)** $\frac{1}{6}$ and $\frac{3}{8}$

2 Fill in the blank space in each of the following:
   (i) $\frac{1}{2} + \frac{1}{4} + \frac{1}{8} = \frac{?}{8}$ **(ii)** $\frac{1}{2} + ? = \frac{3}{4}$ **(iii)** $? + \frac{5}{7} = \frac{13}{14}$ **(iv)** $\frac{1}{6} + \frac{?}{8} = \frac{13}{?}$

Fractions are subtracted in the same way.

Example $\frac{2}{5} - \frac{1}{4} = \frac{8}{20} - \frac{5}{20} = \frac{3}{20}$

Subtract the top numbers this time.

20 is the common denominator.

? **What happens when you add $\frac{3}{20}$ and $\frac{1}{4}$? How does this check your answer?**

? **Work out (a) $\frac{3}{5} - \frac{3}{10}$ (b) $\frac{2}{3} - \frac{1}{7}$. How can you check your answers?**

To work out $1 - \frac{5}{8}$, write 1 as $\frac{8}{8}$.

? **What is $\frac{8}{8} - \frac{5}{8}$? How can you check your answer?**

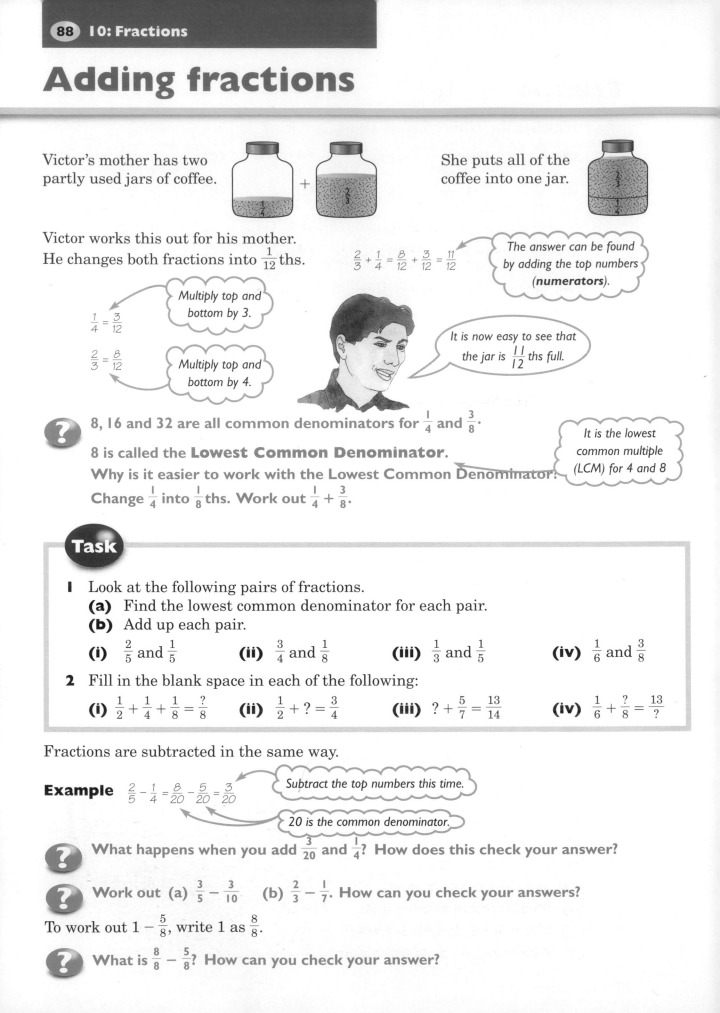

Exercise

1 Work out the following:

(a) $\frac{1}{7} + \frac{2}{7}$ (b) $\frac{1}{4} + \frac{3}{4}$ (c) $\frac{4}{5} - \frac{3}{5}$ (d) $\frac{5}{8} - \frac{3}{8}$

2 The multiples of both 2 and 3 are 6, 12, 18, ...
The lowest of these is 6.

(a) Write down the first three numbers that are multiples of both
   (i)   4 and 5   (ii) 3 and 6   (iii) 4 and 6
   (iv) 5 and 7   (v) 9 and 6.

(b) In each case, (i)–(v), write down the lowest of these numbers.

3 Use the answers to question 2 to help you to work out the following:

(a) $\frac{3}{4} + \frac{1}{5}$ (b) $\frac{5}{6} - \frac{1}{3}$ (c) $\frac{3}{4} + \frac{1}{6}$ (d) $\frac{2}{5} + \frac{3}{7}$ (e) $\frac{7}{9} - \frac{1}{6}$

4 Calculate the following:

(a) $\frac{5}{12} + \frac{7}{12}$ (b) $\frac{3}{7} - \frac{2}{7}$ (c) $\frac{10}{19} - \frac{3}{19}$ (d) $\frac{2}{5} - \frac{1}{10}$

(e) $\frac{2}{5} + \frac{3}{10}$ (f) $\frac{3}{4} - \frac{5}{12}$ (g) $1 - \frac{2}{5}$ (h) $\frac{1}{3} + \frac{1}{4} + \frac{1}{5}$

5 $\frac{1}{8}$th of an iceberg is showing above the water.
What fraction is below the water?

6 Matt paints his bathroom and hall blue.
The bathroom takes $\frac{1}{3}$ of a tin, the hall $\frac{1}{5}$ of a tin.
What fraction of the tin is left?

7 Can all the shampoo be put
into one bottle?

8 Anna has a bar of chocolate.
She eats $\frac{1}{4}$, gives $\frac{1}{5}$ to a friend and $\frac{1}{6}$ to her sister.
What fraction of the chocolate bar is left?

9 Darren, Paul and Bill are standing
for team captain. $\frac{3}{10}$ of the votes are
for Darren.
Paul gets $\frac{3}{8}$ of the votes.
Bill gets the rest of the votes.

(a) What fraction vote for Bill?

(b) Which is the largest fraction?

(c) Who is chosen as team captain?

Finishing off

Now that you have finished this chapter you should be able to:

- find equivalent fractions
- write fractions as percentages
- use equivalent fractions or percentages to compare the size of fractions
- add and subtract fractions.

Review exercise

1 Which of these fractions are equivalent?

$$\frac{3}{4} \qquad \frac{5}{6} \qquad \frac{3}{7} \qquad \frac{6}{8} \qquad \frac{4}{5} \qquad \frac{10}{12}$$

$$\frac{9}{21} \qquad \frac{40}{50} \qquad \frac{1}{3} \qquad \frac{2}{4} \qquad \frac{15}{18}$$

$$\frac{4}{12} \qquad \frac{5}{10} \qquad \frac{50}{60} \qquad \frac{25}{50} \qquad \frac{13}{39} \qquad \frac{16}{20}$$

2 **(i)** Find a common denominator for each pair of fractions.
(ii) Write down each fraction with this denominator, largest first.

(a) $\frac{1}{4}$ and $\frac{3}{8}$ **(b)** $\frac{3}{5}$ and $\frac{4}{7}$ **(c)** $\frac{3}{4}$ and $\frac{5}{6}$ **(d)** $\frac{5}{9}$ and $\frac{2}{3}$

(e) $\frac{2}{5}$ and $\frac{4}{15}$ **(f)** $\frac{2}{3}$ and $\frac{4}{5}$ **(g)** $\frac{5}{12}$ and $\frac{7}{18}$ **(h)** $\frac{1}{6}$ and $\frac{2}{15}$

3 Work out the following:

(a) $\frac{3}{7} + \frac{4}{9}$ **(b)** $\frac{5}{6} - \frac{2}{3}$ **(c)** $\frac{1}{4} + \frac{1}{5} + \frac{1}{10}$ **(d)** $\frac{7}{9} - \frac{5}{18}$

(e) $\frac{1}{6} + \frac{1}{4}$ **(f)** $\frac{3}{8} + \frac{5}{12}$ **(g)** $\frac{2}{3} - \frac{2}{7}$ **(h)** $\frac{7}{12} - \frac{3}{8}$

(i) $\frac{1}{2} + \frac{1}{4} - \frac{5}{8}$ **(j)** $\frac{1}{4} - \frac{9}{16} + \frac{3}{8}$ **(k)** $\frac{1}{6} - \frac{1}{3} + \frac{1}{2}$ **(l)** $\frac{3}{10} - \frac{1}{2} + \frac{2}{5}$

4 Write the following fractions as percentages:

(a) $\frac{1}{2}$ **(b)** $\frac{3}{4}$ **(c)** $\frac{1}{10}$ **(d)** $\frac{3}{10}$ **(e)** $\frac{1}{20}$ **(f)** $\frac{7}{20}$

(g) $\frac{1}{5}$ **(h)** $\frac{2}{5}$ **(i)** $\frac{1}{25}$ **(j)** $\frac{9}{25}$ **(k)** $\frac{1}{50}$ **(l)** $\frac{3}{50}$

5 Here are Brian's end of term test results.

(a) Which is Brian's best mark?

(b) Which is his worst mark?

School Report

Pupil – Brian Jones

Test Results

French $\frac{15}{20}$

English $\frac{25}{50}$

Geography $\frac{44}{80}$

Maths $\frac{48}{60}$

6 The pie chart shows the colours in a box of sweets.

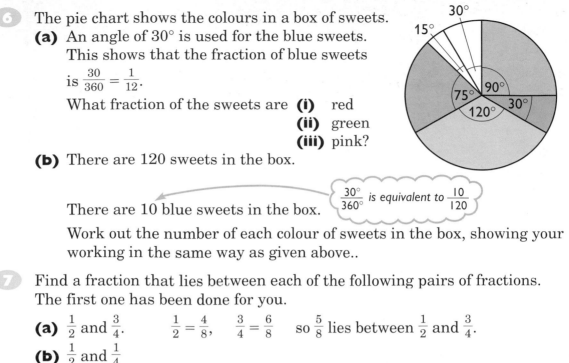

(a) An angle of 30° is used for the blue sweets.
This shows that the fraction of blue sweets
is $\frac{30}{360} = \frac{1}{12}$.
What fraction of the sweets are **(i)** red
(ii) green
(iii) pink?

(b) There are 120 sweets in the box.

$\frac{30°}{360°}$ is equivalent to $\frac{10}{120}$

There are 10 blue sweets in the box.

Work out the number of each colour of sweets in the box, showing your working in the same way as given above..

7 Find a fraction that lies between each of the following pairs of fractions.
The first one has been done for you.

(a) $\frac{1}{2}$ and $\frac{3}{4}$. $\frac{1}{2} = \frac{4}{8}$, $\frac{3}{4} = \frac{6}{8}$ so $\frac{5}{8}$ lies between $\frac{1}{2}$ and $\frac{3}{4}$.

(b) $\frac{1}{2}$ and $\frac{1}{4}$

(c) $\frac{1}{2}$ and $\frac{1}{3}$ (Hint: write each fraction as twelfths this time.)

(d) $\frac{1}{2}$ and $\frac{2}{3}$ **(e)** $\frac{1}{4}$ and $\frac{2}{5}$ **(f)** $\frac{3}{8}$ and $\frac{3}{4}$

8 Michela gets £5 pocket money.
This is how she spends it.

What fraction does she spend on:
(a) Sweets **(b)** Magazines **(c)** Make-up?

Any money left she saves.
(d) What fraction does she save?

Magazines	£1·50
Sweets	50p
Make-up	£2

9 Mr Brown starts his journey with $\frac{1}{2}$ a tank of petrol.
He uses $\frac{1}{3}$ of a tank.
How much petrol has he left?
What fraction must he put in his tank to fill it up?

Activity The table below shows the activities chosen by 75 children in year 8.
Copy and complete the table.

Activity	Number of children	As a fraction	As a percentage
Squash	9	$\frac{9}{75} = \frac{3}{25}$	12%
Computer games	18		
Tennis	15		
Orchestra	27		
Chess	6		
	Total 75	Total 1	Total 100%

Converting units

Lengths

The original units of length came from different parts of the human body.

A foot was the length of a fully grown man's foot.

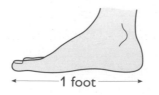

1 foot

Task

Put your thumb by the corner of your exercise book or your file.

Now move it across ...... and again ...... and again.
How many thumbs wide is your book or your file?

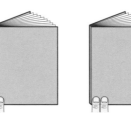

How many thumbs wide is the top of your table or desk?
Why is this more difficult to measure than your book?

Measure the distance from one leg of your table or desk to the next by putting your feet like this and counting.

How many feet across is your table or desk?

The Romans decided that 12 inches are 1 foot.

 Halley is 4 ft 11 inches tall. How many inches is this? How do you work it out?

 The distance from the end of a person's thumb to the knuckle is about an inch.
What is this distance on your thumb?
What is the average distance for your class?

1 metre is approximately 39 inches.

? How many feet are there in a metre? What about in a kilometre?

Exercise

1 The heights of a family are given in feet and inches. Write them in inches.

(a) Dad   6 ft   **(b)** Emily   3 ft   **(c)** Tom   4 ft 7 ins

(d) Mother   5 ft 5 ins   **(e)** James   1 ft 10 ins

2 How many feet are there in these measurements?

(a) The height of a room 120 ins.

(b) The height of a cliff 360 ins.

(c) The wing span of a Pteranodon 264 ins.

3 Edward I defined a yard as 3 feet.

(a) Change these measurements to yards:

   (i)   the length of a cricket pitch 66 ft

   (ii)   the length of a garden 120 ft.

(b) Change these lengths to feet:

   (i)   a Cetisaurus dinosaur 20 yards long

   (ii)   an Ichthyosaur (marine reptile)
      3 yds long.

4 **(a)** 1 metre is about 39 inches.
Is a metre longer than a yard? Explain.

(b) A mile is 1760 yards.
How many inches are there in 1 mile?
How many inches are there in 1500 metres?
Which race is longer, the 1500 metres or the mile?

5 A distance of 5 miles is about the same as 8 km.

(a) Convert to km:

   (i) Barnstaple to Bristol : 160 miles   **(ii)** Oxford to Hereford : 80 miles.

(b) Convert to miles:

   (i) Ledbury to Malvern : 16 km   **(ii)** Birmingham to London : 192 km.

6 Copy and complete the cross-number below.

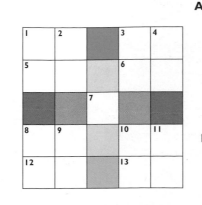

Across 1 Dad's height
     (see question 1)
  3 Emily's height
  5 Inches in 4 ft 4 ins
  6 Millimetres in a centimetre
  7 The length of an Ichthyosaur
  8 4 feet in inches
 10 2 inches less than 2 feet
 12 2 feet in inches
 13 5 feet in inches

Down 1 6 feet 3 ins in inches
  2 Same as 10 across
  3 10 yards 1 foot in feet
  4 Same as 13 across
  8 6 inches less than 4 feet
  9 7 feet in inches
 10 2 feet 2 inches in inches
 11 2 inches shorter than James

Conversion graphs

Jeff and Daisy are on holiday in France.
They see this sign on the motorway. The distances are in kilometres.

| Lyons | 60 |
| Avignon | 280 |

In France and the rest of Europe, distances are measured in kilometres.
In Britain we use miles.
Kilometres are a metric unit, miles are an Imperial unit.

 **Think of some other metric and Imperial measurements.
Which Imperial units are still commonly used in Britain?**

Jeff and Daisy want to know these distances in miles.

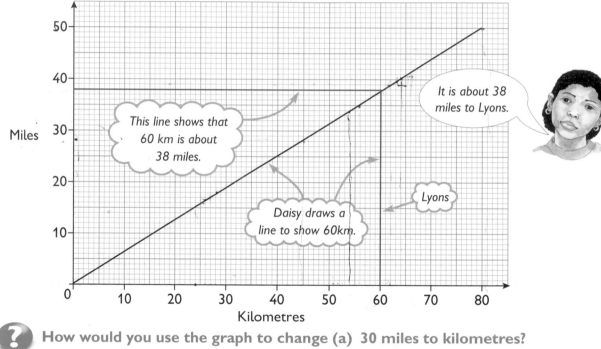

This line shows that 60 km is about 38 miles.

It is about 38 miles to Lyons.

Daisy draws a line to show 60km.

Lyons

 **How would you use the graph to change (a) 30 miles to kilometres?
(b) 40 kilometres to miles?**

Task

During their holiday, Jeff and Daisy keep a record of how far they drive each day,
in miles.

| Monday | 28 | Wednesday | 34 | Friday | 40 |
| Tuesday | 45 | Thursday | 25 | Saturday | 15 |

Use the graph to work out how far they drive each day in kilometres.

 How can you use the graph to find the distance to Avignon in miles?

Exercise

1 Use the conversion graph opposite to change each of these distances to miles.

(a) 80 km **(b)** 64 km **(c)** 56 km **(d)** 24 km

2 Use the conversion graph opposite to change each of these distances to kilometres.

(a) 50 miles **(b)** 25 miles **(c)** 5 miles **(d)** 45 miles

3 This conversion graph is for changing between pounds and kilograms.

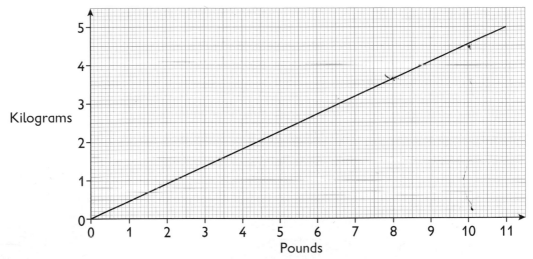

Use the graph to answer the following questions.

(a) A new-born baby weighs 3 kg. What is this in pounds?
(b) A turkey is labelled 5 kg. What is this in pounds?
(c) Laura wants to buy 8 pounds of potatoes. What is this in kg?
(d) A cat basket is suitable for weights of up to 10 pounds.
What is this in kg?

4 This graph converts between pints and litres.

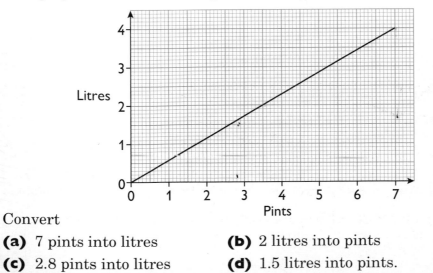

Convert

(a) 7 pints into litres **(b)** 2 litres into pints
(c) 2.8 pints into litres **(d)** 1.5 litres into pints.

Drawing a conversion graph

Jeff and Daisy go shopping during their holiday.

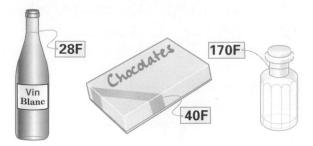

They want to know the cost of each item in pounds and pence.

The exchange rate is £1 = 12 F

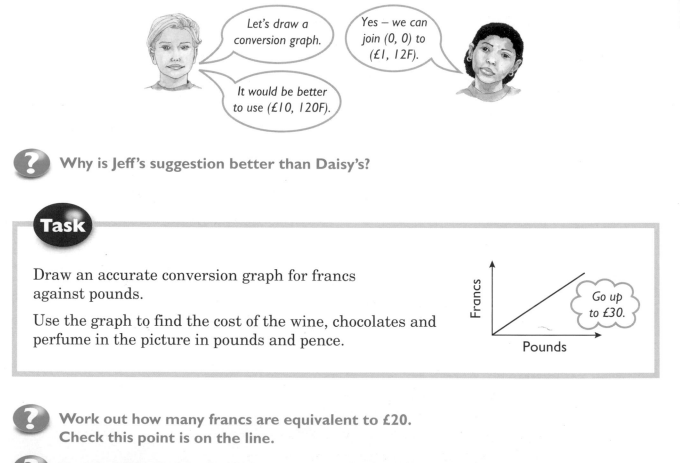

Let's draw a conversion graph.

Yes – we can join (0, 0) to (£1, 12F).

It would be better to use (£10, 120F).

? **Why is Jeff's suggestion better than Daisy's?**

Task

Draw an accurate conversion graph for francs against pounds.

Use the graph to find the cost of the wine, chocolates and perfume in the picture in pounds and pence.

Go up to £30.

? **Work out how many francs are equivalent to £20.**
Check this point is on the line.

? **How can you use a calculator to convert between pounds and francs?**

? **Would this conversion graph be useful for *any* trip to France?**

Exercise

1 Use your conversion graph from the Task to change

(a) these amounts to francs.

(i) £6   **(ii)** £18   **(iii)** £12.50   **(iv)** £3.50

(b) these amounts to pounds

(i) 180 F   **(ii)** 84 F   **(iii)** 270 F   **(iv)** 315 F

2 Chris is going on a business trip in Europe.
He is using euros to pay for all his expenses.
The exchange rate is £1 = 1.6 euros.

(a) Draw a conversion table for pounds and euros.
Your graph should go up to £500.

(b) Chris's hotel bill is 550 euros.
Use your graph to find out what this is in pounds.

(c) The cost of Chris's car hire is 320 euros.
Use your graph to find this in pounds.

(d) Chris's company has allowed £150 for buying petrol.
Use your graph to find this in euros.

3 Petrol is sold in litres. *a metric measure*
It used to be sold in gallons. *an imperial measure*

This conversion graph can be used to convert between litres and gallons.

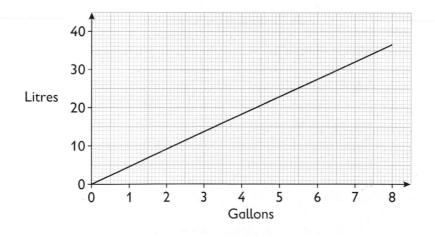

(a) Michelle buys 35 litres of petrol.
How many gallons is this?

(b) Terry's car takes 7.5 gallons of petrol.
Use your graph to convert this to litres.

(c) 1 gallon is equal to 8 pints.

(i) How many gallons are there in 23 litres?
(ii) How many pints are there in 23 litres?
(iii) How many pints are there in 1 litre?

Finishing off

Now that you have finished this chapter you should be able to:
● understand imperial measures ● convert from imperial units to metric units and vice versa ● use a conversion graph ● draw a conversion graph ● make estimates.

Review exercise

Measures	Imperial	Metric	Approximate conversions
Lengths	12 inches = 1 foot 3 feet = 1 yard 1760 yards = 1 mile	10 mm = 1 centimetre 100 centimetres = 1 metre 1000 m = 1 km	1 metre ≈ 39 inches 8 kilometres ≈ 5 miles
Mass	16 ounces = 1 pound 14 pounds = 1 stone 160 stone = 1 ton	1000 mg = 1 gram 1000 g = 1 kg 1000 kg = 1 tonne	1 kg ≈ 2.2 pounds 1 tonne ≈ 1 ton
Capacity	8 pints = 1 gallon	1000 ml = 1 litre	5 litres ≈ 9 pints

1   The egg of a kiwi-bird weighs approximately 0.5 kg.
   A fully grown female bird is about 4 times this weight.
   (a) What is the weight of a fully grown female kiwi?
   (b) Convert this to pounds.

2   **(a)** An elephant has teeth of up to 4.5 kg
      It has 4 of this size.
      What is their total weight?
      Convert this to pounds.
   (b) Each of these teeth is just over 25 cm long.
      How many inches is this?
      Is this more or less than a foot?

3   A small whale contains about 400 gallons of pure oil.
   How many pints is this? Change this to litres.

4   Here are the ingredients for making shortbread.

   5 oz flour   1 oz ground rice   2 oz castor sugar   4 oz butter

   Use the conversion graph opposite to write
   the weights of each ingredient in grams.

   oz is short for ounce

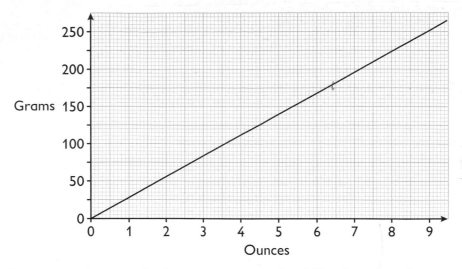

5 Use the conversion graph above to answer the following questions.

(a) A packet of butter is labelled 0.25 kg.
What is this in ounces?

16 ounces = 1 pound (lb)

(b) Paul buys 6.3 oz of cheese.
What is this in grams?

1000 grams = 1 kilogram (kg)

(c) A jar of baby food weighs 200 g.
What is this in ounces?

6 Temperature can be measured in degrees
Fahrenheit (°F) or degrees Celsius (°C).
This conversion graph is for
changing between the two.

(a) What temperature in Fahrenheit
is equivalent to 0°C?

(b) Normal body temperature is 37°C.
What is this in degrees Fahrenheit?

(c) On a very hot summer's day,
the temperature has reached 90°F.
What is this in degrees Celsius?

(d) A comfortable temperature for
a room is about 20°C.
What is this in degrees Fahrenheit?

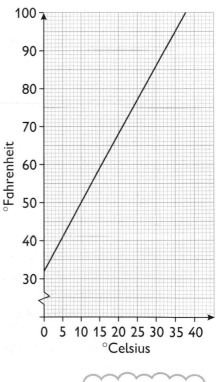

7 The exchange rate for changing British
pounds into German deutschmarks
is £1 = DM3.2.

(a) Draw a conversion graph.
Use your graph to answer the questions below.

*Your graph should
go up to £100.*

(b) (i) Gerry changes £50 into DM.
How much does he get?

(ii) Ellie buys some wine in Germany. It costs DM16.
How much is this in £?

Classifying

Look at these insects.

Some of them have 6 legs, some 8 legs and some more.

 How many ways can you sort these insects?

Triangles can also be sorted in different ways.

 How can you sort triangles?

Task

You can classify triangles by looking at the length of their sides.

Look at this **decision tree diagram**.

Use the diagram to classify the coloured triangles.

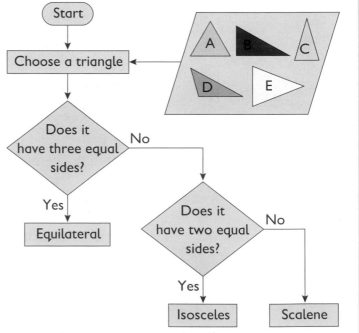

Triangles can also be classified by looking at angles.

 Can a triangle have a reflex angle?
Can a triangle have two right angles?
Can a triangle have three angles of 60°?

Exercise

1 Look at this decision tree diagram.
It classifies triangles by looking at their angles.
Use the diagram to classify the coloured triangles.

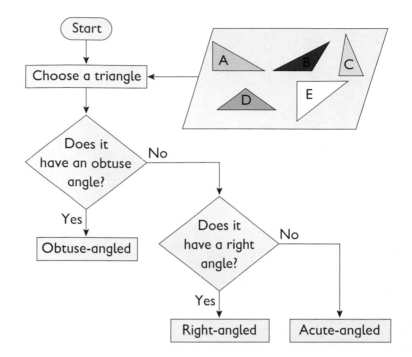

2 Describe fully each of the following triangles using these terms:

> obtuse-angled, right-angled, acute-angled,
> equilateral, isosceles, scalene.

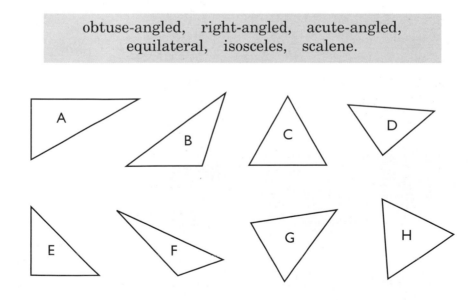

Activity Make a decision tree diagram to sort the
insects on the page opposite.

Shape search

Quadrilateral search

Look at this diagram.

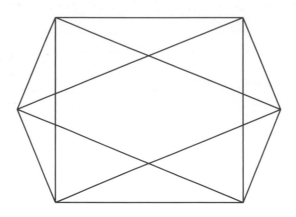

? **Which of these quadrilaterals can you see:**
  (a) square   **(b)** rectangle   **(c)** parallelogram   **(d)** rhombus
  (e) trapezium   **(f)** kite?

? **What other shapes can you find in the diagram?**

Task

Draw each of these quadrilaterals on a poster.

Square   Rectangle   Rhombus   Parallelogram

Trapezium   Kite   Arrowhead

Under each one, say
(a) how many pairs of parallel sides it has   **(b)** which sides are equal
(c) which angles are equal   **(d)** what symmetry it has.

? **Which of these types of quadrilateral can contain a right angle?**
Which of these types of quadrilateral can include a reflex angle?

Exercise

1 Describe each quadrilateral using one of the following terms:

> square, rectangle, rhombus, parallelogram, trapezium, kite, arrowhead, nothing special.

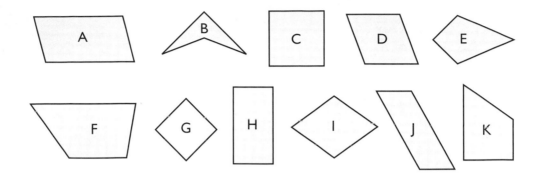

2 Draw x and y axes from 0 to 6.

(a) Plot the points A(1, 6), B(5, 4) and C(5, 2).

(b) Plot D to form
    (i) a parallelogram   **(ii)** a kite
    (iii) a trapezium containing a right angle.

(c) Write down the co-ordinates of D in each case.

3 Look at this decision tree diagram.
Use it to fill the spaces at the bottom with the names of quadrilaterals.

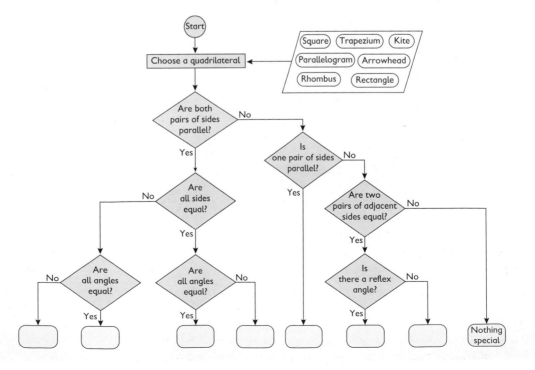

Tessellations

Look at this honeycomb.

It is made of cells fitted together.
The cells **tessellate**.

 What can you say about
(i) the shape of the cells?
(ii) the size of the cells?

 There are no gaps between any of the cells.
How far can the pattern of cells continue?

When *one* shape is repeated to cover a surface this is called *simple* tessellation.
Here are two ways of tessellating a triangle.

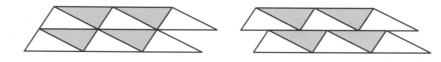

 Are there other ways of tessellating a triangle?

Task

1   Using squared paper, draw a
    rectangle 4 squares by 2.
    Make a tessellation using this shape.

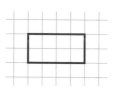

2   Draw a parallelogram on
    squared paper.
    Make a tessellation using this shape.

3   Copy this isosceles trapezium on to
    squared paper.
    Make a tessellation using this shape.

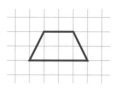

4   Draw a trapezium which is *not*
    isosceles.
    Make a tessellation using this shape.

 Where do you often see patterns of tessellating rectangles?

 Can you tessellate an arrowhead?

Exercise

Copy each of these shapes on to squared paper.
Use it for a tessellation.

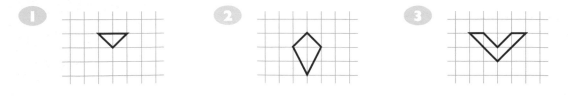

Activity

1 This pattern was created by M C Escher.

Escher was a Dutch artist who lived
from 1898 to 1972.
He used symmetry and transformations
to create pictures.

? **What simple shape is used for this tessellation?**
How is the shape adapted?

Symmetry Drawing E112 by M. C. Escher

2 Look at these three pictures.
The rectangle is transformed into a more interesting shape.

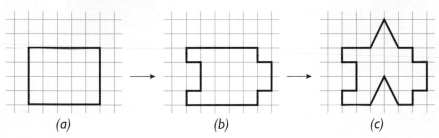

(a)   (b)   (c)

Describe the steps taken.
Make a tessellation using the shape in (c).

3 Escher was inspired by tiling patterns in the Alhambra Palace in Spain.

The Alhambra Palace was built by the
Moors between 1248 and 1354.
It is an example of Islamic art.

Here is a pattern which is found in the
Alhambra Palace.

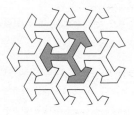

? **What simple shape has been adapted to create this pattern?**

4 On squared paper design your own original shape which will tessellate.
Trace your shape onto card to make a template.
Use your template to 'tile' a piece of paper.
Decorate your tiles.

Solid shapes

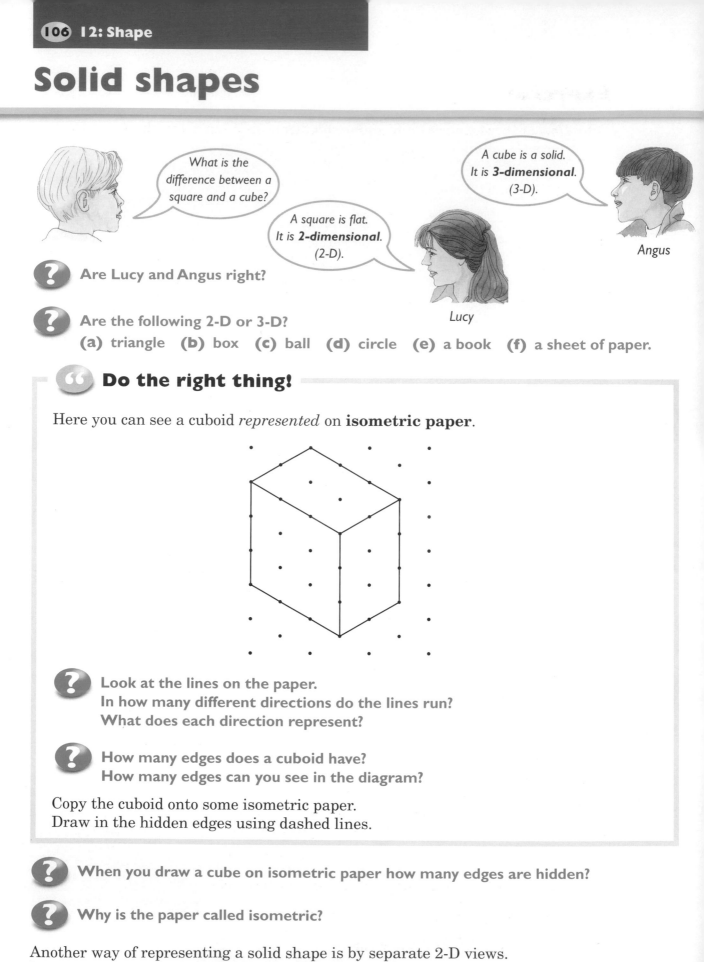

What is the difference between a square and a cube?

A square is flat. It is **2-dimensional**. (2-D).

A cube is a solid. It is **3-dimensional**. (3-D).

Angus

Lucy

? **Are Lucy and Angus right?**

? **Are the following 2-D or 3-D?**
   (a) triangle   **(b)** box   **(c)** ball   **(d)** circle   **(e)** a book   **(f)** a sheet of paper.

" Do the right thing!

Here you can see a cuboid *represented* on **isometric paper**.

? **Look at the lines on the paper.**
   In how many different directions do the lines run?
   What does each direction represent?

? **How many edges does a cuboid have?**
   How many edges can you see in the diagram?

Copy the cuboid onto some isometric paper.
Draw in the hidden edges using dashed lines.

? **When you draw a cube on isometric paper how many edges are hidden?**

? **Why is the paper called isometric?**

Another way of representing a solid shape is by separate 2-D views.
You will meet this in Question 2 opposite.

Exercise

1 Use isometric paper to make 3-D representations of these shapes.

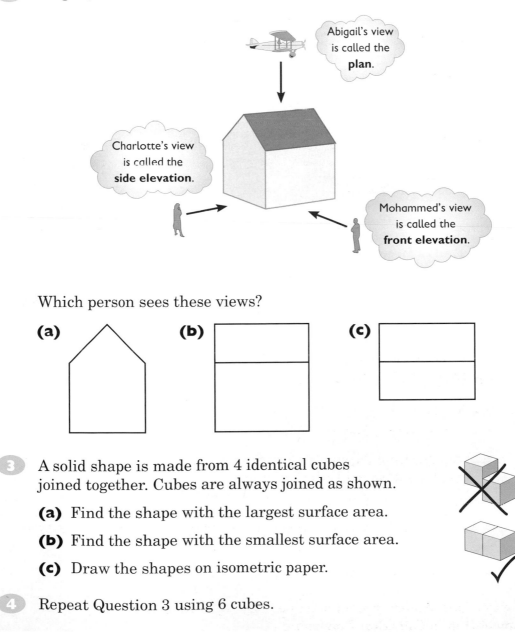

(a)

4 cm
3 cm
2 cm

(b)

1 cm
3 cm
3 cm
1 cm
2 cm

(c)

3 cm
1 cm
2 cm
4 cm
1 cm

2 Abigail, Charlotte and Mohammed view a house from different directions.

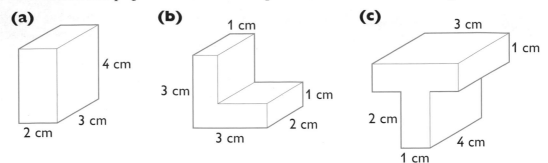

Abigail's view is called the **plan**.

Charlotte's view is called the **side elevation**.

Mohammed's view is called the **front elevation**.

Which person sees these views?

(a)   **(b)**   **(c)**

3 A solid shape is made from 4 identical cubes joined together. Cubes are always joined as shown.

   (a) Find the shape with the largest surface area.

   (b) Find the shape with the smallest surface area.

   (c) Draw the shapes on isometric paper.

4 Repeat Question 3 using 6 cubes.

Finishing off

Now that you have finished this chapter you should be able to:

- classify triangles and quadrilaterals
- make tessellations
- make 2-D drawings of 3-D solids using isometric paper
- draw and use plans and elevations of solid shapes.

Review exercise

1. Write down the name of a triangle having:
   (a) three equal sides (b) two equal angles (c) all sides of different lengths.

2.

   Square
   Rectangle
   Rhombus
   Parallelogram
   Trapezium
   Kite
   Arrowhead

   Jason draws one of the quadrilaterals in the list.
   Holly cannot see what Jason has drawn.

   Holly asks questions to work out what Jason has drawn.

   (a) Holly: 'Does it have any parallel sides?' Jason: 'No.'
       Holly: 'Does it have a reflex angle?' Jason: 'No.'
       Holly: 'It's a kite!'

   Is Holly right? Explain your answer.

   Now they change round and Holly draws a quadrilateral.

   (b) Jason: 'Are all the angles equal?' Holly: 'Yes.'
       Jason: 'Are all the sides equal?' Holly: 'No.'
       Jason: 'It's a rectangle!'

   Is Jason right? Explain your answer.

3. Copy these shapes onto squared paper.
   Use them to make tessellations.

   (a)   (b)   (c)

   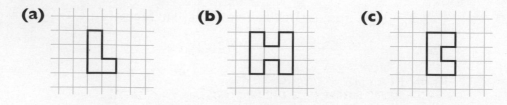

4 Draw these solids on isometric paper.

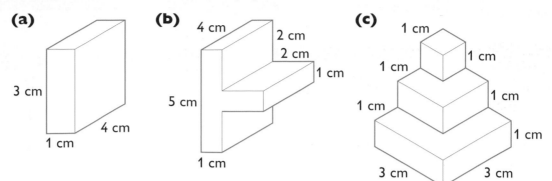

(a)   3 cm   1 cm   4 cm

(b)   4 cm   2 cm   2 cm   1 cm   5 cm   1 cm

(c)   1 cm   1 cm   1 cm   1 cm   1 cm   1 cm   3 cm   3 cm

5 Draw a plan and two elevations of these objects.

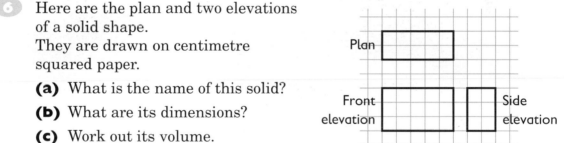

(a)   **(b)**   **(c)**

6 Here are the plan and two elevations of a solid shape.
They are drawn on centimetre squared paper.

(a) What is the name of this solid?

(b) What are its dimensions?

(c) Work out its volume.

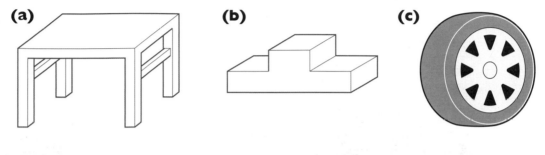

Plan

Front elevation   Side elevation

Activity   Use squared paper to design your own 3-dimensional font.

Make the front face of each letter 3 squares wide and 5 squares high.

A font is a set of letters.

Here is an example.

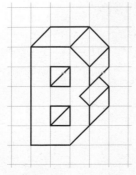

Write your name or a message using your font.

Prime factors

Professor James says

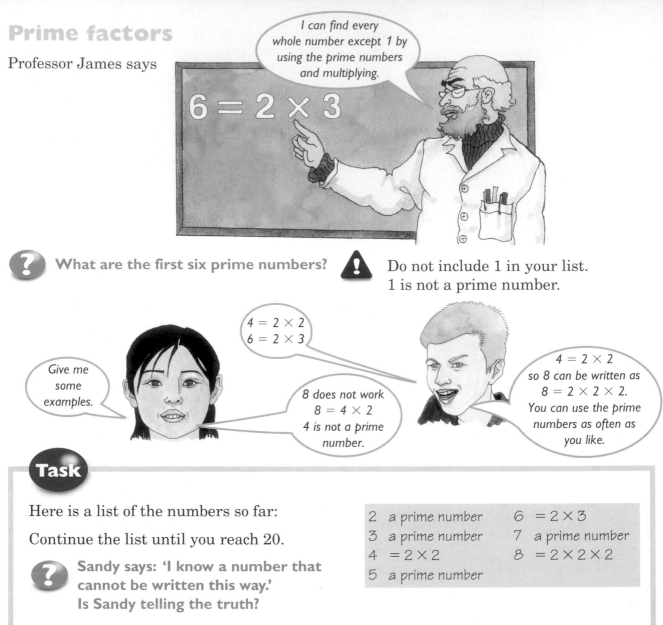

I can find every whole number except 1 by using the prime numbers and multiplying.

$$6 = 2 \times 3$$

? **What are the first six prime numbers?**

! Do not include 1 in your list.
1 is not a prime number.

Give me some examples.

$4 = 2 \times 2$
$6 = 2 \times 3$

8 does not work
$8 = 4 \times 2$
4 is not a prime number.

$4 = 2 \times 2$
so 8 can be written as
$8 = 2 \times 2 \times 2$.
You can use the prime numbers as often as you like.

Task

Here is a list of the numbers so far:

Continue the list until you reach 20.

2	a prime number	6	$= 2 \times 3$
3	a prime number	7	a prime number
4	$= 2 \times 2$	8	$= 2 \times 2 \times 2$
5	a prime number		

? **Sandy says: 'I know a number that cannot be written this way.'**
Is Sandy telling the truth?

Do you agree with what Professor James says?

Products of primes

In the task you wrote each number from 2 to 20 as a **product of its prime factors**.

Write 36 as a product of prime factors like this:

So $36 = 2 \times 2 \times 3 \times 3$

? **Write 56 as a product of prime factors.**

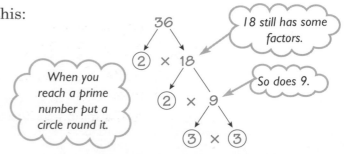

When you reach a prime number put a circle round it.

36
② × 18
② × 9
③ × ③

18 still has some factors.

So does 9.

Exercise

1 Multiply out the following:

(a) $2 \times 2 \times 3$ **(b)** $2 \times 2 \times 2 \times 2$ **(c)** $2 \times 3 \times 3$ **(d)** $2 \times 3 \times 5$

(e) $3 \times 3 \times 5$ **(f)** $3 \times 5 \times 5$ **(g)** $3 \times 5 \times 7$ **(h)** $3 \times 7 \times 11$

(i) 3×13 **(j)** $2 \times 3 \times 11$ **(k)** $2 \times 2 \times 5 \times 5$ **(l)** $3 \times 7 \times 7$

2 Write the following as products of their prime factors.

(a) 21   **(b)** 35   **(c)** 24   **(d)** 25   **(e)** 48

(f) 120   **(g)** 144   **(h)** 39   **(i)** 65   **(j)** 1000

3 Complete this list of the factors of 60.

(a) 1, 2, 3, ..., 60

(b) Write a list of the prime factors of 60.

(c) Write 60 as a product of prime factors.

4 You can write $72 = 2 \times 2 \times 2 \times 3 \times 3$. A shorter way is $72 = 2^3 \times 3^2$.
Rewrite your answers to question 2 using index notation.

5 Multiply out the following:

(a) $2^2 \times 3^2$ **(b)** 3×5^2 **(c)** 2^3 **(d)** 2×7^2 **(e)** $2^3 \times 3^3$

Investigation   The prime factors of a square number can be written in pairs.

Example:

$$36 = (2 \times 2) \times (3 \times 3) \qquad \text{and} \qquad 16 = (2 \times 2) \times (2 \times 2)$$

This is the square of 2×3.   *This is the square of 2×2.*

1 Explain why $3^2 \times 5^2 = 3 \times 3 \times 5 \times 5$ is a square number.
Write down the square root of $3^2 \times 5^2$.

2 Find the square root of:

(a) $2 \times 2 \times 5 \times 5$

(b) $3 \times 3 \times 3 \times 3$

(c) $5 \times 5 \times 7 \times 7$

3 Write down using index notation the square of:

(a) 3×5

(b) $2 \times 3 \times 5$

(c) $2 \times 3 \times 3 \times 7$

4 Write down 3 more products of primes that give square numbers.

Ask a friend to find the square roots of these numbers.

Lowest common multiple

BUSES AVAILABLE FROM THIS STOP

	1b	3a	4
Departing every	5 mins	8 mins	10 mins
First departure	9.00 a.m.	9.00 a.m.	9.00 a.m.

All three buses leave together at 9.00 a.m.

 When is the next time that all three buses leave together?

One way to answer this is to find the
Lowest Common Multiple or LCM of 5, 8 and 10.

This is the smallest number that is a multiple of 5, 8 and 10.

Leroy writes down his answer.

Explain why Leroy's answer is right.

Write down at least three numbers that are multiples of 5 and 10.
At what times can you catch a 1b or a 4 bus but not a 3a?

> *I need the LCM of 5, 8 and 10.*
>
> *Multiples of 5   5, 10, 15, 20, 25, 30, 35, (40,) 45, 50 ...*
> *Multiples of 8   8, 16, 24, 32, (40,) 48, 56, 64 ...*
> *Multiples of 10   10, 20, 30, (40,) 50, 60 ...*
>
> *LCM is 40.*
>
> *So the answer is 9.40 a.m.*

It is the smallest number in all three lists.

Task

1 Find the LCM of the following pairs of numbers:
   (a) 4 and 6   **(b)** 5 and 7   **(c)** 4 and 15   **(d)** 12 and 4   **(e)** 20 and 12

Look carefully at your answers.
Sometimes the LCM of two numbers is simply the product of those numbers.

2 Is the LCM of 5 and 7 given by $5 \times 7 = 35$?

3 Is the LCM of 4 and 6 given by $4 \times 6 = 24$?

Can the LCMs of the other pairs of numbers be found by multiplying them together?

Fractions and the LCM

Sometimes pairs of fractions are written with a common denominator.

 Find the LCM of 6 and 8.
Use your answer to write each of the fractions $\frac{1}{6}$ and $\frac{3}{8}$ with a common denominator.

Exercise

1 Find the LCM of the following pairs of numbers:

   (a) 8 and 12   **(b)** 3 and 6   **(c)** 12 and 18   **(d)** 18 and 2

   (e) 36 and 48   **(f)** 3 and 9   **(g)** 12 and 24   **(h)** 22 and 132.

2 Alan and David are walking side by side.
Alan's stride is 80 cm long and David has a stride of 90 cm.

   (a) Find the LCM of 80 and 90.

They start in step together.

   (b) How far do they walk before they are next in step?

3 The dials below are set at 0.

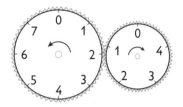

After the left dial has been turned once they will look like this.

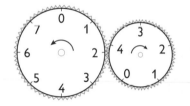

   (a) Draw a diagram to show what they will look like after 2 turns
of the left dial.

   (b) How many turns of the left dial are needed before both
the dials are back to 0?

Activity In a motor race, Alison Falk can
complete the circuit in 5 minutes
but Johnny Sawan takes 6 minutes.

Continue this list to show the times
when these drivers return to the
starting point.

Alison Falk	5, 10, 15, ...
Johnny Sawan	6, 12, 18, ...

How long is it before Alison overtakes Johnny at the starting point?

How many laps is Alison ahead then?

Highest common factor

The class play the common factor game.

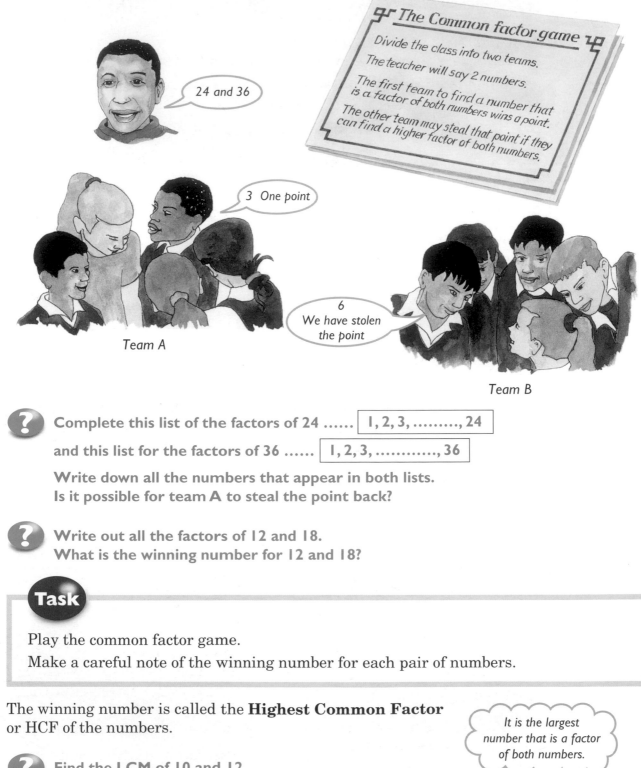

24 and 36

The Common factor game

Divide the class into two teams.

The teacher will say 2 numbers.

The first team to find a number that is a factor of both numbers wins a point.

The other team may steal that point if they can find a higher factor of both numbers.

3 One point

Team A

6
We have stolen
the point

Team B

? **Complete this list of the factors of 24** ...... | 1, 2, 3, ..., 24 |

and this list for the factors of 36 ...... | 1, 2, 3, ..., 36 |

Write down all the numbers that appear in both lists.
Is it possible for team A to steal the point back?

? **Write out all the factors of 12 and 18.**
What is the winning number for 12 and 18?

Task

Play the common factor game.

Make a careful note of the winning number for each pair of numbers.

The winning number is called the **Highest Common Factor**
or **HCF** of the numbers.

*It is the largest
number that is a factor
of both numbers.*

? **Find the LCM of 10 and 12.**
Find the HCF of 10 and 12.
Which is bigger, the HCF or the LCM of two numbers?

Exercise

1 Find the HCF of the following pairs of numbers.

(a) 4 and 6   (b) 6 and 9   (c) 8 and 12   (d) 12 and 18

(e) 3 and 9   (f) 4 and 12   (g) 3 and 5   (h) 7 and 8

(i) 30 and 45   (j) 18 and 72

2 Most of the fractions below can be cancelled down.
Use your answers to Question 1 to help you do this.

(a) $\frac{4}{6}$ (b) $\frac{6}{9}$ (c) $\frac{8}{12}$ (d) $\frac{12}{18}$ (e) $\frac{3}{9}$

(f) $\frac{4}{12}$ (g) $\frac{3}{5}$ (h) $\frac{7}{8}$ (i) $\frac{30}{45}$ (j) $\frac{18}{72}$

(k) Which fractions cannot be cancelled?

(l) What is the HCF of the top and bottom numbers of these fractions?

3 Pete makes rosewood jewellery.
Pieces of wood are joined together to make
bracelets, necklaces and anklets.
All the pieces of wood are the same length.
Look at the poster on the right.

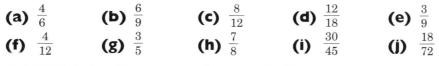

(a) Write down the common factors of
18, 48, 54 and 24.

(b) What are possible lengths for the pieces
of wood?

(c) What length do you think is best?

Pete's Jewellery

Bracelets	18 cm
Necklaces	48 cm
	54 cm
Anklet	24 cm

GUARANTEED TO
BRING YOU LUCK

4 The map shows the route of a charity walk.

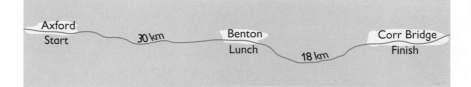

Axford
Start   30 km   Benton
Lunch   18 km   Corr Bridge
Finish

Marshals stand at equally spaced intervals along the route.
There are marshals at the lunch stop, the start and the finish.

(a) Find the HCF of 18 and 30.

(b) What distance is there between each marshal? There are several
possible answers. Give two of them.

(c) What is the smallest possible number of marshals?

Finishing off

Now that you have finished this chapter you should be able to:

- write any number as the product of its prime factors
- find the Lowest Common Multiple of a set of numbers
- find the Highest Common Factor of two numbers
- use the LCM and HCF when solving problems.

Review exercise

1 Multiply out the following:

(**a**) $2 \times 2 \times 3$ (**b**) $2 \times 3 \times 3$ (**c**) $2 \times 5 \times 5$ (**d**) $3 \times 3 \times 5$

(**e**) $2^2 \times 3^2$ (**f**) $3^2 \times 7$ (**g**) $2^3 \times 5$ (**h**) $2^3 \times 7^2$

(**i**) $3 \times 7 \times 11$ (**j**) $2^2 \times 11$

2 Write each of these numbers as a product of its prime factors:

(**a**) 8   (**b**) 15   (**c**) 20   (**d**) 50   (**e**) 70   (**f**) 240

3 Find the LCM of each of the following pairs of numbers:

(**a**) 10 and 15   (**b**) 20 and 30   (**c**) 4 and 12   (**d**) 15 and 20

(**e**) 12 and 18   (**f**) 7 and 8   (**g**) 9 and 11   (**h**) 11 and 15

4 Find the HCF of each of the following sets of numbers:

(**a**) 6 and 8   (**b**) 6 and 9   (**c**) 12 and 16   (**d**) 36 and 42

(**e**) 42 and 70   (**f**) 66 and 121   (**g**) 72 and 36   (**h**) 45 and 90

5 Linda's father services his car every 6000 miles.
Here are some of the checks he carries out.

Check	Required every
Brake fluid	6000 miles
Change oil filter	12 000 miles
Tyres	6000 miles
Wiper blades	18 000 miles
Change timing belt	24 000 miles

Service	6000	12 000	18 000	24 000
check	Brake fluid Tyres	Brake fluid Tyres Oil filter		

(**a**) Continue the table to show all the services up to the 48 000 mile service.

All the checks are carried out at a major service.

(**b**) How often does this happen?

Activity

1 Cut out 6 equal cardboard circles. Label them 3, 4, 6, 9, 12 and 18. Cut evenly spaced notches from the edge of each circle.

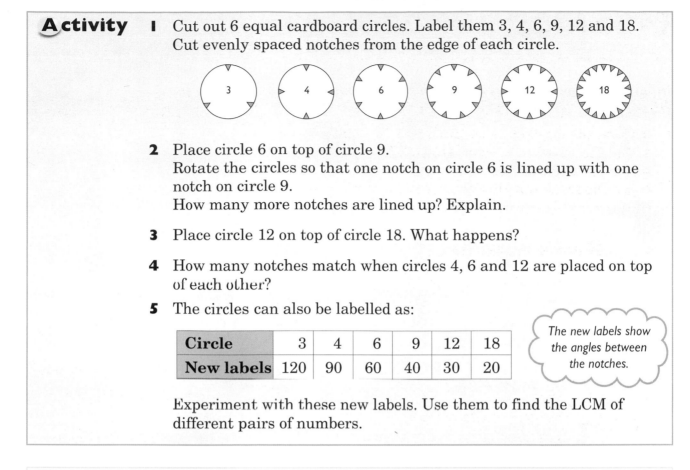

2 Place circle 6 on top of circle 9.
Rotate the circles so that one notch on circle 6 is lined up with one notch on circle 9.
How many more notches are lined up? Explain.

3 Place circle 12 on top of circle 18. What happens?

4 How many notches match when circles 4, 6 and 12 are placed on top of each other?

5 The circles can also be labelled as:

Circle	3	4	6	9	12	18
New labels	120	90	60	40	30	20

The new labels show the angles between the notches.

Experiment with these new labels. Use them to find the LCM of different pairs of numbers.

Investigation   A fraction can be written as a decimal.

The decimal can be exact: $\frac{1}{4} = 0.25$, $\frac{1}{20} = 0.05$

or you can get a recurring decimal: $\frac{1}{3} = 0.333...$ $\frac{1}{7} = 0.1428571428...$

$\frac{1}{16}$ is $1 \div 16$

$$= \frac{0.0625}{16 \overline{)1.0000}}$$

1 Change the following fractions to decimals:
   $\frac{1}{6}, \frac{1}{4}, \frac{2}{5}, \frac{3}{10}, \frac{2}{7}, \frac{3}{25}$ and $\frac{4}{15}$.

2 Enter each of the fractions that produce exact decimals in the table below.

Fraction	Denominator	Product of primes	Prime factors used			
			2	3	5	7
$\frac{1}{4}$	4	2×2	✓			
$\frac{3}{25}$	25	5×5			✓	
$\frac{1}{16}$	16	$2 \times 2 \times 2 \times 2$	✓			

3 What can you say about the denominator of a fraction that can be written as an exact decimal?

Luigi is opening an ice-cream parlour in Avonford.
He asks some people on the High Street a question.

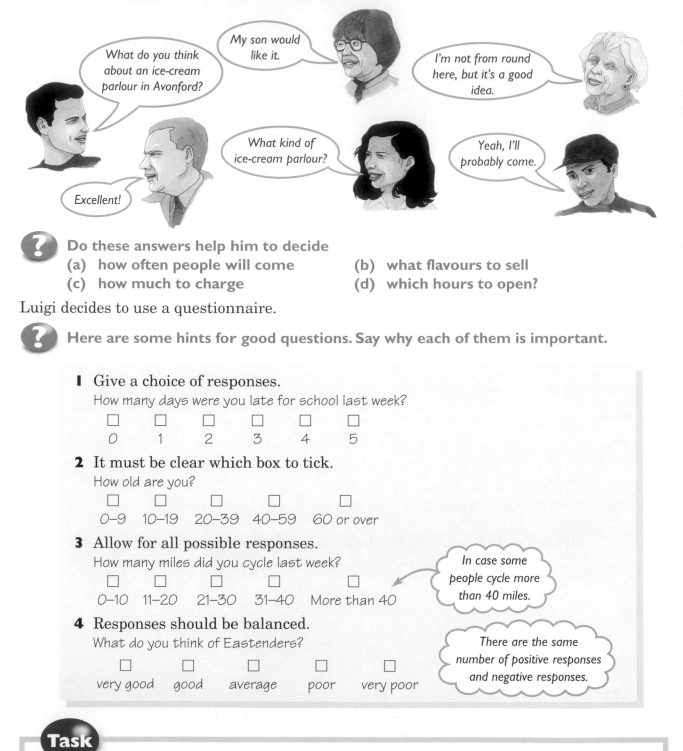

? Do these answers help him to decide
(a) how often people will come
(b) what flavours to sell
(c) how much to charge
(d) which hours to open?

Luigi decides to use a questionnaire.

? Here are some hints for good questions. Say why each of them is important.

1 Give a choice of responses.
How many days were you late for school last week?

☐ ☐ ☐ ☐ ☐ ☐
0 1 2 3 4 5

2 It must be clear which box to tick.
How old are you?

☐ ☐ ☐ ☐ ☐
0–9 10–19 20–39 40–59 60 or over

3 Allow for all possible responses.
How many miles did you cycle last week?

☐ ☐ ☐ ☐ ☐
0–10 11–20 21–30 31–40 More than 40

In case some people cycle more than 40 miles.

4 Responses should be balanced.
What do you think of Eastenders?

☐ ☐ ☐ ☐ ☐
very good good average poor very poor

There are the same number of positive responses and negative responses.

Task

Write down 4 questions for Luigi.

Exercise

1 Gemma has written a questionnaire.
The questions and the responses have got muddled.
Which response goes with which question?

Questions	Responses

Are you married?

☐ never   ☐ sometimes   ☐ always

How many cats do you have?

☐ yes   ☐ no   ☐ don't know

Do you use a hot water bottle?

☐ 0–4999   ☐ 5000–9999   ☐ 10 000–19 999   ☐ 20 000–39 999   ☐ 40 000 or more

How many miles did you drive last year?

☐ yes   ☐ no

Do you think gambling should be banned?

☐ 0   ☐ 1   ☐ 2   ☐ 3   ☐ 4 or more

2 In each of the following cases

(i) state what is wrong with the question
(ii) design a better question.

(a) What do you think of the computer game Crypt Stormer?

☐ excellent   ☐ very good   ☐ quite good   ☐ average

(b) How many packets of crisps do you eat in a week?

☐ 0–5   ☐ 6–10   ☐ 11–15   ☐ 15–20

(c) How many days were you off sick last year?

☐ 0   ☐ 1   ☐ 2   ☐ 4 or more

3 Write down a set of responses to each of the following questions.

(a) How much time did you spend watching T.V. last week?
(b) When was the last time you visited a Health Centre?
(c) How much are you willing to pay for Cable Television each month?

Activity Maya is thinking of starting a lunchtime club.
Design a short questionnaire to help her decide

(a) what kind of club to start
(b) what day to hold it on
(c) whether enough people will attend.

Biased and misleading questions

When writing a questionnaire
always make sure that

- your questions are fair
- you are asking the right people
- the right person is asking
  the question.

I think the pop group Blokezone are brilliant.
What do you think of them?

☐	☐	☐	☐	☐
very good	good	average	below average	poor

 How is the question biased?
How can it be improved?

 What is wrong with these situations?

Do you own a motorbike?

☐	☐
yes	no

Have you ever drawn graffiti?

☐	☐
yes	no

Task

On this page, 3 problems are shown.

1 a question is biased

2 the wrong people are given a question

3 the wrong person asks the question.

Working with a friend, think up one example of each.
Make a poster of the best examples from the class.

It is not easy to design a good questionnaire.

Always try one out on a small group of people first. This is called a **pilot survey**.

Exercise

1 All these questions are biased. Say why. Rewrite them so they are fair.

(a) Sausages taste great, don't they?

☐ Yes   ☐ No

(b) We think fox-hunting should be banned. Do you?

☐ strongly agree   ☐ agree   ☐ neither agree nor disagree   ☐ disagree   ☐ strongly disagree

(c) Why do you think computer games should be banned?

☐ Students play them instead of doing homework   ☐ They are too violent   ☐ Sitting for a long time at a computer is bad for your body

2 You want to find people's views on these subjects.
For each case, write down **(i)** a group of people who are not suitable to ask
(ii) a person who should not ask the question.

(a) Shakespeare's plays

(b) The standard of teaching at St. Meggan's School.

(c) Professional boxing

3 St. John's College is opening a tuck shop.
They want to find out
● what to sell
● when to open
● whether it will make a profit.
This questionnaire has been designed for students to answer.
It is badly written.

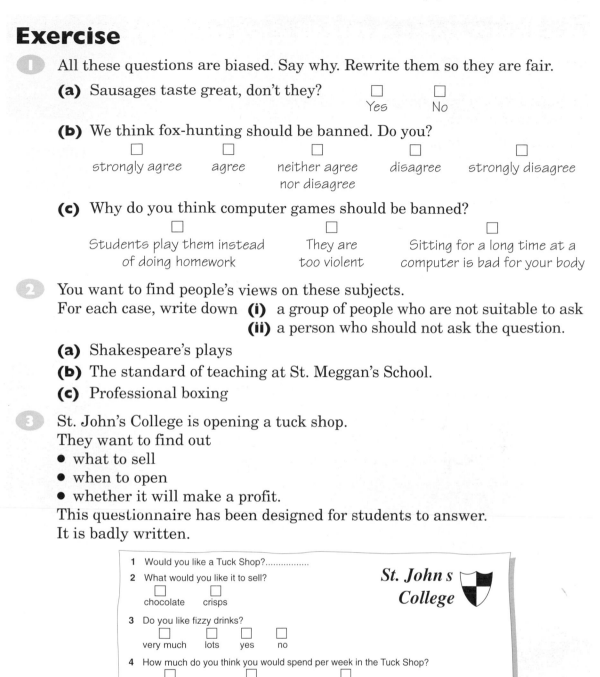

> 1 Would you like a Tuck Shop?.................
>
> 2 What would you like it to sell?
>   ☐ chocolate   ☐ crisps
>
> *St. John's College*
>
> 3 Do you like fizzy drinks?
>   ☐ very much   ☐ lots   ☐ yes   ☐ no
>
> 4 How much do you think you would spend per week in the Tuck Shop?
>   ☐ less than 50p   ☐ between 50p and £1   ☐ between £1 and £2
>
> 5 The Tuck Shop should be open before school.
>   ☐ strongly disagree   ☐ disagree   ☐ agree   ☐ strongly agree
>
> 6 The Tuck Shop should be open at break.
>   ☐ strongly agree   ☐ agree   ☐ disagree   ☐ strongly disagree
>
> 7 You would like the Tuck Shop to be open at lunchtime, wouldn't you?
>   ☐ yes   ☐ no
>
> 8 Do you often visit the local Newsagents?
>   ☐ yes   ☐ no

(a) Write down as many errors as you can find.

(b) Rewrite the questionnaire.

Finishing off

Now that you have finished this chapter you should be able to:

● carry out a survey of your own, following the points given below.

Carry out your own survey

1 Decide what the survey is going to be about.

2 Decide first what you want to find out ...

... and who you are going to ask.

3 Draw up a pilot questionnaire and try it out.

4 Draw up your final questionnaire.

5 Carry out the survey.

6 Collect the results.

7 Write your report. Use the following sections.

Aim	What were you trying to find out from your questions?

Method	Who did you ask? How did you choose them? Who asked them?

Questionnaire	Include a copy of your questionnaire.

Results	Give the results of each question as a frequency table and a data display.

Conclusions	What are the answers to your questions? Could you have done anything better?

Ratio and proportion

Dan is cooking Tuna and Cheddar Stuffed Peppers.
His recipe serves **4 people**.

For one person the quantity of breadcrumbs is $\frac{100}{4} = 25$ g.

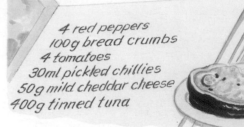

4 red peppers
100g bread crumbs
4 tomatoes
30ml pickled chillies
50g mild cheddar cheese
400g tinned tuna

 What are the quantities of the other ingredients for one person.

 **One day Dan makes the meal for 1 person, but he puts in 30 ml of pickled chillies.
Is this too much or too little?
What will it taste like?**

> **These quantities must all be kept in proportion.**
>
> When the amount of one ingredient is divided by 4, all the others must be too. Otherwise the flavour will be altered.

Task

Dan also makes a dessert.

Work out the quantities for one person.

Dan is actually cooking the Stuffed Peppers and Peach Melba for 8 people.

> *This is proportion again.
> One ingredient is multiplied by 8 so the others must be too.*

Peach Melba (serves 6)

6	meringue nests
300g	fresh raspberries
36g	castor sugar
600g	peach slices

 What quantities of food does he need for each course?

 **How does finding the amount for one person help you?
This is called the unitary method.**

Exercise

1. Mrs. Roberts is making up party bags for Serena's party.
   There will be 30 people.
   (a) A six-pack of chocolate wheels costs 60p.
      (i) How much does one cost?
      (ii) How much do 30 cost?
   (b) A five-pack of Star bars costs £1.50.
      (i) How much is one Star bar?
      (ii) How much are 30 bars?
   (c) A pack containing 10 mini-rolls costs £2.00.
      (i) How much is one mini-roll?
      (ii) How much are 30 mini-rolls?

2. A pack of three video tapes costs £9.00.
   (a) How much does one tape cost?
   (b) How much do five tapes cost?

   VHS tape 180 minutes
   £9.00

3. Roses are priced at £4.00 for a bunch of eight.
   What is the cost of 24 roses?

4. Christmas cards are wrapped in packs of ten.
   Each pack costs £5.00.
   The shopkeeper sells the cards separately at the same rate.
   What is the cost of 8 cards?

5. Here is a recipe for 30 truffles.
   (a) How much of each ingredient
   is in each truffle?
   (b) How much is needed to make
      (i) 20 truffles?
      (ii) 50 truffles?

   Main ingredients
   150 ml double cream
   375 g dark chocolate
   30 g butter
   30 ml brandy
   15 ml chopped stem ginger

   Finishing
   15 ml cocoa powder
   60 g white chocolate

6. A survey is carried out on 20 robins' nests.
   They have laid a total of 80 eggs.
   About how many eggs would you expect to find in
   (a) one nest
   (b) 300 nests?

7. In water, two moles of hydrogen (H_2) combine with one mole of oxygen (O_2)
   to make two moles of water (H_2O).

   $$2H_2 + O_2 \rightarrow 2H_2O$$

   How many moles of hydrogen combine with
   (a) 4 moles of oxygen?
   (b) 6 moles of oxygen?
   (c) How many moles of H_2O are produced in each case?

Ratios

David makes a toy for his baby sister.
It has 3 boxes A, B and C.

Each box is a cube with one face missing.
It is an open box.

You can make them into a tower or a nest.

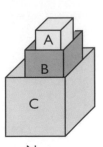

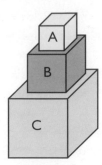

Tower   Nest

Task

The smallest box A is a 4 cm cube.

1 Draw the net accurately.

2 Include flaps so you can stick it together.

3 Cut it out and make it.

4 The other two boxes have sides
5 cm (B) and 6 cm (C).
Make them too.

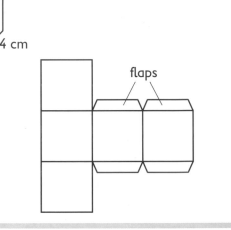

4 cm

4 cm

4 cm

flaps

? **The boxes are made into a nest.**
What is the gap between A and B?
What is the gap between B and C?

The ratio of the sides of cubes A and C is $4\,\text{cm} : 6\,\text{cm}$
$$= 2\,\text{cm} : 3\,\text{cm}$$

This can be cancelled down like a fraction.

? **What is the ratio of the sides of cube A : cube B?**
Is the ratio of the sides of cubes B and C the same?

The ratio can be written the other way round.

Side C : Side A = 3 : 2

The order matters. It must match the order of the words.

You can also write all these ratios together.

Side A : Side B : Side C = $4\,\text{cm} : 5\,\text{cm} : 6\,\text{cm}$

? **Can you cancel down 4 : 5 : 6?**

? **What is the ratio of** **(a)** **the surface areas?** **(b)** **the volume of the three boxes?**

Exercise

1. In a box there are 20 pink and 30 white tissues.
   (a) Write down the ratio, pink tissues : white tissues.
   (b) Simplify your answer.

2. A shop sells boxes of plain and milk chocolates.
   One box contains 3 plain and 9 milk chocolates.
   (a) Write down the ratio, plain chocolate : milk chocolate.
   (b) Simplify your answer.

   All the other boxes have the same ratio, plain : milk
   (c) A box contains 27 milk chocolates.
   How many plain chocolates does it have?
   (d) Another box contains 12 plain chocolates.
   How many milk chocolates does it have?

3. A florist puts 4 yellow and 8 white roses together in a bunch.
   (a) Write down the ratio of yellow : white roses.
   (b) Simplify your answer.

   She makes other bunches with the same ratio, yellow : white
   (c) One bunch has 24 yellow roses.
   How many white roses does it have?
   (d) Another bunch has 16 white roses.
   How many yellow roses does it have?

4. Simplify the following ratios.
   Some have different units. You must change them to the same units first.
   (a) 20 : 30   **(b)** 5 : 10   **(c)** 12 : 4
   (d) 24 : 32   **(e)** £16 : £12   **(f)** 40 hours : 24 hours
   (g) 4 : 8 : 6   **(h)** 35 : 25 : 50   **(i)** 75p : £1.25
   (j) 2 hours : 30 minutes   **(k)** 30 minutes : 2 hours
   (l) 9 km : 4000 m   **(m)** 2 km : 2.5 km

5. Fred is painting the outside doors and windows of the houses on an estate.
   All the houses are the same. He uses 6 tins of paint on 4 houses.
   (a) How many tins of paint does he need for 36 houses?
   (b) He buys 15 tins of paint. How many houses can he do with them?

6. Marsh gas (methane) consists of one mole of carbon and 2 moles of hydrogen.
   (a) Write down the ratio, moles of carbon : moles of hydrogen.
   (b) How many moles of hydrogen combine with 3 moles of carbon?
   (c) How many moles of carbon combine with 16 moles of hydrogen?

Sharing in a given ratio

Tom, Alex and Julie buy a set of 60 old football programmes between them. The set costs £180.

Tom pays £30. Alex pays £60. Julie pays £90.

Tom

That is 20 programmes each.

Not fair!

Alex

Julie

 Why does Julie say 'Not fair'?
How many programmes should each person get?

 Task

Find how many programmes each person should get. Use both these methods.

Method 1 (Unitary Method)

60 programmes cost £180.

(a) How much is one programme?

(b) Tom spent £30. How many programmes does he get?

(c) What about Alex and Julie?

Method 2 (Unitary Ratio)

The money they spend is in the ratio

Tom : Alex : Julie = 30 : 60 : 90
                       1 : 2 : 3

Tom has 1 share, Alex has 2 shares and Julie has 3 shares.

$1 + 2 + 3 = 6$, so there are 6 shares in all.

6 shares = 60 programmes
1 share   = ... programmes

Tom has 1 share   or ... programmes
Alex has 2 shares or ... programmes
Julie has 3 shares or ... programmes

 How can you check your answers?

 Miss Ferrera, Ms Ramesh and Mr Smith start a business together.
Miss Ferrera invests £200 000, Ms Ramesh £300 000 and Mr Smith £500 000.
In the first year they make £20 000 profit.
How much does each of them get?

Exercise

1 Divide £24 between two people in the ratio 1 : 5.
How much does each person get?

2 Divide 1 m (100 cm) of wood in the ratio 7 : 3.
How long is each piece?

3 A school fete raises £1400.
It is shared between the school and a charity in the ratio 4 : 3.
How much does each receive?

4 Pastry is made with twice as much flour as fat by weight.

(a) What is the ratio of flour to fat?

(b) The flour and fat together weigh 240 g.
How much flour is there?
And how much fat?

5 Ninety girls are asked for their
favourite sport.
The answers are shown in the
pie chart.

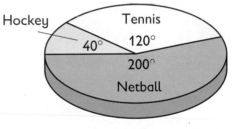

(a) Write down the ratio of the angles,
netball : hockey : tennis.

(b) Simplify this ratio.

(c) How many girls like each sport best?

(d) Check your answer.

6 180 people are asked their favourite of these four channels.

The answers were

Space Sports 1	90
UK Bronze	30
Charley Cinema	25
Film Seven	35

(a) Write down the ratio of
Space Sports 1 : UK Bronze : Charley Cinema : Film Seven

(b) Simplify it.

(c) Divide 360° (a complete circle) in the above ratio.

(d) Draw a pie chart to show these answers.

Finishing off

Now that you have finished this chapter you should be able to:

- write down a ratio
- simplify a ratio
- use the unitary method and direct proportion
- divide a quantity in a given ratio

Review exercise

1 Simplify the following ratios:

(a) $15 : 20$

(b) $35 : 40$

(c) $24 : 16$

(d) $12 : 16 : 20$

(e) $30 : 50 : 45$

(f) $63 : 56 : 28$

(g) $2 : 4$

(h) $6 : 3$

(i) $8 : 2$

(j) $5 : 30$

2 Simplify these ratios. Change them to the same units first.

(a) $10p : £1$

(b) $25 \, cm : 1 \, m$

(c) $2 \, km : 100 \, m$

(d) $3 \, days : 1 \, week$

(e) $20 \, m : 1 \, km$

(f) $500 \, ml : 1 \, litre$

(g) $20 \, seconds : 1 \, minute$

(h) $1 \, day : 12 \, hours$

3 Divide £32 between Terry and Grant in the ratio $7 : 9$.

4 Divide £48 000 between Mr Beech, Mrs Cook and Ms David in the ratio $8 : 5 : 3$.

5 A school raises £3000 in aid of charity.
The money is divided between Cancer Research and a hostel for the homeless in the ratio $3 : 2$.
How much does each charity receive?

6 The scale of a model tractor is $1 : 32$.

(a) The diameter of a large back wheel on the model is 8 cm.
What is the diameter of a back wheel on a real tractor?

(b) The diameter of a small front wheel on the real tractor is 128 cm.
What is the diameter of a front wheel on the model tractor?

7 The scale on a plan is 1 : 100.

(a) Find the actual distance represented by 3 cm on the plan.

(b) An object's real length is 25 m.
How long is it on the plan?

8 The scale on a map is 1 : 10 000.

(a) Find the actual distance represented by 4 cm on the map.

(b) Two places are 2.5 km apart.
How far apart are they on the map?

9 A map scale is given as 1 : 1 000 000.

(a) On the map Manchester and Liverpool are 5.6 cm apart.
How far is it from Manchester to Liverpool really?

(b) On the map Cambridge to Guildford is 14.4 cm apart.
How far is it from Cambridge to Guildford really?

10 The ingredients for Soft Fruit in Summer Sauce are

This serves 8 people.

(a) Work out the quantities for one person.

(b) Work out the quantities for 6 people.

11 90 teenagers are asked to vote for their favourite pop group.
The votes are

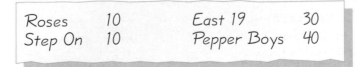

| Roses | 10 | East 19 | 30 |
| Step On | 10 | Pepper Boys | 40 |

(a) Write down the ratio
Roses : Step On : East 19 : Pepper Boys
Simplify it.

(b) Divide 360° (a complete circle) in this ratio.

(c) Draw a pie chart to show these votes.

16 Using formulae

Asha replaces the broken glass in the roof of her greenhouse.
She works out the total area of the glass needed.

? **What is the shape of the broken piece?**

Asha works out the area of the piece by using
the **formula**:

Area of a rectangle = lw

This means l × w.

? **What do *l* and *w* stand for?**

Asha substitutes the values of l and w into the formula.
She writes

Area of glass   = lw
l = 1 and w = 2
So area of the rectangle = 1 x 2
                = 2
  So I need 2m² of glass

*Area is measured
in square units.
Here it is m².*

Asha wants to make sure that the
temperature in her greenhouse is 77°F.

She uses the formula $C = \dfrac{5 \times (F - 32)}{9}$

*Her thermometer only
has a Celsius scale.*

? **What do *C* and *F* stand for?**

*This converts
from Fahrenheit to
Celsius.*

? **Look at the thermometer.**
Does Asha have to change the heating in her greenhouse?

Task

1 Kofi grows tropical vegetables in his greenhouse.
   He needs to keep them at 86°F.
   Use the formula given above to convert this to Celsius.

2 Kofi wants to keep a ready reckoner in his greenhouse.
   What answers does he get when he converts the
   following temperatures to Celsius?

   (a) 50°F   **(b)** 100°F   **(c)** 0°F

°F	°C
100	
80	
60	
40	
20	
10	
0	
−10	
−20	
−30	
−40	
−50	

? **What is −40°F in Celsius? What do you notice?**

Exercise

1 Find the value of $7a + 4b - 3c$ when:

(a) $a = 2$, $b = 5$ and $c = 4$

(b) $a = 6$, $b = -2$ and $c = 1$

(c) $a = 1$, $b = 0.5$ and $c = 5$

(d) $a = 10$, $b = 0.5$ and $c = 5$

(e) $a = -2$, $b = -3$ and $c = 7$

(f) $a = 6$, $b = -7$ and $c = -2$

2 In Rugby Union the formula to work out the total score is $S = 5t + 2c + 3g$

(a) What do S, t, c and g stand for?

(b) What is the total score when:

(i) $t = 2$, $c = 1$ and $g = 8$

(ii) $t = 10$, $c = 2$ and $g = 3$

> In Rugby Union
> A try = 5 points
> A conversion = 2 points
> A goal kick = 3 points

3 **(a)** Kerry drives for 2 hours on the motorway at 100 km per hour.

Use the formula   Distance = Speed × Time

to work out how far she has travelled.

(b) On another journey she travels 300 km in 2 hours.

(i) What is her speed?

(ii) Is she within the speed limit of 112 kilometres per hour?

(c) On the return journey she travels 400 km.
Her speed is 80 kilometres per hour.
How long does the journey take?

Investigation   Look at this rectangle.

Write down a formula for

(a) the perimeter of the rectangle.

(b) the area of the rectangle.

The rectangle is skewed to make a parallelogram.

(c) Is the area of the parallelogram

(i) bigger

(ii) smaller

(iii) the same as the rectangle?

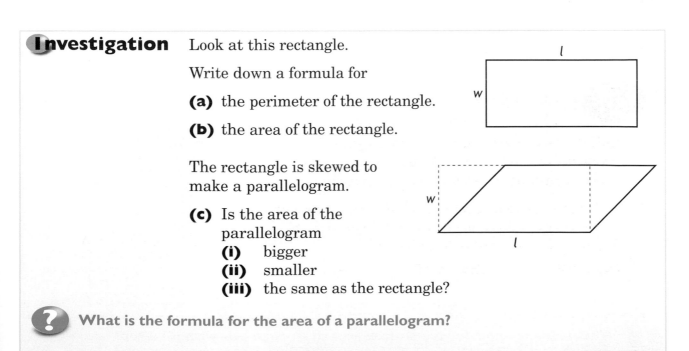

? What is the formula for the area of a parallelogram?

Using formulae to solve problems

Pia and Hans work for a food company.
One day their supervisor, Mr Smith, calls them into his office.

I want you to design a box for a new cereal. It must hold 8,000 cm³.

Pia's box

Hans' box

The formula for the volume of a box is $V = lwh$

Volume is measured in cubic units. Here it is cm³.

 What is the volume of Pia's box?
Look at Hans' box. Its volume is 8000 cm³. What is its width?

Pia colours her box. The area for the green face is 40 cm × 8 cm = 320 cm².

 What are the areas of the blue face and the red face?
How many faces has the box got altogether?

Pia writes
   The formula for the surface area is 2hw + 2hl + 2lw

 Explain the formula.

 How much cardboard does Pia need for her box?
How much cardboard does Hans need?

 Task

1   Design two more boxes with a volume of 8000 cm³.

2   Use the formula to work out the surface area of each box.

 What is the best design?

The best design has the smallest surface area.

 What is the formula for the surface area of an open box without a top?

Exercise

1 A company work out its profit using the formula:

Profit = Sales − Costs

(a) In one week the company sells £8000 of goods. The total costs are £3500.
How much profit does the company make?

(b) Next week the profit is £5000. Costs stay the same.
What are the sales?

(c) What must the costs be to satisfy
the Boss? Is this realistic?

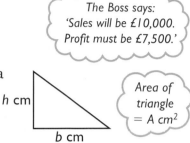
The Boss says:
'Sales will be £10,000.
Profit must be £7,500.'

2 **(a)** Write down the formula for finding the area
of this triangle.

(b) What is the area when $h = 5$ and $b = 8$?

(c) Find h when $b − 6$ and $A − 18$.

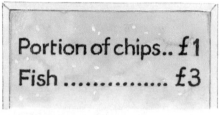
h cm

b cm

Area of
triangle
= A cm²

3 Tom and Mark buy some fish and chips. They only have a £20 note.
Tom writes down the change from the £20 as the formula: $C = 20 − p − 3f$

(a) What do C, p and f stand for?

(b) Jamie and David buy 3 portions
of chips and 4 of fish.
How much change do they get?

(c) Phoebe buys 5 portions of chips
and some fish. She gets £3 change.
How much fish does she buy?

(d) Stella does not want any fish. How many portions of chips can she
buy for £20?

Portion of chips.. £1

Fish £3

4 A rectangular garden pond has fencing round it.

(a) How wide is the pond? How long is the pond?

(b) What is the formula for the perimeter of
a rectangle?

(c) How much fencing is used?

(d) The island in the middle is 2 m long and
1 m wide.
Work out the surface area of the water in the pond.

(e) The pond is 0.5 m deep. Work out the volume of water.

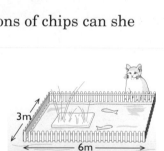
3m

6m

Investigation

Jamie is organising a party. He wants to get some invitation cards from the local
printers. The printers work out the cost of the cards using the formula

Cost (in pence) = 25 × number of cards + 50

They write it down as: $C = 25n + 50$

Jamie's bill is £8.

(a) What is the value of C?

(b) How many cards are printed?

Jamie's sister, Stephanie, wants a bigger party. The cost of her cards is £12.

(c) How many people does she invite to her party?

Finishing off

Now that you have finished this chapter you should be able to:

- understand what a **formula** is
- use formulae expressed in words and symbols
- substitute numbers into a formula
- use formulae to solve problems.

Review exercise

1 Find the value of $3a + 5b$ when:
(a) $a = 2$ and $b = 5$ (b) $a = -1$ and $b = 3$ (c) $a = -5$ and $b = -6$

2 Find the value of $2s + 4t$ when:
(a) $s = 1$ and $t = 10$ (b) $s = 4$ and $t = -1$ (c) $s = -5$ and $t = -6$

3 Find the value of $x + 2y + 3z$ when:
(a) $x = 6$, $y = 3$ and $z = 1$ (b) $x = 10$, $y = -20$ and $z = 50$
(c) $x = 15$, $y = 5$ and $z = -7$ (d) $x = 12$, $y = 5$ and $z = 0$

4 Find the value of $2d - 3e + 5f$ when:
(a) $d = 1$, $e = 1$ and $f = 1$ (b) $d = 6$, $e = -1$ and $f = 1$
(c) $d = 2$, $e = 2$ and $f = 2$ (d) $d = 5$, $e = 1$ and $f = 2$

5 The speed limit on motorways is 70 mph.
A police car notices a car doing 128 km h^{-1}.
To work out the driver's speed,
they use the formula

$$\text{Speed in mph} = \frac{5 \times \text{speed in km h}^{-1}}{8}$$

Is the driver speeding?

This converts kilometres per hour into miles per hour.

6 (a) Write down the formula for the area of this triangle.

The area of the triangle is 24 cm^2. The base is 16 cm.
(b) What is its height?

h

b

7 Look at this cube.
(a) How many faces does it have?
(b) How many edges does it have altogether?
(c) Write down a formula for the area of one face.
(d) Work out a formula for the total area of all the faces.
(e) Each edge is 4 cm long. What is the total area of the cube?

l

l

l

8 Ranjana wants to order some shirts for the school rugby team.
They cost £9 per shirt plus £5 overall postage.
(a) How does she work out the cost of 5 shirts?
(b) Write down a formula for the cost of the shirts.
(c) Use your formula to work out the cost of 12 shirts.
(d) How many shirts does Ranjana get for:
    (i) £86   **(ii)** £68   **(iii)** £113?

9 Robert wants to hire a car.

(a) How much does it cost to hire a car for 1 day?
(b) Write down a formula for the cost of hiring a car for n days.
(c) Robert decides to hire the car for one week. How much does he pay?
(d) Ruth hires a car. It costs her £105.
How many days does she hire the car for?

Investigation

Qamar and Rebecca are going on holiday to Kuala Lumpur.
They want to convert pounds into the local currency. There are 4 Ringgits to £1.

 Write down a formula to work out how many Ringgits they get for £P.

1 How many Ringgits do they get for £200?

2 On the way back, they spend a weekend in Bombay.
Here the currency is in Rupees. There are 50 Rupees to £1.
The Bureau of Exchange at the airport charges 400 Rupees commission.
How many Rupees do they get for £60?

Investigation

Zoe, Yuri, Xavier and Wan are trying to find the value of $-5e + 3f$ when $e = -4$ and $f = -2$.

| Zoe writes: −26 | Yuri gets: 14 | Xavier's answer is: 26 | Wan works out: −14 |

? Who is right? Where have the others gone wrong?

17 **Measuring**

Perimeter, area and volume

Eric's silly morning

After his breakfast at eighteen-oh-five,
Eric jumps into his car,
Nineteen square inches the distance to drive,
It's not exactly too far.

A ten litre parking space, easy to fit,
Four kilograms from the front door,
Ten metres in volume, is the smart lift,
But what is the size of its floor?

The top of his desk is rectangular,
Three metres, the length of one side,
And with Eric's great mountain of paper,
It has to be two litres wide.

? **What is silly about Eric's morning?**

Task

1 Rewrite the rhyme as a sensible *story*.

2 Eric's office has a rectangular floor 8 m long and 6 m wide. The office is 2.5 m high.
Work out

(a) the area   **(b)** the volume

3 Eric buys a new computer desk.
Here is its plan.
Work out

(a) the perimeter   **(b)** the area

4 The floor of the lift is square with an area of 4 m².
The volume of the lift is 12 m³.
Work out

(a) the length and width of the floor of the lift

(b) the height of the lift.

Perimeter of a rectangle = $2(l + w)$
Perimeter is measured in length units eg cm

Area of a rectangle = length × width = $l \times w$
Area is measured in square units eg cm²

Volume of a cuboid = length × width × height
Volume is measured in cubic units eg cm³

Exercise

1 Work out the perimeter of these rectangles.

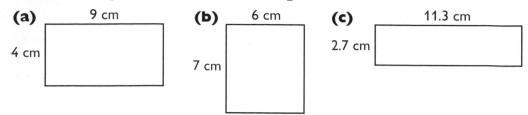

(a) 9 cm
4 cm

(b) 6 cm
7 cm

(c) 11.3 cm
2.7 cm

2 Work out the area of each rectangle in Question 1.

3 A square has a side 25 m long. Find its perimeter.

4 A window is 120 cm high and 100 cm wide. Find its area.

5 The diagram shows Sara's lounge.
Work out

(a) the value of x

(b) the value of y

(c) the area of the lounge.

3 m
1 m y m
x m
3 m
5 m

6 Find the area of these shapes.

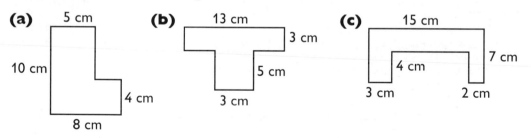

(a) 5 cm
10 cm
4 cm
8 cm

(b) 13 cm
3 cm
5 cm
3 cm

(c) 15 cm
7 cm
4 cm
3 cm   2 cm

7 Find the volume of these solids.

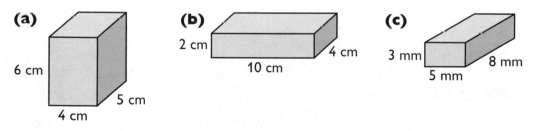

(a) 6 cm
5 cm
4 cm

(b) 2 cm
10 cm
4 cm

(c) 3 mm
5 mm
8 mm

More areas

This picture shows the stairs and front door in Anna's house.

? **What shapes can you see in this picture?**

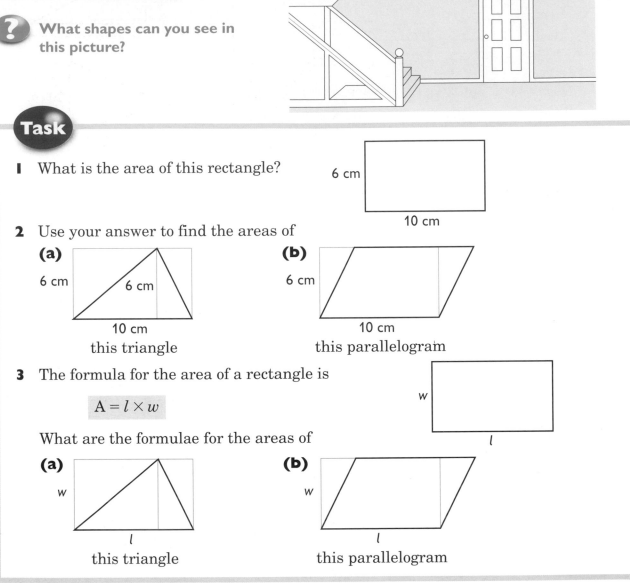

Task

1   What is the area of this rectangle?

6 cm

10 cm

2   Use your answer to find the areas of

(a)

6 cm

6 cm

10 cm

this triangle

(b)

6 cm

10 cm

this parallelogram

3   The formula for the area of a rectangle is

$$A = l \times w$$

What are the formulae for the areas of

w

l

(a)

w

l

this triangle

(b)

w

l

this parallelogram

? Another way of writing the formula for the area of a triangle is $A = \frac{1}{2}bh$
What do A, b and h stand for?

Anna wants to make the stairs safe for her young child.
She fixes this piece of wood to the stair posts.

? Explain how you would find the area of this piece of wood.

This picture shows the end of Anna's house.

? Explain what method you would use to find the area of it.

Exercise

Find the areas of these shapes.

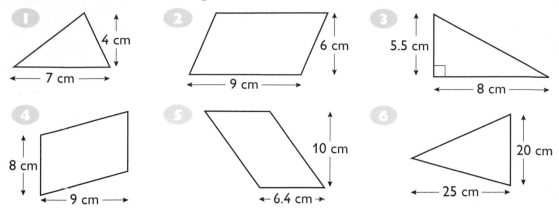

① 4 cm / 7 cm

② 6 cm / 9 cm

③ 5.5 cm / 8 cm

④ 8 cm / 9 cm

⑤ 10 cm / 6.4 cm

⑥ 20 cm / 25 cm

Investigation   Look at this island.

The squares are 1 km by 1 km.

?   **Why can't you find its area exactly?**

?   **What is the area of the green shape?**

?   **What is the area of the black shape?**

?   **Complete the following.**
   'The area of the island is bigger than … km²
   and smaller than … km².'

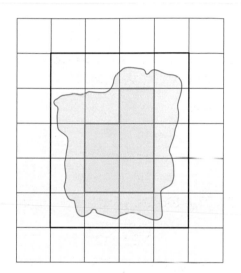

Estimate the area of the island.

Now estimate the areas of these islands.

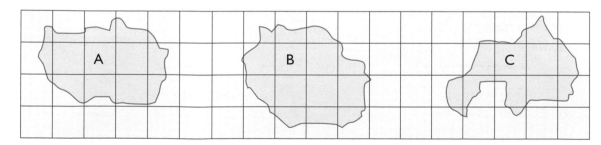

A   B   C

Activity   Here is a trapezium.
   You have two of these.

   How can you arrange them to make a
   parallelogram?
   What is the area of this parallelogram?
   Deduce the area of the trapezium.

   How else could you find the area of this trapezium?

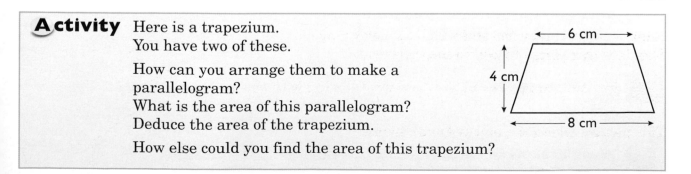

6 cm / 4 cm / 8 cm

Volume and surface area

Make a list of objects in the classroom which are cuboids.

Here is the net of a cuboid.
Each rectangle makes a face of the cuboid.

 What is the area of the bottom face?
What is the area of the top face?

The volume of the box tells you how much the box contains.

 What is the volume of the box?
What does the surface area tell you?

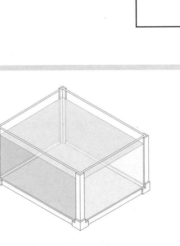

8 cm
5 cm
2 cm
Bottom
Top

Task

You are designing a fish tank.
It does not have a top.

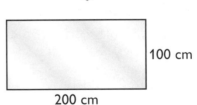

You have a sheet of clear plastic
which is 2 m by 1 m.

100 cm

200 cm

You also have edging strip and
corner pieces.

1 Show how you are going to cut up the plastic.
2 What area is wasted?
3 What length of edging strip do you need?
4 How many corner pieces do you need?
5 Work out the volume of your tank.

? **Which member of the class has the tank with the greatest volume?**

? **What is the surface area of the fish tank?**

Exercise

1. Work out the volume of these cuboids.

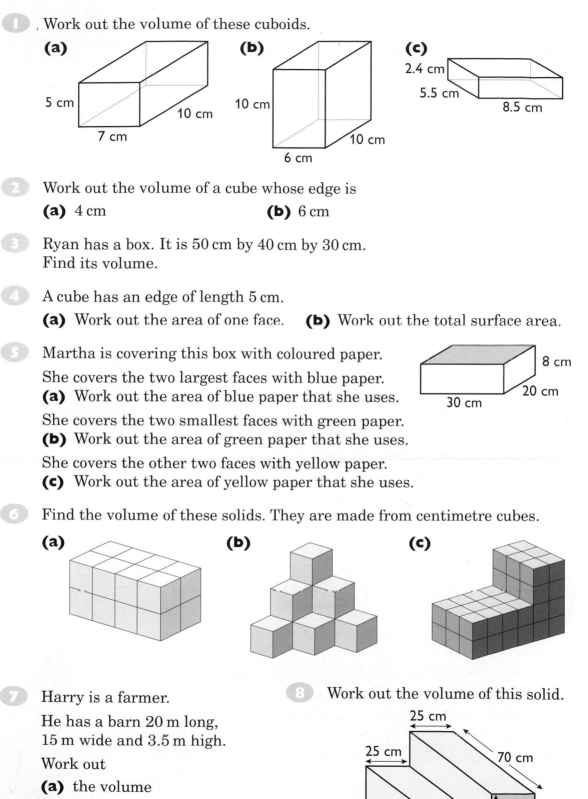

(a)
5 cm
10 cm
7 cm

(b)
10 cm
10 cm
6 cm

(c)
2.4 cm
5.5 cm
8.5 cm

2. Work out the volume of a cube whose edge is
   (a) 4 cm   **(b)** 6 cm

3. Ryan has a box. It is 50 cm by 40 cm by 30 cm.
   Find its volume.

4. A cube has an edge of length 5 cm.
   (a) Work out the area of one face.   **(b)** Work out the total surface area.

5. Martha is covering this box with coloured paper.

   She covers the two largest faces with blue paper.
   (a) Work out the area of blue paper that she uses.

   She covers the two smallest faces with green paper.
   (b) Work out the area of green paper that she uses.

   She covers the other two faces with yellow paper.
   (c) Work out the area of yellow paper that she uses.

   8 cm
   20 cm
   30 cm

6. Find the volume of these solids. They are made from centimetre cubes.

   (a)   **(b)**   **(c)**

7. Harry is a farmer.
   He has a barn 20 m long,
   15 m wide and 3.5 m high.
   Work out
   (a) the volume
   (b) the floor area.

8. Work out the volume of this solid.
   25 cm
   25 cm
   70 cm
   20 cm
   20 cm

Finishing off

Now that you have finished this chapter you should be able to:

- work out the area of a rectangle, triangle and parallelogram and shapes made up from these
- work out the volume of a cuboid and shapes made up from cuboids
- work out the surface area of a cuboid
- use correct units for length, area and volume.

Review exercise

1 Work out the perimeter and area of each of these rectangles.
(a) Length 7 cm, width 2 cm
(b) Length 9 mm, width 3 mm
(c) Length 17 inches, width 10 inches
(d) Length 5.5 m, width 2.3 m

2 An underpass is 40 feet long and 8 feet high.

Jake is painting both walls.
A tin of paint covers 120 square feet.

How many tins does Jake need?

3 Find the area of these shapes.

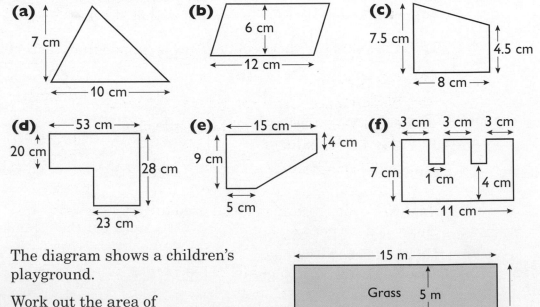

4 The diagram shows a children's
playground.

Work out the area of
(a) the sand-pit
(b) grass.

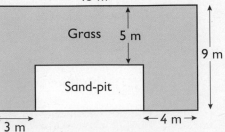

5 Estimate the area of each of these islands.
The squares represent square miles.

6 Work out the volume of these cuboids.

(a) Length 6 cm, width 4 cm, height 3 cm

(b) Length 30 mm, width 25 mm, height 20 mm

(c) Length 1.5 m, width 1 m, height 1.3 m

(d) Length 42.3 cm, width 27.5 cm, height 18.2 cm

7 Work out the surface area of the cuboids in Question 6.

8 Brandon is making concrete.

He is going to concrete a
rectangular area 8 m long
and 5 m wide to a depth
of 0.1 m.

What volume of concrete does
he require?

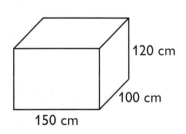

9 Natasha's water tank is shown in the diagram.
It is full of water.

(a) Work out the volume of water in the tank.

(b) Given that 1000 cm^3 = 1 litre write down
the volume in litres.

The tank is made of metal.
It has no top.

(c) Work out the area of metal used to make the tank.

120 cm

100 cm

150 cm

Investigation Draw as many different rectangles as you can with a
perimeter of 16 cm.
Each side must be a whole number.

Work out the area of each rectangle.

 Which rectangle has the greatest area?

 **Percentages**

? There are 600 boys and 600 girls at Avonford High School.
How many do sports?
How many do dancing?

> A percentage is another way of writing a decimal.

Task

Here is a chart for converting between percentages, decimals and fractions. Make your own copy, 20 cm long and 8 cm wide. (You can use graph paper.) Fill in the missing numbers.

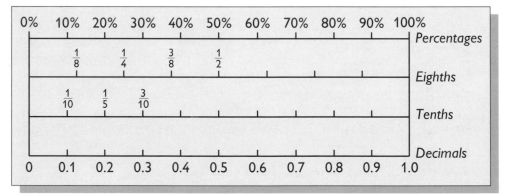

Set your friends some questions to do with it, like 'Roughly, what is $\frac{3}{8}$ as a percentage?'

42% can be written as a fraction $\quad 42\% = \frac{42}{100} = \frac{21}{50}$

... or as a decimal $\quad\quad\quad\quad\quad 42\% = 0.42$

Similarly $\quad\quad\quad\quad\quad\quad 28\% = \frac{28}{100} = \frac{7}{25}$

$\quad\quad\quad\quad\quad\quad\quad\quad 28\% = 0.28$

> Remember that percentage means out of 100

> Cancelling down.

 In 0.42 the 4 means four tenths. What does the 2 mean?

Remember: to change fractions or decimals to percentages multiply by 100% (a whole one)

$\frac{2}{5} = \frac{2}{5} \times 100\% = 40\%$ $\quad\quad\quad\quad\quad 0.37 = 0.37 \times 100\% = 37\%$

Exercise

1 Convert these percentages to fractions.

    (a) 50%   **(b)** 75%   **(c)** 80%   **(d)** 10%   **(e)** 64%

    (f) 35%   **(g)** 14%   **(h)** 5%   **(i)** 8%   **(j)** 3%

2 Convert these percentages to decimals.

    (a) 25%   **(b)** 60%   **(c)** 74%   **(d)** 8%   **(e)** 9%

    (f) 12.5%   **(g)** 1%   **(h)** 2.5%   **(i)** 3.2%   **(j)** $\frac{1}{2}$%

3 Convert these fractions to percentages.

    (a) $\frac{1}{5}$ **(b)** $\frac{2}{5}$ **(c)** $\frac{3}{5}$ **(d)** $\frac{4}{5}$ **(e)** $\frac{3}{10}$

    (f) $\frac{9}{20}$ **(g)** $\frac{3}{100}$ **(h)** $\frac{8}{25}$ **(i)** $\frac{1}{40}$ **(j)** $\frac{1}{1000}$

4 Convert these decimals to percentages.

    (a) 0.5   **(b)** 0.25   **(c)** 0.13   **(d)** 0.04   **(e)** 0.7

    (f) 0.23   **(g)** 0.01   **(h)** 0.99   **(i)** 0.53   **(j)** 0.155

5 Change these percentages to fractions.

    (a) $37\frac{1}{2}$%   **(b)** $87\frac{1}{2}$%   **(c)** $62\frac{1}{2}$%   **(d)** 50%   **(e)** 75%

6 Write these fractions **(i)** as percentages   **(ii)** as decimals

    (a) $\frac{1}{3}$ **(b)** $\frac{2}{3}$ **(c)** $\frac{1}{9}$ **(d)** $\frac{2}{9}$ **(e)** $\frac{5}{9}$

7 Copy and complete this table.

Fraction	Decimal	Percentage
$\frac{1}{2}$		
	0.25	
		75%
$\frac{1}{10}$		

These are useful to know. You should learn them.

More percentages

AVONFORD STAR
Famous Football Club In Credit

Falmouth City gave details of their finances at their Annual General Meeting yesterday. 'Ticket Sales provided 40% of our income,' says spokesperson Linda Leeroy. 'Our total income for the season is £60 million.'

Other sources of income are TV, sponsorship, shop sales and catering.

Look at these figures.

40% comes from the ticket sales

So other sources come to $(100 - 40)\% = 60\%$

> 100% represents $\frac{100}{100}$ or 1.
> It is the whole amount.

Ticket sales

40% of £60 million

$\frac{40}{100} \times £60$ million $= £24$ million

Other sources

60% of £60 million

$\frac{60}{100} \times £60$ million $= £36$ million

 Task

The percentage income for Falmouth City is shown in the bar chart.

(a) Look at the bar chart. Write the information as a table.

(b) Check the total percentage amounts to 100%.

(c) Work out how much money comes from each source. Check that the total is £60 million.

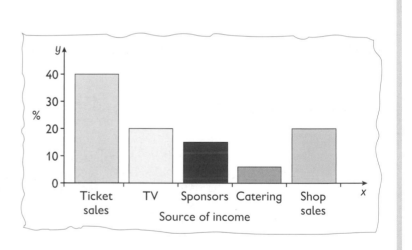

The shop sales for kits comes to £3 million.

Fraction for kit sales $= \frac{£3 \text{ million}}{£60 \text{ million}}$

Percentage kit sales $= \frac{3}{60} \times 100\% = 5\%$

What percentage of City's income is this?

 ? **What percentage of the income from shop sales comes from kits?**

Exercise

1 Find
   (a) 20% of £300
   (b) 3% of £5000
   (c) 10% of 220 km
   (d) 1% of 250 kg

2 Write these as percentages.
   (a) 16 out of 50
   (b) 5 kg out of 200 kg
   (c) 3 inches out of 12 inches
   (d) 4 litres out of 25 litres

3 A sweater is made from 80% acrylic. The rest is wool.
   What percentage is wool?

4 A skirt is 70% lambswool, 20% angora and the rest is polyamide.
   What percentage is polyamide?

5 Brass is made up of 66% copper. The rest is zinc.
   What percentage is zinc?

6 Stella scores 48 marks out of a possible 80 in a French test.
   What is this as a percentage?

7 Simon scores 32 marks in the same test.
   What is his percentage?

Investigation The pie charts show the contents of one type of cheese and of eggs.

1 Copy and complete the answer to
'What percentage of the cheese is protein?'

Fraction of protein $= \frac{90}{360}$ ← *Remember there are 360° in a circle.*

% of protein $= \frac{90}{360} \times 100\%$

$= \boxed{}$

2 What percentage of eggs is protein?

Selina eats 200 g of cheese and
2 eggs, each of 60 g

How much protein does she eat?

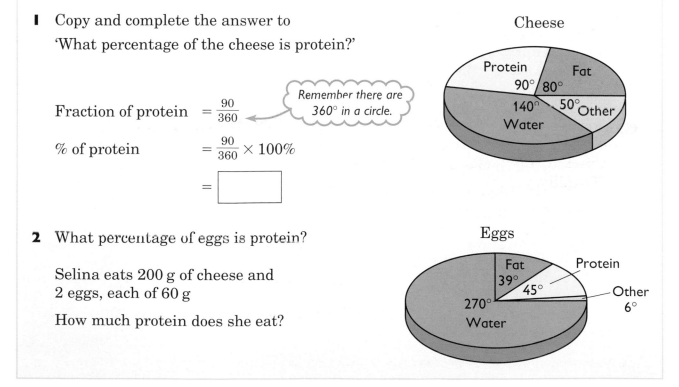

Cheese

Eggs

Everyday percentages

AVONFORD TIMES

Local nurses

Nurses at Avonford Hospital say they need a 4% pay increase to meet the rise in the cost of living.

AVONFORD TIMES

Avonford nurses accept 3% increase

This is less than the 4% they had wanted.

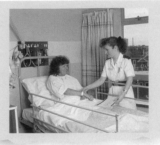

Anneka works in the Accident and Emergency Department of Avonford Hospital. She was earning £21 000 before the rise.

She writes

$$3\% \text{ of } 21\,000 = \frac{3}{100} \times 21\,000$$
$$= £630$$
$$\text{New salary} = £(21\,000 + 630) = £21\,630$$

Anneka's friend Terry says he can work it out quicker.

He writes

$$100\% + 3\% = 103\%$$
$$103\% \text{ of } £21\,000$$
$$\frac{103}{100} \times £21\,000 = £21\,630$$

 Which method is easier, Anneka's or Terry's?

 Anneka is not happy with the 3%. She says '4% is much more'.
How much more is 4% for Wanda?

Task

Make a poster showing everyday use of percentages.
You may use newspapers, magazines, leaflets and brochures.

William bought a new bicycle 3 years ago. It cost £400.
Now it has lost 30% of its value.

What is its value now?

$$30\% \text{ of } £400 = \frac{30}{100} \times £400$$
$$= £120$$

Its value is £400 − £120 = £280

I have lost £120

Exercise

1 These people work for Avonford Zoo. They are all given a 3% pay increase. Work out the new salary for

(a) Abigail, a trainee, who earned £13 000

(b) Alka, the big cats' keeper, who earned £18 000

(c) Alf, the maintenance man, who earned £15 000.

2 A car goes down in value by 20% after 1 year. Work out the value of these cars which are all 1 year old.

(a) a Fiat Brava; new price was £8500

(b) a Peugeot 406; new price was £13 700

(c) a Peugeot 806; new price was £17 000

(d) a Vauxhall Astra Coupe; new price was £16 250

3 **SALE 10% off**

Find the sale price of these items.

(a) £40   (b) £65   (c) £32

4 30% of a Tropical Fruit drink is made from juices of orange, lemon, pineapple and apricot.

How much of these juices is in

(a) a 1 litre bottle   (b) a 350 ml glass   (c) a 2.5 litre jug?

5 Edward buys a guitar. Its price is £300. He pays for it in instalments. He also pays a deposit of 35% first.

(a) How much deposit must he pay?

Then he makes 12 monthly payments of £20 each.

(b) What is the total of all 12 monthly payments?

(c) How much does he pay altogether?

(d) How much more than £300 is this?

Finishing off

Now that you have finished this chapter you should be able to:

- understand that percentages, fractions, and decimals are equivalent forms of the same number
- find a percentage of a quantity
- express one quantity as a percentage of another
- use percentages to solve problems such as percentage increase and decrease.

Review exercise

1 Eva scores these marks in tests.
Convert them to percentages.

(a) French $\frac{15}{20}$ **(b)** Maths $\frac{20}{25}$ **(c)** RE $\frac{6}{10}$ **(d)** Science $\frac{36}{40}$ **(e)** IT $\frac{39}{50}$

2 Convert these percentages to fractions in their lowest terms.

(a) Sale 25% off **(b)** 10% deposit required

(c) Music exam: distinction 80% **(d)** Deposit of 30% required

3 Convert these decimals to percentages.

(a) 0.55 **(b)** 0.72 **(c)** 0.6 **(d)** 0.255

4 **(a)** 35 of the 500 people on a train travel first class.
What percentage of the people travel first class?

(b) 700 people are given an injection. 49 of them get a slight temperature.
What percentage of the people get a temperature?

(c) 44 people out of 80 buy a programme at a rugby match.
What percentage of the people buy a programme?

5 A shop receives 700 light bulbs. 1% of them are faulty.
How many of the light bulbs are faulty?

6 A shop buys 500 batteries.
2% of them are faulty.
How many batteries are faulty?

7 A tub of fruit fool consists of 8% lemon.
The tub contains 120 g of fruit fool.
How many grams of lemon are there in
the tub?

8 Sam buys a keyboard priced at £550.
He pays the shopkeeper a deposit of 30% of the price of the keyboard.
How much deposit does he pay?

9 Helen buys a guitar priced at £180.
First she pays a deposit of 30%.

(a) How much deposit does she pay?

(b) She then makes 12 monthly payments
of £13 each. How much do these
payments come to altogether?

(c) What is the total of the deposit and the
12 monthly instalments?

(d) How much extra does she pay for the guitar?

10 12 out of 60 calculators have flat batteries within two years.
What percentage is this?

11 9 out of 30 pupils attain full marks in a Mathematics test.
What percentage of pupils is this?

12 12 textbooks out of 150 are thrown away at the end of the school year.
Some of their pages are no longer there.
What percentage is this?

13 The price of the following items goes up by 20%.
What are the new prices?

(a) CD £15   **(b)** jeans £45

(c) video recorder £250   **(d)** football ticket £25

14 These items go down in value by the percentage shown.
What is the new value of each item?

(a) Bicycle £300, down 20%.

(b) Guitar £440, down 25%.

(c) Model car £30, down 50%.

Reflection symmetry

Look at each picture.

It is **symmetrical**.

This type of symmetry is called **reflection symmetry** (or mirror symmetry).

? **Where is the line of symmetry (or mirror line) in each picture?**

Task

On a grid draw your own picture of an animal, butterfly or bird which has reflection symmetry.

This is how you can complete a drawing with two lines of symmetry.

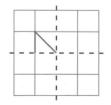

First reflect in the vertical line of symmetry.

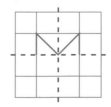

Then reflect in the horizontal line of symmetry.

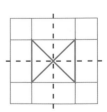

? **Now do these reflections in a different order.**
First reflect in the horizontal line, then in the vertical.
What do you notice?

Exercise

1. Which of these objects have reflection symmetry?

   (a)   **(b)**   **(c)**   **(d)**

2. Copy each of these shapes and draw all the lines of symmetry.
   Some do not have any symmetry.

   (a)

   isosceles triangle

   (b)

   rectangle

   (c)

   kite

   (d)

   L-shape

   (e)

   rhombus

   (f)

   *quadrant
   (quarter of a circle)*

3. Copy the figures which have lines of symmetry.
   Draw on the lines of symmetry.

   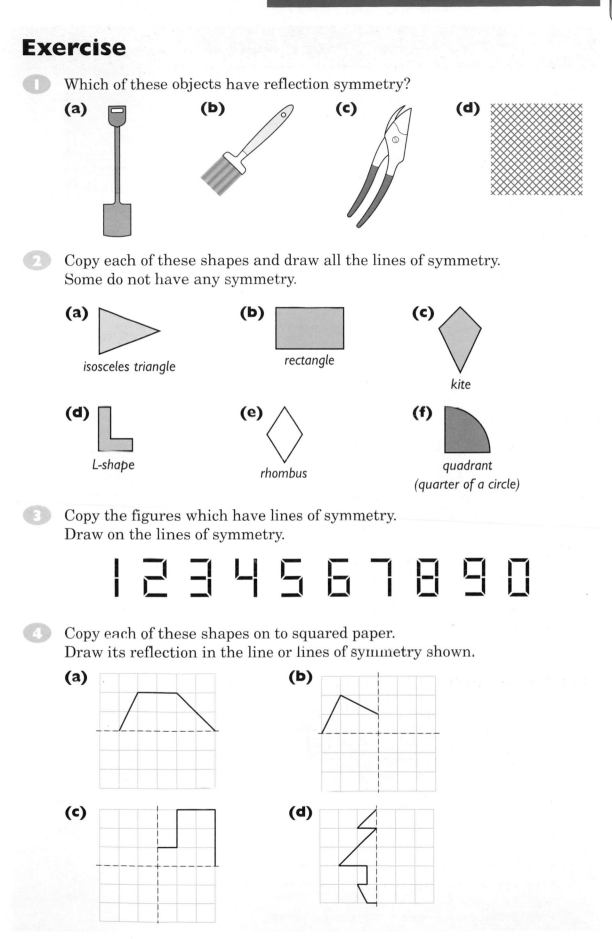

4. Copy each of these shapes on to squared paper.
   Draw its reflection in the line or lines of symmetry shown.

   (a)   **(b)**

   (c)   **(d)**

Rotational symmetry

Look at this letter S.

It has no reflection symmetry.

A barred spiral galaxy showing the letter S.

 Does it have **rotational symmetry**?

Copy this letter onto tracing paper. Turn the tracing through 180° (half a turn).

 What do you find?

Centre of rotation

S has **rotational symmetry of order 2**.

 Task

Follow these instructions to construct a regular octagon (8 sides).
You will need a ruler, a pair of compasses and a protractor.

1 Draw a circle with centre O. Construct triangle OAB with angle 45° at O.

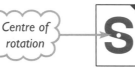

2 Construct triangle OBC with angle 45° at O.

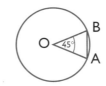

3 Continue drawing triangles in this way until you complete the octagon.

What is the order of rotational symmetry of a regular octagon?

This diagram shows a regular hexagon in a circle centre O.

4 What is the size of angle *x*?

5 Draw the circle and construct the hexagon.

What is the order of rotational symmetry of a regular hexagon?

OPQ is an isosceles triangle.
Rotate it about O so that OP lies on OQ.
Keep on doing this.
Do you always get a regular polygon?

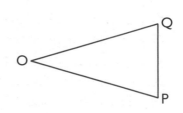

 Explain when you get a regular polygon.

Exercise

1 Which of these playing cards have rotational symmetry?

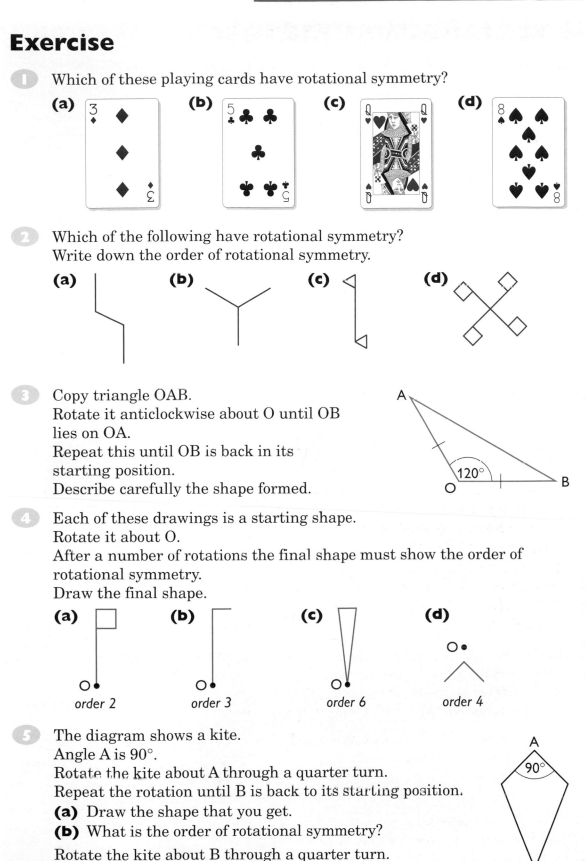

(a)   **(b)**   **(c)**   **(d)**

2 Which of the following have rotational symmetry?
Write down the order of rotational symmetry.

(a)   **(b)**   **(c)**   **(d)**

3 Copy triangle OAB.
Rotate it anticlockwise about O until OB
lies on OA.
Repeat this until OB is back in its
starting position.
Describe carefully the shape formed.

4 Each of these drawings is a starting shape.
Rotate it about O.
After a number of rotations the final shape must show the order of
rotational symmetry.
Draw the final shape.

(a) *order 2*   **(b)** *order 3*   **(c)** *order 6*   **(d)** *order 4*

5 The diagram shows a kite.
Angle A is 90°.
Rotate the kite about A through a quarter turn.
Repeat the rotation until B is back to its starting position.
(a) Draw the shape that you get.
(b) What is the order of rotational symmetry?

Rotate the kite about B through a quarter turn.
Repeat the rotation until A is back to its starting position.
(c) Draw the shape that you get.
(d) What is the order of rotational symmetry?

Using reflection and rotational symmetry

In the Task on page 156 you rotated
an isosceles triangle to produce
a regular octagon.

This octagon also has line symmetry.

? **How many lines of symmetry
does it have?**

**Copy the diagram and draw on
the lines of symmetry.**

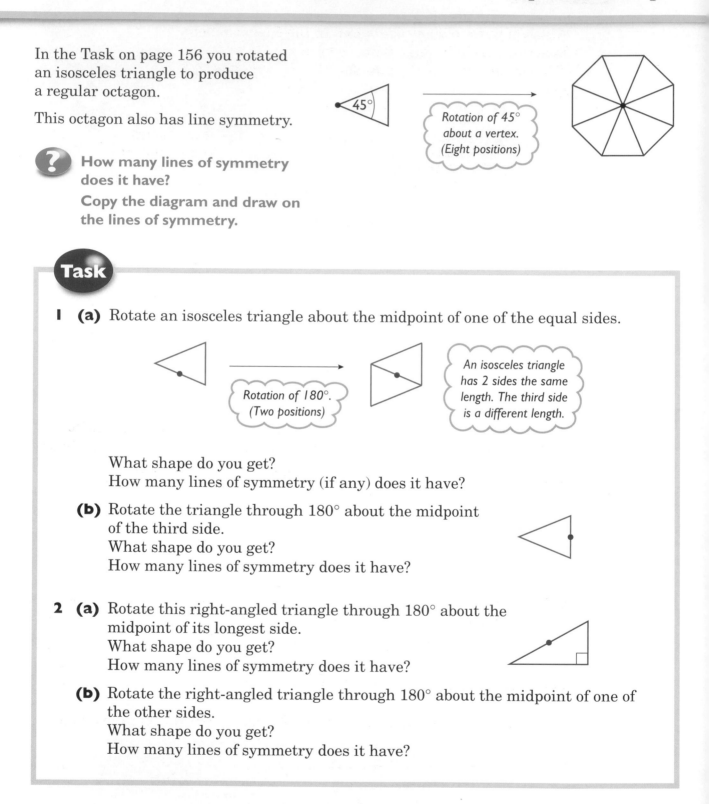

Rotation of 45°
about a vertex.
(Eight positions)

Task

I (a) Rotate an isosceles triangle about the midpoint of one of the equal sides.

Rotation of 180°.
(Two positions)

An isosceles triangle
has 2 sides the same
length. The third side
is a different length.

What shape do you get?
How many lines of symmetry (if any) does it have?

(b) Rotate the triangle through 180° about the midpoint
of the third side.
What shape do you get?
How many lines of symmetry does it have?

2 (a) Rotate this right-angled triangle through 180° about the
midpoint of its longest side.
What shape do you get?
How many lines of symmetry does it have?

(b) Rotate the right-angled triangle through 180° about the midpoint of one of
the other sides.
What shape do you get?
How many lines of symmetry does it have?

In the Task you rotated shapes to form new shapes.
The new shapes do not always have reflection symmetry.

Exercise

1 An equilateral triangle is rotated in the following way.
Describe carefully what shape is formed.
(This is the same method used at the top of page 158.)

(a)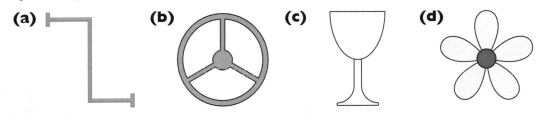

*Rotation of 60°
about a vertex.
(Six positions)*

(b)

*Rotation of 180°
about the midpoint
of a side.
(Two positions)*

(c) How many lines of symmetry do each of the new shapes have?

2 Which of these shapes have both reflection symmetry and rotation symmetry?

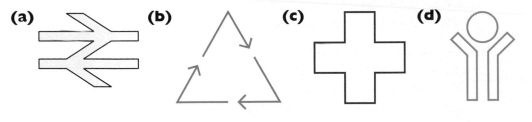

(a) **(b)** **(c)** **(d)**

3 Some of the shapes below have reflection symmetry, some have rotational symmetry and some have both. Describe fully the symmetry of each shape.

(a) **(b)** **(c)** **(d)**

4 **(a)** Explain how this trapezium can be rotated to produce a hexagon.

(b) How many lines of symmetry does this hexagon have?

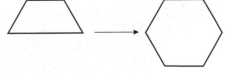

(c) Draw a hexagon with one line of symmetry.

5 **(a)** Explain how a trapezium can be rotated to produce a parallelogram.

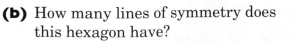

The parallelogram does not have reflection symmetry.

(b) **(i)** Draw a parallelogram that does have reflection symmetry.

(ii) What is it called?

Finishing off

Now that you have finished this chapter you should be able to:

- recognise reflection symmetry
- draw lines of symmetry
- reflect a shape in a line of symmetry
- recognise rotational symmetry
- write down the order of rotational symmetry
- complete a diagram so that it has a particular kind of symmetry.

Review exercise

1 Which of the following shapes have reflection symmetry?
Copy them and draw in the lines of symmetry.

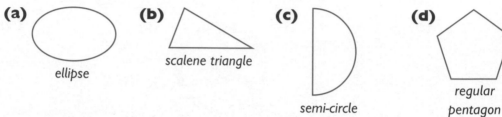

(a) ellipse **(b)** scalene triangle **(c)** semi-circle **(d)** regular pentagon

2 Copy each of these shapes onto squared paper.
Draw its reflection in the line or lines of symmetry shown.

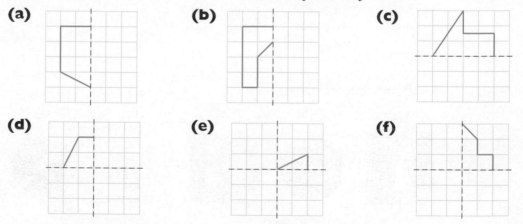

(a) **(b)** **(c)**

(d) **(e)** **(f)**

3 Give three reasons why each of the following pictures do not have
a vertical line of symmetry.

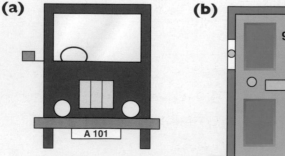
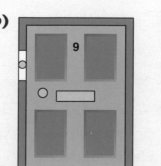
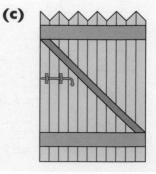

(a) **(b)** **(c)**

4 Which of the following have rotational symmetry?
Write down the order of rotational symmetry.

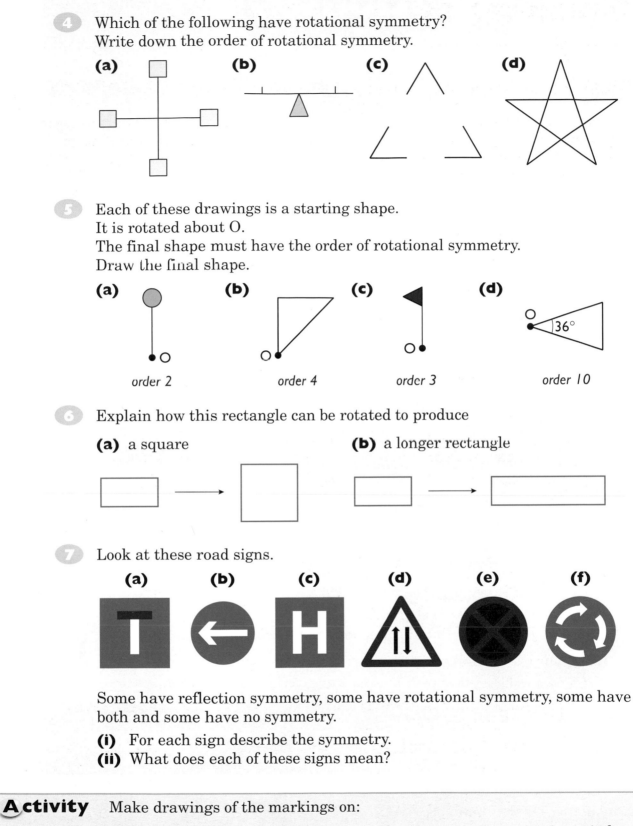

(a)   **(b)**   **(c)**   **(d)**

5 Each of these drawings is a starting shape.
It is rotated about O.
The final shape must have the order of rotational symmetry.
Draw the final shape.

(a)   **(b)**   **(c)**   **(d)**

order 2   *order 4*   *order 3*   *order 10*

6 Explain how this rectangle can be rotated to produce

(a) a square   **(b)** a longer rectangle

7 Look at these road signs.

(a)   **(b)**   **(c)**   **(d)**   **(e)**   **(f)**

Some have reflection symmetry, some have rotational symmetry, some have both and some have no symmetry.

(i) For each sign describe the symmetry.
(ii) What does each of these signs mean?

Activity   Make drawings of the markings on:

(a) a football pitch   **(b)** a squash court   **(c)** a rounders pitch
(d) the pitch or court for a sport of your choice.

In each case describe the symmetry.

Solving equations

Stuart and Debbie are playing the Think Of A Number game.

I think of a number.

Multiply it by 4.
Subtract 6.
The answer is 22.

 What is the inverse operation of subtract 6?
What is the inverse operation of multiply by 4?

Stuart writes

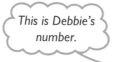 This is Debbie's number.

$$4n - 6 = 22$$
$$4n - 6 + 6 = 22 + 6$$
$$4n = 28$$
$$4n \div 4 = 28 \div 4$$
$$n = 7$$

Add 6 to both sides
Tidy up
Divide both sides by 4

 Work out $4 \times 7 - 6$. How does this help you check your answer?
Does it matter whether Stuart adds 6 first or divides by 4 first? Why?

 Task

Play your own game of Think Of A Number with a partner.

You think of a number.
Describe it like Debbie did.
Your friend works the number out.
Your friend writes out the working like Stuart did.

Then your friend thinks of a number.

Ranjana and her family go to Avonford Theme Park for the day.

Adults cost £14 each.

Ranjana writes the equation $4c + 28 = 60$

AVONFORD THEME PARK

Entrance Fee
2 adults and 4 children £60

 What does c stand for?
Solve Ranjana's equation.
How much does it cost for one child to go to the theme park?

Exercise

In this exercise set out your work carefully as Stuart did.

1 Solve these equations.

(a) $p + 7 = 13$ (b) $k - 12 = 3$

(c) $f - 10 = 4$ (d) $4a = 16$

(e) $h - 5 = 6$ (f) $3s = 18$

(g) $b + 3 = 8$ (h) $5r = 20$

(i) $g - 8 = 12$ (j) $7n = 42$

2 Solve these equations.

(a) $5x + 6 = 16$ (b) $11j - 11 = 22$

(c) $3a - 7 = 14$ (d) $2n - 10 = 4$

(e) $10 + 3f = 19$ (f) $3b - 15 = 3$

(g) $12 + 7g = 33$ (h) $4k - 18 = 2$

(i) $5p - 12 = 8$ (j) $4c - 30 = 10$

3 This is Jenny.

I think of a number.

Multiply it by 3.

Subtract 8.

The answer is 19.

(a) Write an equation to help you find Jenny's mystery number.

(b) Solve your equation.

(c) Check your answer.

4 Petra and her family are going to the cinema.
Part of the sign is missing.
Petra pays £25 for 2 adults and 5 children.

(a) Write an equation showing this information.

(b) Solve your equation.

(c) Check your answer.

Avonford Cinema

14.35 Performance

Drinks & Popcorn available in the Foyer at all times

ADULTS £5
CHILDREN £

Equations with an unknown on both sides

Emma wants to buy CDs from her local shop with her birthday money.

I can buy 4 CDs and have £2 change or 3 CDs and £9 change.

 You can write this as $4c + 2 = 3c + 9$.
Explain this equation.

Cyrus wants to know the cost of one CD.

He writes

$$4c + 2 = 3c + 9$$

Subtract 3c from both sides	$4c + 2 - 3c = 3c + 9 - 3c$
Tidy up	$c + 2 = 9$
Subtract 2 from both sides	$c + 2 - 2 = 9 - 2$
	$c = 7$

3c − 3c = 0

So 1 CD costs £7.

He checks his answer.

$$4c + 2 = 3c + 9$$
$$4 \times 7 + 2 = 3 \times 7 + 9$$
$$28 + 2 = 21 + 9$$
$$30 = 30$$

✓

 How much money was Emma given for her birthday?

 You are solving the equation $5n - 3 = 32 - 2n$.
What steps do you take?

Task

Work in a group of three. Each of you chooses two of the following equations.
Make a poster explaining

(a) how to solve your equations   **(b)** how to check your answers.

$$4x - 3 = x + 6$$
$$4t - 8 = 22 - t$$
$$4 + 3b = 2b + 6$$
$$10 - 3p = 12 - 5p$$
$$6 + 3n = 21 - 2n$$
$$3r - 21 = r - 19$$

 Look at the posters from other groups.
Can you follow how they have solved their equations?

Exercise

1   Solve the following equations.

(a) $2n + 1 = n + 3$ (b) $3p - 2 = 2p + 1$

(c) $1 + 4r = 2r + 5$ (d) $3b - 2 = 4 + b$

(e) $10 + 2f = 15 - 3f$ (f) $3 + 3w = 10 - 4w$

(g) $5k - 1 = 2k + 2$ (h) $15 - x = 23 - 2x$

(i) $12 - 3c = 18 - 5c$ (j) $4m - 3 = 5 + 2m$

2   Mercy is buying some bananas from the local shop.

I can buy 5 bananas with 10 p change or 3 bananas with 50 p change.

(a) Write down an expression for the cost of 5 bananas with 10p change.

(b) Write down an expression for the cost of 3 bananas with 50p change.

(c) Make an equation using your two expressions.

(d) Solve your equation.

(e) What is the cost of 1 banana?

(f) Check your answer.

(g) How much money does Mercy have?

3   Tim and Brad are having an argument about this equation.

$$7x - 8 = 19 - 2x$$

I think x = 4.

No you are wrong. x = 3.

Tim   Brad

(a) How can you check who is right?   You do not need to solve the equation.

(b) Who is right?

(c) Show how to solve the equation.
    Explain your method at each stage.

Solving equations with brackets

Mick and Tania are playing a game of Equation Bingo.
They take turns drawing an equation from a pile.

They have a Bingo card each to fill in with the answers.
The winner is the first one to have a complete row or column.

This is Tania's Bingo card.

8	1	4
3	5	9
7	2	6

This is Mick's Bingo card.

1	3	5
4	2	13
8	7	10

Tania draws this equation from the pack:

$$5(x+3) - 2x = 27$$

 **The equation has +, − and brackets.
Which do you work out first?**

Tania writes

$$5(x+3) - 2x = 27$$

Multiply out the brackets $\quad 5x + 15 - 2x = 27$
Tidy up $\quad\quad\quad\quad\quad\quad 3x + 15 = 27$
Subtract 15 from both sides $\quad 3x + 15 - 15 = 27 - 15$
$\quad\quad\quad\quad\quad\quad\quad\quad 3x = 12$
Tidy up
Divide both sides by 3 $\quad 3x \div 3 = 12 \div 3$
$\quad\quad\quad\quad\quad\quad\quad\quad x = 4$

*Remember BIDMAS.
What does it stand for?*

 How can you check that x = 4 is right?

Both Mick and Tania cross 4 off their Bingo cards.

Mick draws the next equation: $\quad 4(p-2) = 2p + 10$

 Solve this equation. Whose card is crossed off?

 Tania wins next time. What number came up? Write down a suitable equation.

Task

Play your own game of Equation Bingo with a friend.

 How can you be sure that no one cheats?

Exercise

1 Solve these equations.

(a) $4(d + 2) = 20$

(b) $5(h - 3) = 15$

(c) $5(x + 4) = 20$

(d) $3(y - 4) = 18$

(e) $2(3x + 1) = 20$

(f) $3(2m - 4) = 12$

(g) $7(b + 2) - 3b = 18$

(h) $4(3x - 2) - 7x = 2$

(i) $2(5a - 3) + 8 - 4a = 44$

(j) $3(p + 2) + 2p = 36$

(k) $5(q - 1) - 4q = 9$

(l) $7(r + 3) - 31 = 81$

2 Solve these equations. Check your answers for each equation.

(a) $2(b + 3) = b + 7$

(b) $3(x + 1) = 2x + 5$

(c) $5(x - 4) = 2x + 1$

(d) $4(2a + 1) = 5a + 7$

(e) $5(f - 1) = 4f + 1$

(f) $3(x + 2) = 2(x + 3)$

(g) $5(x + 2) = 2(x + 20)$

(h) $10(x + 1) = 5(x + 3)$

(i) $7(x - 1) = 2(x + 4)$

(j) $3(3g - 8) = 2g - 3$

(k) $4(2e + 3) = 7e + 2$

(l) $5(3n - 2) = 10n$

Activity Wan and Lee play a game of Equation Bingo.
The first to get a line is the winner.

Wan's card

1	8	10
9	13	4
5	6	3

Lee's card

13	4	6
12	5	9
1	10	8

Solve the following equations and work out who wins the game.
Check your answers.

1 $5(x - 2) + 3x = 14$

2 $9c + 7 - 3c = 19$

3 $3 + 4p - 2p = 13$

4 $10r - 4 = 3(r + 1)$

5 $5(n + 1) = 65$

6 $2k - 14 = 2$

7 $3(2b - 5) = 4b - 7$

8 $6d = 4(5 + d)$

Using equations to solve problems

Lulu works at a rescue centre for pets.
She feeds the dogs.
Every day she gives each small dog b biscuits.
A large dog gets 2 more biscuits than a small dog.

? **How many biscuits does a large dog receive?**

There are 6 small dogs and 4 large dogs at the
rescue centre. They get 38 biscuits altogether.

You can write $6b + 4(b + 2) = 38$

? **Explain this equation.**
Solve the equation.
How many biscuits does a small dog get? What about a large dog?

Task

Here are some expressions.

| $A = x - 4$ | $E = 3x$ | $I = 4x$ | $L = x + 6$ | $P = x - 1$ | $S = 2x$ | $W = 3 - x$ | $Z = x + 4$ |

Write down the letter for each of the following. They spell a name. What is the name?

(6 more than x)   (4 less than x)   (Double x)   (Twice x)   (4 times x)   (3 times x)

□ □ □ □ □ □

Task

Sheuli, Vronnie and Halley are given £85 between them. Halley is given £h.

I have £5 more than Halley.

Sheuli

I was given twice as much as Halley.

Vronnie

Halley

(a) Write down expressions for:
   (i) Sheuli's money   **(ii)** Vronnie's money   **(iii)** the total for the three friends.

(b) Write down an equation. Solve it to find h.

(c) How much is each of them given?   **?** **How can you check your answers?**

Exercise

1 Hoddel wants to find the weight of some identical parcels.
She uses weighing scales.

She writes: Weight of left side = 5p + 4

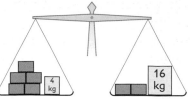

(a) What does p stand for?

(b) Write down an expression for
the weight of the right hand side.

(c) Form an equation.

(d) Solve your equation to find the weight of one parcel.

(e) Check your answer.

2 Sergio thinks of a
mystery number, x.

*I think of a number.
I multiply it by 4 and add 2.
The answer is four more than
twice my number.*

(a) Write down expressions for:
  (i) 'I multiply my number by 4 and add 2'
  (ii) '4 more than twice my number'.

(b) Form an equation.

(c) Solve your equation to find Sergio's mystery number.

3 Peter is the penguin keeper at Avonford Zoo.
He is designing a new enclosure for the penguins. It must fit around the
penguin pond.
Here are his two designs. Measurements are in metres.

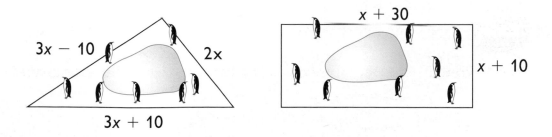

(a) Write down expressions for the perimeters of the enclosures.
Simplify them.

(b) Both penguin enclosures have the same perimeter of fencing.
Write down an equation for x.

(c) Solve your equation to find x.

(d) What are the dimensions of each penguin enclosure?

(e) How much fencing will Peter need for both fencing enclosures?

Finishing off

Now that you have finished this chapter you should be able to:

- solve an equation with an unknown on one side
- solve an equation with an unknown on both sides
- use equations to solve problems.

Review exercise

1 Solve the following equations.

    (a) $y + 5 = 9$ **(b)** $2n = 12$

    (c) $t - 3 = 11$ **(d)** $4m = 16$

    (e) $10 + a = 12$ **(f)** $18 = 3k$

    (g) $2 + r = 7$ **(h)** $5t = 45$

2 Solve the following equations.

    (a) $4n + 7 = 15$ **(b)** $3t - 12 = 3$

    (c) $4 + 3d = 19$ **(d)** $7q - 24 = 4$

    (e) $2f - 7 = 3$ **(f)** $4k + 8 = 24$

    (g) $6h - 5 = 1$ **(h)** $3(6 + 2r) = 30$

3 Solve the following equations.

    (a) $5t + 8 = 4t + 18$ **(b)** $3n - 5 = 7 - 3n$

    (c) $4(g + 1) = 3g + 9$ **(d)** $2(p - 2) = p - 1$

    (e) $3(x + 2) = 2x + 13$ **(f)** $10 - 3r = 12 - 5r$

    (g) $3(2h - 3) = 4h + 3$ **(h)** $2(5 - k) = 12 - 4k$

4 Tim is buying some fish and chips.
He pays £12 for 3 portions of fish and
3 portions of chips.

    (a) Write down an equation to show
        this information.
        Use f to show the cost of
        one portion of fish.

    (b) Solve your equation to work out the price of one portion of fish.

    (c) Check your answer.

5 Keiran is buying pencils.

I can buy 6 pencils with 28p change or 4 pencils with 52p change.

(a) Write down an expression for buying
(i) 6 pencils with 28p change
(ii) 4 pencils with 52p change

(b) Form an equation.

(c) Solve your equation to find the cost of one pencil.

(d) Check that you have solved the equation correctly.

(e) How much money does Keiran have?

6 Alexandra is weighing some tins of soup using scales.
The soup tins are all the same.
Each weighs m kg.

Alexandra writes: $4m + 5 =$

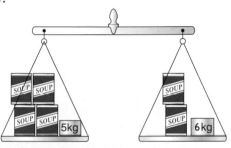

(a) How should Alexandra finish off this equation?

(b) Solve the equation to find the weight of one tin of soup.

(c) Check you have solved the equation correctly.

(d) What is the total weight on the left hand side of the scales?

7 Oliver and Susan are trying to solve this equation.

$$10n - 18 = 2(7 - 3n)$$

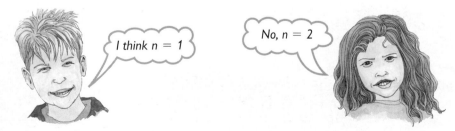

I think n = 1

No, n = 2

(a) Without solving the equation check who is right.

(b) Solve the equation, writing out the answer.

Activity Design your own set of 10 Equation Bingo cards.

The equations should have answers 1, 2, 3, ..., 9, 10.

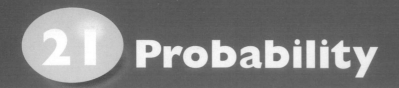

21 Probability

Using equally likely outcomes

Avonford School is holding a summer fete.
There is a raffle at the fete.
500 tickets are sold.

Amy buys a ticket
for the raffle.

Each of the 500 tickets is **equally likely**
to win the prize.

The probability that Amy's ticket wins is 1 in 500, or $\frac{1}{500}$.

Tom buys 3 tickets.

The probability that Tom wins is $\frac{3}{500}$.

Tom has 3 chances
of winning.

 What is the probability that Amy does not win?
What is the probability that Tom does not win?

The pupils in Class 8B are organising a game for the fete.
They are using a die with 10 faces numbered from 1 to 10.

 What is the probability of winning in this game?
What is the probability of losing? Is the game fair?

CLASS 8B
10p to throw dice
WIN 20p
if you score
8 or more

 Task

Play the game 30 times.
Work out how much money you spend and how much you win.
Collect the results from the whole class.

? **How much profit is made?**

? **Think of some more games using dice that Class 8B could use.**
Which ones would make the most money?

 You know the probability that something will happen.
How can you find the probability that it will not happen?

For example, there is a
60% chance it will
rain tomorrow.

Exercise

1 Stephen throws a normal 6-sided dice. What is the probability that he gets:

(a) 1   **(b)** 6

(c) an odd number   **(d)** 5 or more?

2 Sunil is using this 8-sided spinner in a game.
What is the probability that he gets:

(a) yellow

(b) red

(c) 1

(d) a green 4

(e) a red or yellow number 3 or 4

(f) a green 2?

3 Jayne picks a card out of a normal pack of 52 cards.
Find the probability that her card is:

(a) the Seven of Diamonds   **(b)** an Ace

(c) not an Ace   **(d)** a spade

(e) not a spade   **(f)** a King, Queen or Jack?

4 In the National Lottery balls are selected at random by a machine.
They are numbered from 1 to 49.

What is the probability that
the first ball selected is:

(a) the number 42

(b) an odd number

(c) greater than 30

(d) a multiple of 3

(e) not a multiple of 3

(f) a prime number

(g) not a prime number?

5 Zoë and Anna are playing a game with cards numbered from 1 to 12.

(a) Zoë takes a card and says: 'You win if you get a prime number, otherwise I win.'
Is Zoë's game fair? Explain your answer.

(b) Anna takes a card and says: 'I win if I get a prime number, you win if you get a multiple of 3. Otherwise it's a draw.'
Is Anna's game fair? Explain your answer.

(c) Think of a way to make the game fair.

Probability scales

 How do you think each person decides on these probabilities? How accurate do you think they are?

These probabilities can be shown on a probability scale like this.

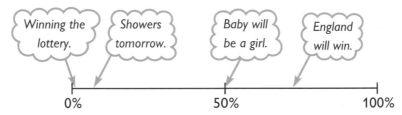

 What does a probability of 0% or 0 mean? What does a probability of 100% or 1 mean?

Task

1 Think of an event which can be described by each of these words.
   likely   unlikely   certain   impossible   very likely   very unlikely   evens

2 Decide on a probability for each event. Write it as a percentage.

3 Draw a probability scale and mark your events on the scale.

4 Make a class poster with a number line and the most interesting events on it.

 How good do you think your probability estimates are?

Some probabilities can be worked out exactly, using equally likely outcomes.

Other probabilities are only estimates.

> Amy knows she has 1 chance in 500 of winning the raffle.

> The chance is only about 1 in 100 for it to snow on Christmas day.

 Think of 3 events where you work out the probabilities using equally likely outcomes.

 Think of 3 events where the probabilities are estimates.

Exercise

1 Choose one of these words to describe each of the events below.

> certain   impossible   likely   very likely
> unlikely   very unlikely   evens

(a) Someone you know will win the lottery this week.

(b) A baby will be born a boy.

(c) You will watch TV tonight.

(d) You will get a 7 when you throw an ordinary die.

(e) You will live to be 100 years old.

Think of events to match the two remaining words you haven't used.

2 Copy this probability scale. Mark each of the events from Question 1 on it.

```
0%              50%              100%
```

Think of three more events of your own. Mark them on the probability scale.

3 Hassan is carrying a basket of shopping.

Hassan drops the basket outside in the car park.

(a) Which item is most likely to break?

(b) Which item is least likely to break?

(c) Draw a probability scale. Mark each item on it to show how likely it is to break.

4 Estimate the probability of each of the following events. Write it as a percentage.

(a) You will have three or more children.

(b) You will use a computer some time in the next week.

(c) Man will discover time travel in the next hundred years.

(d) It will rain tomorrow.

Draw a probability scale and mark each event on it.

5 Look at the list of events below. For each one write down either 'I can work out the exact probability using equally likely outcomes', or 'I can only estimate the probability'.

(a) You will get a head when you toss a coin.

(b) It will snow on Christmas Day this year.

(c) Liverpool will win the next FA Cup.

(d) You will get a six when you throw a die.

(e) A drawing pin which you toss will land point down.

Estimating probability

In the game Pass the Pigs two small model pigs are thrown in the air.
You score points according to how they land.

You cannot work out a probability here.

The different positions the pigs land in are not equally likely.

*But, you can make an **estimate** for the probabilities by carrying out an experiment.*

Emily throws one of the pigs 50 times.
Here are her results.

Side	31
Back	9
All four feet	6
Front feet and snout	3
One front foot and snout	1

From these results, the **relative frequency** of a pig landing on its side is

It lands on its side 31 times … out of 50 throws

$\frac{31}{50}$ or 0.62

Relative frequency is used as an estimate of probability.

Emily throws the pig again. There is a probability of 0.62 that the pig will land on its side.

? **Emily throws the pig another 50 times. Will it land on its side exactly 31 times again? How accurate is the estimated probability of 0.62?**

Task

To make a biased die

(a) copy this net of a die onto squared paper and cut it out.

(b) attach a small piece of blu-tack to the inside of one face.

(c) stick the net together.

Throw your die 50 times and write down the results.
Use your results to estimate the probability of each number coming up.

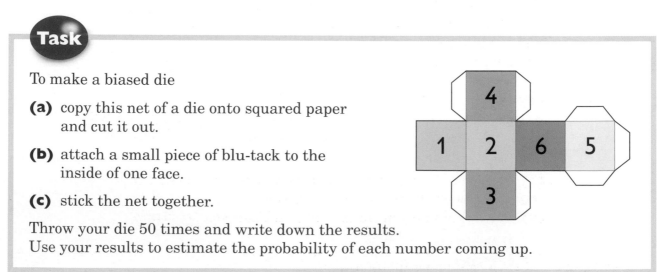

? **What results did you expect?**
How can you make your probability estimates more reliable?

Exercise

1. Laura tosses a drawing pin 50 times.
   It lands point up 22 times.
   (a) Estimate the probability that the drawing pin will land point up. Use the above results.
   (b) How many times does the drawing pin land point down?
   (c) Estimate the probability that the drawing pin will land point down.

2. Paul is carrying out an opinion poll before a local election.
   He asks 80 people which candidate they intend to vote for.
   (a) Estimate the probability that the next person he asks says Joe.
   (b) Estimate the probability that the next person he asks says Mary.
   (c) 2000 people vote in the local election. From Paul's opinion poll, how many people do you expect to vote for each candidate?

   Joe Wilson 32
   Mary Smythe 38
   Fred Jones 10

3. Martin thinks his die is biased. He thinks that the number six does not come up as often as the other numbers.
   He throws the die 120 times. Here are his results.

Score	1	2	3	4	5	6
Frequency	26	18	24	18	19	15

   (a) How many times should each number come up if the die is fair?
   (b) From Martin's results, estimate the probability of getting a six.
   (c) Do you think that the die is fair?

4. Gemma, Simon and Julie have three coins.
   They know that one of the coins is biased.
   They take one coin each, and toss it a number of times.
   Here are their results.

Gemma	Coin A	Heads 21	Tails 29
Simon	Coin B	Heads 61	Tails 39
Julie	Coin C	Heads 90	Tails 110

   (a) How many times did each of them toss their coin?
   (b) Whose results are the most reliable?
   (c) Which coin do you think is biased? Can you be sure?

Activity   Toss a coin yourself 100 times.
Record the results.
Compare them with the results in Question 4.

Finishing off

Now that you have finished this chapter you should be able to:

- find the probability of an event using equally likely outcomes
- understand that the probabilities of an event happening or not happening add up to 1
- describe events using words such as certain, impossible, likely, unlikely and evens
- put events in order of probability
- mark events on a probability scale
- say whether a game is fair or unfair
- understand that an experiment may have different outcomes
- use an experiment to estimate probabilities.

Review exercise

1 Aisha throws a die with 8 faces, numbered 0 to 7.
What is the probability that the number she gets is

(a) 0   **(b)** not 0

(c) 5 or more   **(d)** an odd number

(e) a square number   **(f)** not a square number?

2 Matt and Anna are playing a game of 'Battleships'.
Anna has drawn this diagram. The coloured squares represent ships.

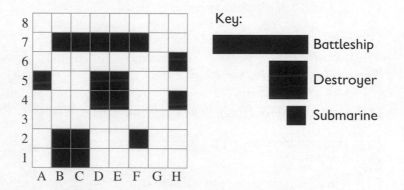

Anna chooses a square at random, without looking at the diagram.
What is the probability that she

(a) hits one of Matt's ships

(b) hits the battleship

(c) hits a destroyer

(d) hits a submarine

(e) does not hit a ship?

3 Charlotte and James are playing with a die. It has 10 faces.
Look at the following games. Is the game fair?
If it is not fair, say who is more likely to win?
(a) Charlotte wins if they get 5 or more.
(b) Charlotte wins if they get an odd number.
(c) James wins if they get a multiple of 3.
(d) James wins if they get a prime number.
(e) Charlotte wins if they get less than 5.

4 Dave lives on a busy main road. One morning he carries out a survey of
the vehicles passing his house between 10 and 11 a.m.
Here are his results.

Car	Lorry	Motorcycle	Van	Bus/Coach
43	18	11	16	7

(a) How many vehicles are in Dave's survey?
(b) Estimate the probability that the next vehicle that passes Dave's
house after 11 a.m. is a car.
(c) Estimate the probability that the next vehicle that passes Dave's
house after 5 p.m. is a lorry.
(d) How reliable are your answers to (b) and (c)? Explain.

5 Maxine plants 80 marigold seeds. 64 of the seeds germinate.
Maxine's friend Sue plants 200 similar marigold seeds.

Maxine's tray   Sue's tray

(a) Estimate the probability that one of Sue's seeds, chosen at random,
will germinate.
(b) Estimate the probability that one of Sue's seeds, chosen at random,
will not germinate.
(c) How many of Sue's seeds do you think will germinate?

6 **(a)** Write down an event which has probability 0.
(b) Write down an event which has probability 1.
(c) Write down an event which has probability $\frac{1}{2}$.

7 Estimate the probabilities of each of the following events.
Explain how you decide on each probability.
(a) Man will land on the moon again in the next 10 years.
(b) You will live to be 100 years old.
(c) You will eat chips sometime in the next week.
(d) You will watch TV for more than one hour tonight.
(e) It will snow sometime next January.

Show your answers on a probability scale.

22 Number patterns

Working systematically

Look at this diagram.

You can move from the red circle to either of the other circles.
You can only move downwards.

 There is one path from the red circle to the green circle.
How many circles are there in the bottom row?

Look at the second diagram.

 How many paths are there from the
red circle to the blue circle?
How many circles are there in the bottom row?

Look at the third diagram.

 How many paths are there from the
red circle to the yellow circle?
How many circles are there in the
bottom row?

 What pattern can you see?

Task

1 Copy the third diagram.

2 Move from the red circle to each of the other circles.
How many different paths can you find?

3 Add another row of circles to the bottom of the pattern.
How many different paths are there to these new circles?
Write the numbers in your new circles.

 What is the easiest way of finding them?

4 Find the total of each row in the triangle.
What do you notice?
What is special about these numbers?

It helps to be systematic.

 How can you be systematic in the Task?

This pattern of numbers is called Pascal's Triangle.
Pascal's Triangle has many different number patterns.

 Look at the diagonal lines. What patterns do you find?

Investigation

The Tower of Hanoi is a
mathematical puzzle.
There are three pegs and several
discs as shown.

The aim is to move all of the discs
onto another peg.
The rules are:

> You can only move one disc at a time.
>
> You must not put a larger disc
> on top of a smaller disc.

*You should take as
few moves as possible.*

1   Make your own Tower of Hanoi by cutting out discs from card.

2   Start with 2 discs. How many moves do you need?

3   Show that it cannot be done in fewer moves.

4   How many moves are needed with
    (a) 2 discs
    (b) 3 discs?
    Fill in the table.

Number of discs	Number of moves needed
1	
2	
3	
4	
5	

5   Explain how you have done this investigation systematically.
    How has it helped you?

Investigation

Look at this addition sum.

There are 10 letters. Each letter stands for one
(and only one) of the 10 numbers
1, 2, 3, 4, 5, 6, 7, 8, 9, 0.

```
  W R M G M T Y
  H M H T M T K
  -------------
  M I K T O G K Y
```

1   Replace all the letters by their numbers.
    Complete this table.

Number	1	2	3	4	5	6	7	8	9	0
Letter										

2   You can solve this problem systematically.
    Write down how you do this, step by step.

Making predictions

Pearl is laying a garden path around her pond.
Her paving stones are regular hexagons.
The side of each paving stone has a length of 1 foot.

 How many sides does a hexagon have?

Here are the first three stages
of Pearl's design.

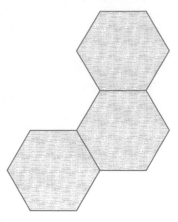

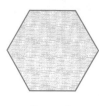

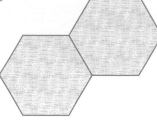

Stage 1   *Stage 2*   *Stage 3*

Pearl makes a table giving the perimeter
of her path at different stages.

 **What is the perimeter for each of the
next three stages?**
How can you check your answer?

Stage	Perimeter (in feet)
1	6
2	10
3	14

Pearl writes

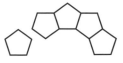

> At each stage the perimeter is 4 more
> than the one before.
> So, the perimeter of the 4th stage = 6+3×4 =18 ✓
>   5th stage = 6+4×4 =22 ✓
>   6th stage = 6+5×4 =26 ✗

Pearl has got the 6th stage wrong. Why?
How many paving stones does Pearl need to complete her path?
What is the shape of the pond?

Task

Kwame is laying a path around his lawn, using regular
pentagon slabs.

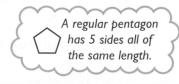

1 Cut out pentagons from card. Put them together to make a model of the path.
2 Each stone has sides of 1 foot. Find the perimeter of each stage.
3 Make a table of your results.

Describe the pattern in the table.
What shape is the lawn?

> A regular pentagon
> has 5 sides all of
> the same length.

Exercise

1 Avonford High School's canteen uses trapezium-shaped tables.
Each table can seat 7 people. The tables are laid out in long lines.

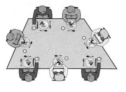 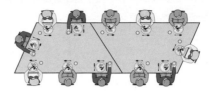

Stage 1 (1 table)   *Stage 2 (2 tables)*

(a) Draw the next 2 stages.

(b) Fill in this chart.

Number of tables	Number of seats
1	7
2	12
3	
4	
5	

(c) Predict how many people can sit at:

(i) 6 tables   **(ii)** 8 tables
(iii) 10 tables.

(d) How many people can sit at a line of 20 tables?

2 Alex is laying a straight garden path using regular octagonal paving stones.
Each side is 1 foot long.

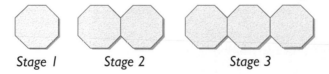

Stage 1   *Stage 2*   *Stage 3*

(a) Draw the next 3 stages.
(b) Make a table showing the perimeter of the first 5 stages.
(c) How do you find the perimeter of the next stage?
(d) Predict the perimeter of the 9th and 10th stages.

Investigation   At a wedding reception, the caterers use tables like this, in lines.

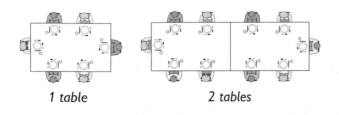

1 table   *2 tables*

The tables are set out as in the diagram opposite.

All the seats are filled.

How many people attend the wedding reception?

(3 tables)

(10 tables)

Finding the rule

Paddy is making a tiling pattern on his bathroom floor.
Each layer of tiles has a different design.

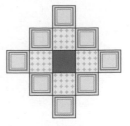

Starting design

Layer 1
4 new tiles

Layer 2
8 new tiles

 How many new tiles are needed for layer 3?

Paddy makes this table.

Layer no.	No. of new tiles needed
1	4
2	8
3	
4	
5	

 What are the missing numbers in Paddy's table?

Paddy notices that the number of tiles is 4 more for each new layer.

He writes

It is the 4 times table.
The rule is T = 4 L

This is the rule
in English.

This is in
algebra.

 What do *T* and *L* stand for?
How many new tiles are there in layer 10?

Task

1 Draw the first 3 layers with this starting design. Use squared paper.
2 Find a rule for the number of tiles for the next layer.
3 Make a table like the one above.
4 How many new tiles are needed for layer 10?

This is a true story.
The first time Jezebel was pregnant, she had one kitten.
Next time she had 2, then 4 and then 8.

 What do you notice about these numbers?
Guess what happened next.

Exercise

1 **(a)** Draw the first 3 layers for this tiling design.

(b) How many new tiles are needed for each layer?

(c) Make a table of your results.

(d) Which times table is the rule based on?

(e) Find the formula.

(f) How many new tiles are needed for layer 10?

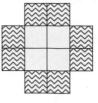

Layer 1

2 **(a)** James has a round cake.
He cuts right across the cake, through the middle.
How many pieces of cake are there after
(i) 1 cut **(ii)** 2 cuts **(iii)** 3 cuts **(iv)** n cuts?

(b) Sarah has a chocolate roll.
She cuts it into slices.
How many pieces of roll are there after
(i) 1 cut **(ii)** 2 cuts **(iii)** 3 cuts **(iv)** n cuts?

Investigation

1 Look at these tiling patterns.

(i)  **(ii)**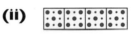

In each case

(a) draw the first 3 layers.

(b) copy and complete this table.

Layer	Number of new tiles
1	
2	
3	
4	
5	
10	

(c) find a rule for the number of new tiles needed.

2 Predict the rule for
this starting design.

Activity

Draw 2 of your own tiling patterns, for 3 layers each.

Make a poster of your favourite designs.

On your poster explain how you found the rule in each case.

Sequences

Jane and Peter are playing a game.

Jane writes down a **sequence**:   5, 10, 15, 20, ...

Peter has to find the rule for Jane's sequence.

He writes

> *A sequence is a list of numbers like this.*

$$+5 \qquad +5 \qquad +5$$
$$5 \qquad 10 \qquad 15 \qquad 20$$
$$1\times5 \quad 2\times5 \quad 3\times5 \quad 4\times5$$

> *The **difference** is 5. So you add 5 each time.*

? **How do you work out:**
(a) **the 10th term**   **(b)** **the 50th term**   **(c)** **any term?**
What formula do you use to find these numbers?

Peter writes down   *It is the 5 times table. The nth term is 5n.*

? **What is the *n*th term of the sequences:**
(a) **3, 6, 9, 12, 15, ...?**   **(b)** **4, 8, 12, 16, 20, ...?**

Now Peter writes down a new sequence: 3, 7, 11, 15, ...

Jane wants to find the *n*th term of Peter's sequence.

She writes

> *So the sequence is always 1 less than the 4 times table. The nth term is 4n − 1.*

$$+4 \qquad +4 \qquad +4$$
$$3 \qquad 7 \qquad 11 \qquad 15$$
$$1\times4 \quad 2\times4 \quad 3\times4 \quad 4\times4$$
$$4 \qquad 8 \qquad 12 \qquad 16$$
$$-1 \qquad -1 \qquad -1 \qquad -1$$
$$3 \qquad 7 \qquad 11 \qquad 15$$

> *The difference is 4*

> *It is the 4 times table*

> *This is the formula for the sequence.*

? **What is the *n*th term of the sequence 3, 5, 7, 9, 11, ...?**

Task

1   Write down the *n*th term of a sequence of your own. Put it on one side.
2   Write down the first 5 terms of your sequence. Give them to a friend.
3   Ask your friend to work out the *n*th term of your sequence.

Exercise

1 Write down the next three terms for each of the following sequences.

(a) 5, 10, 15, 20, ..., ..., ...,

(b) 1, 4, 9, 25, 36, ..., ..., ...,

(c) 1, 2, 4, 8, ..., ..., ...,

(d) 36, 33, 30, 27, 24, ..., ..., ...,

(e) 2, 5, 8, 11, 14, ..., ..., ...,

(f) 256, 128, 64, 32, ..., ..., ...,

For each sequence, write down, in English, how you find the next term.

2 Find the 10th term of each of the following sequences.

(a) 3, 5, 7, 9, ...   **(b)** 4, 7, 10, 13, ...   **(c)** 1, 5, 9, 13, ...

3 Write down the first four terms of the sequences with nth terms.

(a) $3n + 4$ **(b)** $2n - 1$ **(c)** $n - 3$

4 Find an expression for the nth term.

(a) 2, 4, 6, 8, ...   **(b)** 3, 6, 9, 12, ...

(c) 3, 5, 7, 9, ...   **(d)** 2, 5, 8, 11, 14, ...

For each of these sequences, write down how you find the next term.

5 Denise thinks of the following sequence.   5, 7, 9, 11, ...

(a) What are the next three terms of her sequence?

(b) What is the 20th term of the sequence?

(c) Find the nth term of the sequence.

(d) Use your formula to find the 50th term.

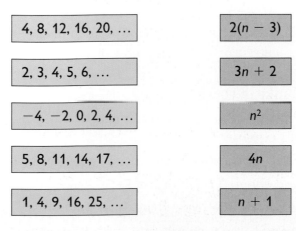

6 Match the following sequences with their nth terms.

4, 8, 12, 16, 20, ...		$2(n - 3)$
2, 3, 4, 5, 6, ...		$3n + 2$
−4, −2, 0, 2, 4, ...		n^2
5, 8, 11, 14, 17, ...		$4n$
1, 4, 9, 16, 25, ...		$n + 1$

Finishing off

Now that you have finished this chapter you should be able to:

● work systematically to solve problems
● generate terms of a sequence with a rule
● describe the rule for a sequence
● find the nth term of a sequence.

Review exercise

1 **(a)** Alison is making some patterns out of matchsticks.

Pattern 1   Pattern 2   Pattern 3

(i) Draw the next two patterns.

(ii) Copy and complete the following table.

Pattern, n	1	2	3	4	5
Number of matches, M	4				

(iii) How many matches are added each time?

(b) How many matches are needed for the
(i) 6th pattern   **(ii)** 10th pattern   **(iii)** 100th pattern?

(c) Find the formula for the number of matchsticks needed for pattern number n.

(d) Now repeat parts (a)–(c) for the following matchstick patterns.

Pattern 1   Pattern 2   Pattern 3

2 Write down the first five terms of each of the sequences with nth terms:
(a) $3n + 4$ **(b)** $n^2 + 1$ **(c)** $5 - 2n$

3 Paul thinks of this sequence.

2, 6, 10, 14, …

(a) What are the next three terms of his sequence?

(b) What is the 20th term of the sequence?

(c) Find the nth term of the sequence.

(d) Use your rule to find the 50th term.

4 A snail is crawling up a wall 20 m high.
During the day it goes up 4 m but at night it slips down 1 m.
(a) Write down the first ten terms in this sequence for the snail's journey.
(b) How long does it take the snail to reach the top of the wall?

5 A sequence begins with the numbers 1, 2, ...

(a) Find 2 different ways of continuing this sequence.

(b) For each, draw a table like this.

Sequence number	Answer
1	1
2	2
3	
4	
5	
10	

Investigation Here are four sequences from everyday life.

31, 28, 31, 30, 31, ...

1, 2, 3, ..., 10, 11, 12, 1, 2, ...

1, 2, 3, ..., 58, 59, 60, 1, 2, 3, ...

S, M, T, W, ...

What do they refer to?
Give the next three terms of each.

Investigation Robin and Shomeet collect pebbles from the beach.
When they get home they play a game.
They take it in turns to add pebbles to the pattern.

Robin   *Shomeet*   *Robin*   *Shomeet*

(a) Write down the number of pebbles in each of these patterns.

(b) How many pebbles are there in the next three patterns?

These numbers are called **triangular numbers**.

The formula for triangular numbers is $\dfrac{n(n + 1)}{2}$

(c) Use this formula to find:
(i) the 10th
(ii) the 20th
(iii) the 50th triangular numbers.

> *This is the nth triangular number.*

Addition and subtraction

Andy's van carries 4 crates.

Their total weight may not exceed 4 tonnes.
Andy does calculations like this.

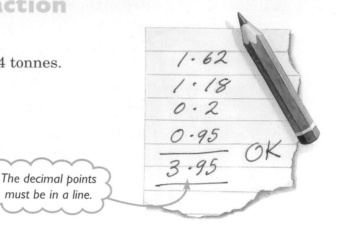

1.62
1.18
0.2
0.95
3.95 OK

The decimal points must be in a line.

Task

Andy has 12 loads to take one day.
They are

| 1.63 | 0.85 | 1.15 | 0.37 | 1.60 | 1.23 |
| 0.33 | 1.36 | 0.64 | 0.77 | 1.01 | 1.06 |

He makes 3 journeys. How does he load them?

A marathon is 42.2 km long.
Yvette takes 2 hours 36 minutes
33 seconds for the race.

The picture shows Yvette passing
a marker.

Don't give up now!

42.2
−30.4
11.8

FINISH

 How long, in minutes and seconds, does Yvette still have to run?

Exercise

1 Work out

(**a**) $1.4 + 2.3$ (**b**) $3.6 + 2.41$ (**c**) $4.5 + 1.49$ (**d**) $4.5 + 1.61$

(**e**) $12.4 + 0.23$ (**f**) $9.9 - 2.8$ (**g**) $6.2 - 0.1$ (**h**) $6.2 - 0.3$

(**i**) $1 - 0.8$ (**j**) $2.01 - 0.04$ (**k**) $3.27 - 0.01$ (**l**) $2 - 0.03$

2 Work out the widths and lengths of these pictures.

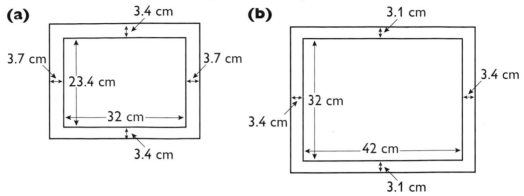

(**a**) 3.4 cm, 3.7 cm, 3.7 cm, 23.4 cm, 32 cm, 3.4 cm

(**b**) 3.1 cm, 32 cm, 3.4 cm, 3.4 cm, 42 cm, 3.1 cm

3 Three TV programmes are 1.5 hours, 0.5 hours, 15 minutes.

(**a**) How much time is this altogether?

(**b**) Will all three programmes fit onto one 3-hour video tape?

4 Three other programmes are 35 minutes, 1.2 hours and $1\frac{1}{4}$ hours.

(**a**) How much time is this altogether?

(**b**) Will all three programmes fit onto one 3-hour video tape?

5 Two teams take part in a 4×100 m relay race.
Here are the runners' times, in seconds.

Team A: Allotey 10.21; Brew 10.07; Mensah 10.13; Annan 10.02
Team B: Le Boeuf 10.19; de Court 10.25; Pascal 10.10; de Gaulle 10.01

(**a**) Which team wins? (**b**) What is the winning margin?

6 Karen sticks a painting onto a wall.
The sizes are given in the picture.

(**a**) The painting is in the middle,
left to right.
How much space is there each side?

(**b**) The painting is 50 cm from the top
of the card.
How much space is underneath it?

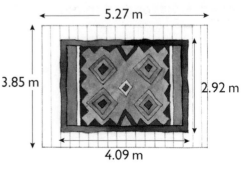

5.27 m, 3.85 m, 2.92 m, 4.09 m

7 Jonas weighs 124.5 kg. His doctor says, 'You must lose weight. You should
be 85 kg.' Jonas goes on a diet.
After 1 month Jonas weighs 119.6 kg.

(**a**) How much weight has he lost? (**b**) How much more must he lose?

Multiplication and division

THE AVONFORD STAR

Dream Match

Giantkillers Avonford Town have been drawn at home to Manchester United in the 3rd round of the FA Cup.

Tickets will cost £16.50 with half price for children and senior citizens.

It's going to cost over £100.

Nonsense. It is just 4.5 × 16.5

You will have £25.75 left from £100.

How do you know where to put the decimal point?

 How does Mum get 4.5?
How do you work out 4.5 × 16.5?
Is Mary's figure of £25.75 right?

Task

1 320 cars use this car park.
   How much do they pay?

2 The coaches pay £716.10.
   How many coaches are there?

BIG MATCH PARKING

Cars **£6.25**

Coaches **£32.55**

 What is the best way to work out the number of coaches in part 2 of the Task?

You can use a calculator and do 716.1 ÷ 32.55.

Another way is to work in pence. $\dfrac{£716.10}{£32.55} = \dfrac{71610p}{3255p} = \ldots\ldots$

Remember $\dfrac{71610}{3255}$ means $71610 \div 3255$

 What is the answer?

Working in pence is easier. All the numbers are whole numbers.

Task

Work out

(a) 8×2 **(b)** 8×0.2 **(c)** 0.8×2 **(d)** 0.8×0.2 **(e)** 8×0.02

(f) $\dfrac{8}{2}$ **(g)** $\dfrac{0.8}{2}$ **(h)** $\dfrac{8}{0.2}$ **(i)** $\dfrac{0.8}{0.2}$ **(j)** $\dfrac{0.8}{0.02}$

Write down, in your own words, rules for multiplying and dividing decimals.

Exercise

1 (a) 3.2×10 (b) 3.2×100 (c) 3.2×1000

     (d) 0.51×10 (e) 0.51×100 (f) 0.51×1000

     (g) 0.06×10 (h) 0.06×100 (i) 0.06×1000

2 (a) 0.3×8 (b) 0.5×6 (c) 8.4×5

     (d) 0.14×6 (e) 0.06×4 (f) 0.16×9

3 (a) 0.07×3 (b) 0.07×30 (c) 0.07×8

     (d) Now use your answers to parts (b) and (c) to find: 0.07×38

4 (a) 0.2×0.1 (b) 0.3×0.2 (c) 0.4×0.3

     (d) 0.7×0.5 (e) 0.6×0.8 (f) 0.6×0.1

5 (a) 0.05×0.1 (b) 0.04×0.2 (c) 0.03×0.7

     (d) 0.04×0.06 (e) 0.03×0.07 (f) 0.02×0.08

6 (a) $6.4 \div 2$ (b) $5.3 \div 5$

     (c) $7.2 \div 8$ (d) $0.64 \div 4$

     (e) $0.24 \div 4$ (f) $0.0096 \div 6$

     (g) $5.6 \div 7$ (h) $0.00324 \div 9$

7 (a) $4.2 \div 0.1$ (b) $4.2 \div 0.01$

     (c) $4.2 \div 0.001$ (d) $0.57 \div 0.1$

     (e) $0.63 \div 0.01$ (f) $0.08 \div 0.001$

     (g) $0.46 \div 0.01$ (h) $3.9 \div 0.1$

8 (a) $6.4 \div 0.2$ (b) $0.55 \div 1.1$

     (c) $0.35 \div 0.07$ (d) $0.084 \div 0.06$

     (e) $0.084 \div 0.3$ (f) $0.12 \div 0.02$

     (g) $2.75 \div 0.5$ (h) $0.044 \div 0.8$

9 Tickets at a concert cost £2.35 each.

     (a) One night 123 people attend. How much do they pay in total?

     (b) Another night the ticket sales are £352.50. How many people attend?

10 (a) Convert 2.3 m into   (i) cm   (ii) mm

     (b) Convert 6.1 m into   (i) cm   (ii) mm

Finishing off

This was a revision chapter.
Now that you have finished it you should be able to:

● add, subtract, multiply and divide decimals more confidently.

Revision exercise

1 Work out

    (a) $1.6 + 2.3$ **(b)** $6.2 + 1.8$ **(c)** $4.02 + 3.652$

    (d) $1.61 + 3.9$ **(e)** $2.6 + 3.02 + 0.04$ **(f)** $0.2 + 0.02 + 0.22$

    (g) $2.5 - 1.3$ **(h)** $4.3 - 3.6$ **(i)** $2.6 + 0.44 - 0.03$

    (j) $0.1 - 0.01$ **(k)** $5 - 0.4$ **(l)** $20 - 0.03$

2 Find the totals of these weights.

    (a) 6.3, 4.4, 2.1, 5.0 tonnes   **(b)** 4.9, 3.9, 3.3, 7 grams   **(c)** 16.2, 4.8, 3.12 kg

3 Peter's computer keyboard is 45.3 cm wide.
His mouse mat is 23.2 cm. His table is 69.5 cm long.

Can Peter fit his keyboard and his mouse mat on his table, side by side?

4 **(a)** How much material is left from 4.5 m after 2.8 m has been cut from it?

    (b) How much paint is left in a 3-litre tin after 1.7 litres has been used?

    (c) How much change is given from £15 after £13.84 has been paid?

    (d) How much further must a 1500 metre runner go once he has completed $3\frac{1}{2}$ laps of 400 m?

5 Cars and lorries are packed in rows on a ferry.
Each row is 20 m long.
Find the total length of these cars to see if they will fit into a 20 m row.

    (a) Mercedes 3.58 m, Range Rover 4.7 m, Saab 4.62 m, Vauxhall 4.11 m

    (b) Renault 3.78 m, Nissan 4.19 m, Volkswagen 3.53 m, Jaguar 4.85 m, Ford 3.63 m

    (c) Toyota 3.61 m, Peugeot 3.84 m, Rover 3.99 m, Fiat 3.33 m, Fiesta 3.84 m

6 Work out

(a) 0.3×7 (b) 1.8×6 (c) 0.4×10

(d) 2.9×0.2 (e) 3.8×0.5 (f) 6.3×0.6

(g) 1.2×0.09 (h) 5.7×0.04 (i) 16.9×0.003

7 Work out

(a) $0.4 \div 0.1$ (b) $0.4 \div 2$ (c) $0.8 \div 0.2$

(d) $3.6 \div 0.3$ (e) $13.8 \div 0.002$ (f) $2.4 \div 0.5$

(g) $0.72 \div 2.4$ (h) $2.4 \div 0.12$ (i) $0.59 \div 0.005$

8 Work out

(a) 1.3×1.2 (b) 5.2×2.4 (c) 0.65×1.3

(d) 0.72×4.7 (e) 0.65×1.5 (f) 0.83×0.16

(g) 4.3×0.37 (h) 0.38×0.65 (i) 0.009×0.0011

9 Work out

(a) 8.3×2 (b) 8.3×20 (c) 8.3×6

(d) Use (b) and (c) to find 8.3×26

(e) 7.1×6 (f) 7.1×60 (g) 7.1×3

(h) Use (f) and (g) to find 7.1×63

(i) 14.3×5 (j) 14.3×50 (k) 14.3×2

(l) Use (j) and (k) to find 14.3×52

10 (a) Find each of the areas A, B, C and D in the diagram.

(b) Use your answers to find the area of the whole rectangle.

(c) Multiply 4.5×2.5. Explain how your answer is a check for parts (a) and (b).

11 A photograph is placed in the middle of a piece of card. It leaves a border all round.

(a) Find the area of the card.

(b) Find the area of the photograph.

(c) Use your answers to find the area of the border.

12 (a) Write 2.34 m in   (i) cm   (ii) mm.

(b) Write 632 cm in   (i) m   (ii) km.

24 Transformations

Do you remember?

A **transformation** is a movement of shape.
Congruent shapes are the same size and shape.

Here are two types of transformation.

Translation

Look at triangles A and B.

You can slide A onto B.
This is called a translation.

The translation 6 right and 2 up maps A to B.

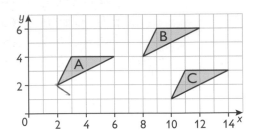

 What translation maps B to A?

What translation maps (i) B to C (ii) C to A?

Reflection

Here are two reflections.

When a shape is reflected it is 'flipped over'.

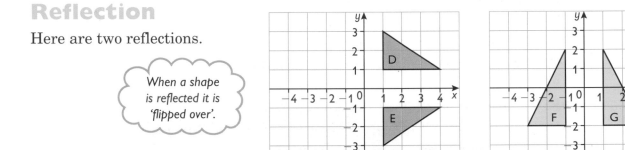

 Describe the reflection which maps (i) D to E (ii) F to G?

 Look at the triangles in these diagrams. Which of them are congruent to each other?

Task

James is designing a quilt cover.
He wants pictures of angels on it.
This diagram shows part of his design.

I Draw and label axes from −10 to 10.

Copy the diagram onto your grid.

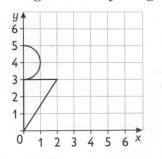

2 Reflect the triangle in
  (a) the *x* axis
  (b) the *y* axis
  (c) the *y* axis and then the *x* axis.

3 Reflect the semicircle in the *y* axis.
Now you have a complete angel.

4 Translate the angel (a) 7 right and 2 down (b) 7 left and 2 up.

Make your own quilt cover pattern using reflections and translations.

 What transformation is equivalent to reflection in x followed by reflection in y?

Exercise

1 Look at this wallpaper pattern
   of repeated cars.
   Car A is mapped to C by a
   translation of 4 right and 1 down.

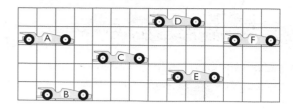

(a) Describe the translations
    which take
    (i) A to B   **(ii)** A to D
    (iii) C to D   **(iv)** E to D
    (v) C to B   **(vi)** B to E
    (vii) F to E   **(viii)** F to A

(b) Two of these translations are the same as D to C. Which are they?

2 Draw and label x and y axes from -5 to $+5$.
   Plot the following points and join them to form a parallelogram. Label it P.
   $(1, 1), (2, 3), (5, 3), (4, 1)$

(a) Reflect P in the y axis. Label it A.

(b) Reflect A in the x axis. Label it B.

(c) Reflect B in the y axis. Label it C.

(d) Reflect C in the x axis. Describe what happens.

Investigation Hannah is playing a computer game.
She is shooting down aeroplanes with a gun (G).

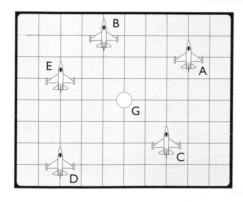

She will move the gun 3 right and 2 up to shoot down A.

This takes $3 + 2 + 1 = 6$ keystrokes.   *For shooting*

From A she moves the gun to B, C, D and E.

(a) Describe the moves from
    (i) A to B   **(ii)** B to C   **(iii)** C to D   **(iv)** D to E.

(b) How many keystrokes does Hannah use in total?

(c) How can you shoot down all five aeroplanes using fewer
    keystrokes than Hannah?

Rotation

Look at these clocks.

? **How many degrees does the minute hand rotate from**

One turn = 360°

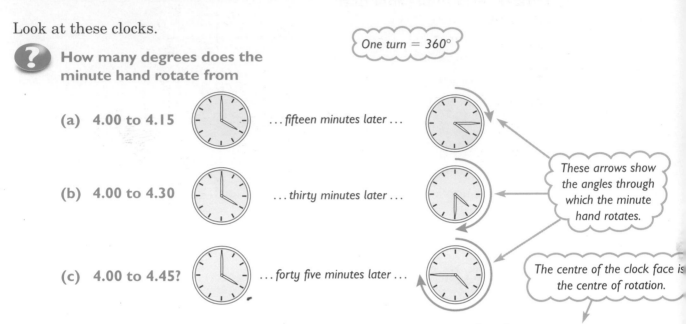

(a) **4.00 to 4.15** ... fifteen minutes later ...

(b) **4.00 to 4.30** ... thirty minutes later ...

(c) **4.00 to 4.45?** ... forty five minutes later ...

These arrows show the angles through which the minute hand rotates.

The centre of the clock face is the centre of rotation.

The movement of the minute hand is a **rotation**, through an angle, about a centre.

Task

Look at this table. It shows part of Anna's day.
Copy and complete it.

Activity	Start time	Minute hand rotates	Finish time
Breakfast	8.00	180°	
Bus to work	8.45		9.00
Open post	9.30		10.15
Coffee break		90°	11.00
Meeting		270°	12.15
Lunch	12.25	180°	
Bus home	1.05	90°	

In the diagram the red triangle (**object**) is rotated through 90° anticlockwise about O to form the green triangle (**image**).

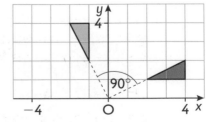

The red triangle and the green triangle are congruent.

? **What does congruent mean? Is Jack right?**

Exercise

1. Describe each of the following rotations.

   (a) A to B

   (b) A to C

   (c) A to D

   (d) B to A

   (e) D to B

   (f) C to B

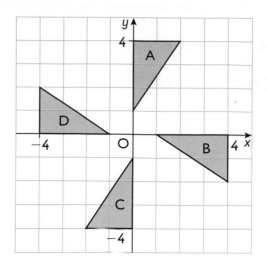

2. Copy the grid and draw shape C.

   (a) Rotate C, about O, through

   (i) 90° clockwise. Label it D.

   (ii) 180°. Label it E.

   (iii) 270° clockwise. Label it F.

   (b) Which of these shapes are congruent to C?

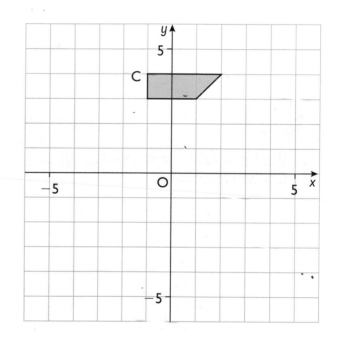

Activity The diagram shows the path of an aeroplane looping the loop.

(The aeroplane flies horizontally, goes round in a vertical circle and then continues horizontally.)

On squared paper

(i) design your own aeroplane

(ii) draw the aeroplane in the six positions shown in the diagram.

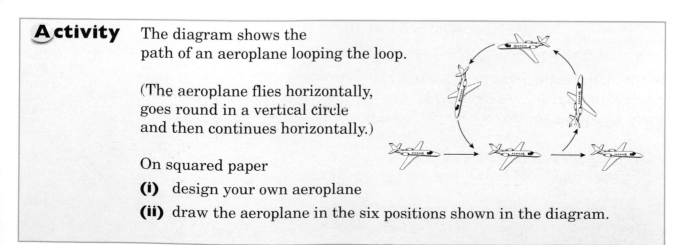

Enlargement

Look at these triangles.

 Which triangles are congruent to triangle A?

Explain why triangles A and B are not congruent.

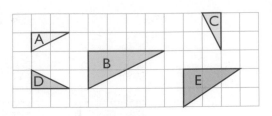

Task

Look at these two model cars.
The angles marked in
yellow are used in part 3.

1 Copy and complete
this table.

Measurement of	Red car	Blue car
Length of car	3.5 cm	
Height of car		
Diameter of wheel		
Length of aerial		

2 Compare the measurements of the two cars.

3 Copy and
complete this
table.

Measurement of angle between	Red car	Blue car
Aerial and roof	30°	
Bonnet and front windscreen		
Rear window and boot		
Bottom and rear wheel arch		

4 Compare the angles in the two cars.

The blue car is an **enlargement** of the red car.
The **scale factor** is 2.

? **A shape is enlarged. The scale factor is two.**
What happens to (a) the lengths and (b) the angles?

? **Look at the triangles at the top of the page.**
Is B an enlargement of A?
Is E an enlargement of A?

Exercise

1 Write down the scale factor of enlargement of each of these signs.

(a)   **(b)**   **(c)**   **(d)**

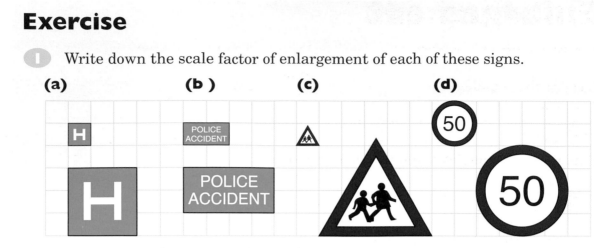

2 Copy each of these shapes onto a grid and enlarge it by a scale factor of 3.

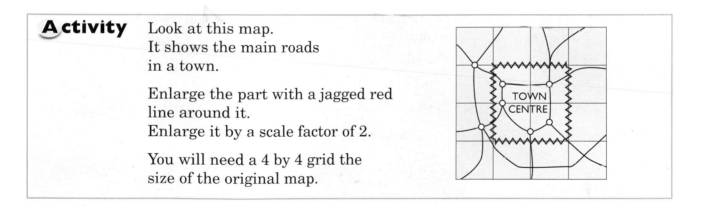

Activity   Look at this map.
It shows the main roads
in a town.

Enlarge the part with a jagged red
line around it.
Enlarge it by a scale factor of 2.

You will need a 4 by 4 grid the
size of the original map.

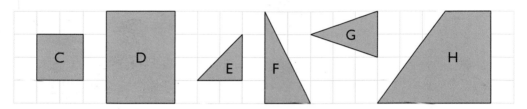

Investigation   Here is (a) a drawing of a coffee table (it is an elevation)
                      (b) a photograph of a coffee table.

Caitlin made the drawing in Design and Technology.
Does the photograph match Caitlin's drawing? Explain your answer.

Finishing off

Now that you have finished this chapter you should be able to:

- recognise rotations, reflections, translations and enlargements
- rotate, reflect, translate and enlarge simple shapes
- understand the meaning of the word congruent.

Review exercise

1   Describe fully the following transformations.

   (a) A to C

   (b) A to G

   (c) B to D

   (d) D to F

   (e) C to H

   (f) G to C

   (g) E to A

   (h) H to G

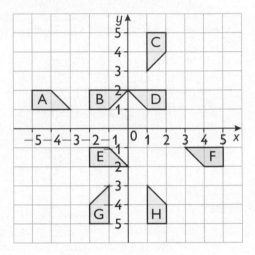

2   On the grid below there are five different shapes and their enlargements.

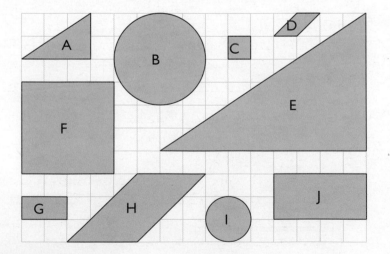

   (a) Match the shapes.

   (b) Name the shapes.

   (c) Work out the scale factor of enlargement for each shape.

3 Draw and label axes from −5 to 5 on centimetre squared paper.
The points (−4, 4), (−2, 4) and (−2, 3) are joined to make triangle T.

(a) Draw triangle T.

(b) Reflect T in the x axis. Label it B.

(c) Rotate T through 90° clockwise about the origin. Label it C.

(d) Translate T 5 right and 3 down. Label it D.

(e) The points (−2, −2) (4, −2) and (4, −5) are joined to make triangle E.
Draw triangle E.

(f) Triangle E is an enlargement of T.
What is the scale factor of enlargement?

(g) Which triangles are congruent to triangle T?

Activity   Look at these four triangles.

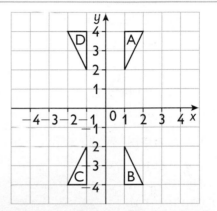

Copy and complete the following table.

Triangle	Reflected in x axis	Reflected in y axis	Rotated through 180° about O
A	B		
B		C	
C			A
D			

1 Do a reflection and a rotation ever give the same result? Explain your answer.

2 Triangle A reflected in the x axis maps to B.
Triangle B reflected in the y axis maps to C.
What single transformation maps A to C?

3 Triangle E has vertices (2, 1), (4, 1) and (4, 2). Draw triangle E.
What transformation maps A to E?

4 (a) Reflect triangle E in the x axis. The image is F.

(b) Rotate triangle E through 180° about O. The image is G.

(c) Reflect triangle E in the y axis. The image is H.
What do you notice?

The first letters of the words in this list spell **BIDMAS**.
How does this word help you?

Brackets
Index
Divide
Multiply
Add
Subtract

Multi-stage calculations

Daniel and Jo are using their calculators to work out

$$\frac{2.2}{4.4 + 1.1}$$

No it's 1.6.

The answer is 0.4.

You are wrong.
$\frac{2.2}{4.4 + 1.1}$ *is roughly* $\frac{2}{4 + 1} = 0.4$
1.6 can't be right.

Daniel is right. What is Jo's mistake?

In many calculations you work out the answer to one bit of the sum.
Then you use it for the next bit. There are three ways of doing this.

" Do the right thing!

Use your calculator to work out $\frac{3.9}{4.3 - 1.6}$.

1 Using brackets

| 3.9 | ÷ | (| 4.3 | − | 1.6 |) | = |

2 Using the memory

Work out 4.3 − 1.6 first | 4.3 | − | 1.6 | = |

To store it in the memory press | M+ | or | STO |

Clear the screen | AC |

Now work out | 3.9 | ÷ | MR | or | RCL | = |

3 Using the answer button
(Not all calculators have this.)

Work out 4.3 − 1.6

| 4.3 | − | 1.6 | = |

⚠ Do *not* clear the screen.

Now work out

| 3.9 | ÷ | ANS | = |

Explain why the calculator sequence | 2.4 | + | 3.1 | ÷ | 4.2 | × | 1.6 | = |

does not give the correct answer to $\frac{2.4 + 3.1}{4.2 \times 1.6}$

Use two of the methods above to find the correct answer.

Exercise

1 Use the brackets on your calculator to work out the following:

(a) $2.1 \times (3.9 + 8.7)$ **(b)** $3.4 \div (8.2 + 4.6)$ **(c)** $(67 + 93) \times (104 - 67)$

(d) $(8.1 + 3.6)^2$ **(e)** $\dfrac{86 + 72}{16}$ **(f)** $(5.9 + 3.2) - (1.1 + 2.7)$

2 Each of the following calculations is wrong.
In each case find the correct answer.
Then explain how the printed answer can be found.

(a) $\dfrac{45 + 36}{1.8 + 3.6} = 48.6$ **(b)** $\dfrac{45 + 36}{1.8 + 3.6} = 68.6$

(c) $(1.2 + 3.6)^2 = 14.16$ **(d)** $\dfrac{14 - 6.8}{25} = 13.728$

3 Find an approximate answer to each of the following. Then use your calculator to find the exact answer.

(a) $\dfrac{64}{2.7 + 1.3}$ **(b)** $\dfrac{83.6 + 42.4}{12.1}$ **(c)** $\dfrac{82 \times 8}{6.1 - 4.0}$

(d) $\dfrac{102 + 394}{52}$ **(e)** $\frac{1}{2}$ of $(62 + 97)$ **(f)** $\frac{3}{4}$ of $(8.2 + 4.5 + 7.2)$

Activity

16 × 25 = 400
I can work that out more quickly in my head than on a calculator.

Ali

Me too. I just add 2 noughts and divide by 4.

Sue

1 Work these out with a friend. One of you uses a calculator.
The other uses Ali's and Sue's method. $8 \times 25,$ $12 \times 25,$ $6 \times 25,$ 25×25
Who is quicker?

2 Suggest quick ways to multiply by 5, 50 and 250.
3 Write some multiplication sums involving these numbers.
4 Challenge a friend. Your friend works with a calculator. You use your head.
Who is quicker?

Investigation

You should get the answer 7.

1 Do the sum $7 + 3 \div 3 - 1$ on your calculator.
Write down the order of operations to get this answer.

2 Now try   **(a)** $7 + 3 \div (3 - 1)$ **(b)** $(7 + 3) \div (3 - 1)$
How many different answers can you get by placing
brackets in different places?

Do not move the positions of the numbers or the operations +, ÷ and −.

3 Investigate what happens when you place brackets
in these sums: **(a)** $9 - 6 \div 3 + 1$ **(b)** $8 + 4 \times 2 - 1$

Fractions

Find the fraction button on your calculator.

Press [3] [a$\frac{b}{c}$] [4]. Write down the display.

This is how your calculator shows $\frac{3}{4}$.

> *A mixed number contains a whole number and a fraction.*

Press [2] [a$\frac{b}{c}$] [4] [a$\frac{b}{c}$] [5]

Your calculator shows the mixed number $2\frac{4}{5}$.

Enter the following fractions into your calculator.

$\frac{1}{2}$ $\frac{2}{5}$ $\frac{5}{12}$ $\frac{11}{25}$ $1\frac{2}{3}$ $7\frac{4}{13}$

Write down the display each time. Clear the screen between each fraction.

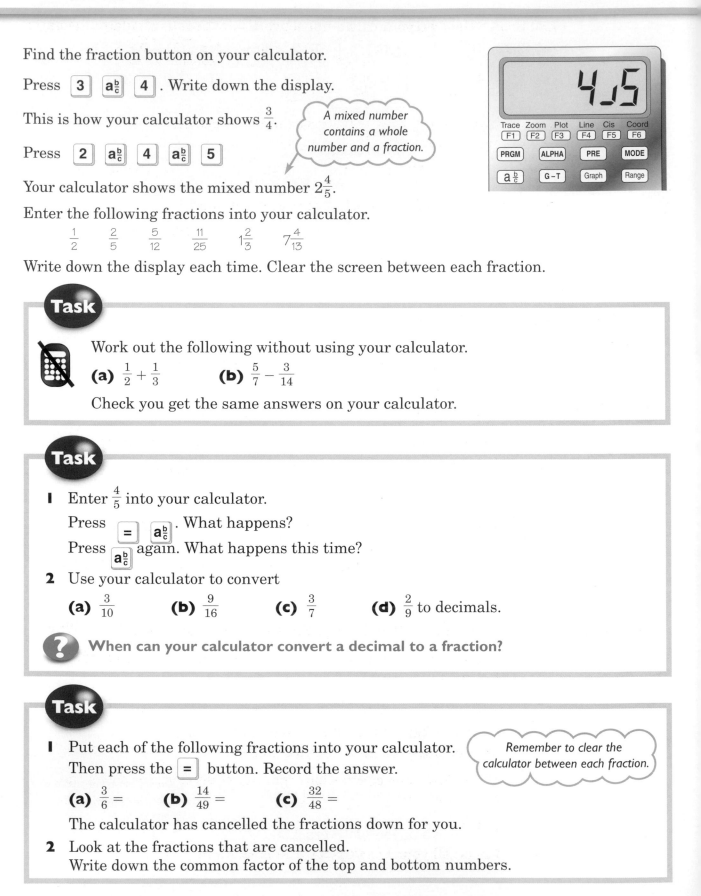

Task

Work out the following without using your calculator.

(a) $\frac{1}{2} + \frac{1}{3}$ **(b)** $\frac{5}{7} - \frac{3}{14}$

Check you get the same answers on your calculator.

Task

1 Enter $\frac{4}{5}$ into your calculator.

Press [=] [a$\frac{b}{c}$]. What happens?

Press [a$\frac{b}{c}$] again. What happens this time?

2 Use your calculator to convert

(a) $\frac{3}{10}$ **(b)** $\frac{9}{16}$ **(c)** $\frac{3}{7}$ **(d)** $\frac{2}{9}$ to decimals.

? When can your calculator convert a decimal to a fraction?

Task

1 Put each of the following fractions into your calculator.
Then press the [=] button. Record the answer.

> *Remember to clear the calculator between each fraction.*

(a) $\frac{3}{6} =$ **(b)** $\frac{14}{49} =$ **(c)** $\frac{32}{48} =$

The calculator has cancelled the fractions down for you.

2 Look at the fractions that are cancelled.
Write down the common factor of the top and bottom numbers.

Exercise

1 Write down the fractions shown in each of the following calculator displays:

(a) $\boxed{2 \lrcorner 5}$ (b) $\boxed{11 \lrcorner 12}$ (c) $\boxed{1 \lrcorner 1 \lrcorner 2}$

(d) $\boxed{2 \lrcorner 7 \lrcorner 9}$ (e) $\boxed{10 \lrcorner 1 \lrcorner 5}$

2 Cancel down the following fractions as much as possible.
Use your calculator to check your answers.

(a) $\frac{5}{10}$ (b) $\frac{3}{9}$ (c) $\frac{10}{15}$ (d) $\frac{36}{90}$

3 (a) Work out the following without your calculator:

(i) $\frac{3}{15} + \frac{7}{9}$ (ii) $\frac{8}{15} - \frac{2}{5}$ (iii) $\frac{4}{7} + \frac{5}{14}$ (iv) $\frac{3}{4} + \frac{7}{8}$

(b) Now use your calculator to check your answers.

Investigation   Enter the mixed number $1\frac{2}{3}$ into your calculator.

Press $\boxed{\text{SHIFT}}$ or $\boxed{\text{2nd}}$ $\boxed{a\frac{b}{c}}$ and write down the display

Why do you think the term top-heavy is used?

This is the top-heavy fraction $\frac{5}{3}$. It is equivalent to $1\frac{2}{3}$.

Use your calculator to convert the following to top-heavy fractions.

(a) $1\frac{4}{5}$ (b) $2\frac{1}{3}$ (c) $3\frac{4}{7}$ (d) $4\frac{1}{4}$

Look carefully at your answers.

Write a set of instructions to convert a mixed number to a top-heavy fraction without using a calculator.
Ask a friend to test your instructions on the mixed number $5\frac{3}{4}$.

Investigation   Work out $7 \div 2$ and $7 \times \frac{1}{2}$. You should get the same answer. Why?

Write down a multiplication that is equivalent to each of the following:

(a) $5 \div 4$ (b) $11 \div 5$ (c) $15 \div 7$ (d) $22 \div 6$

Work out $30 \div 5 \times 3$, $30 \times 3 \div 5$ and $\frac{3}{5} \times 30$.
Why do these all give the same answer?

Write down two calculations that are equivalent to each of the following:

(e) $16 \div 5 \times 4$ (f) $\frac{4}{7} \times 12$ (g) $22 \times 5 \div 11$

Check all your answers on your calculator.

Indices

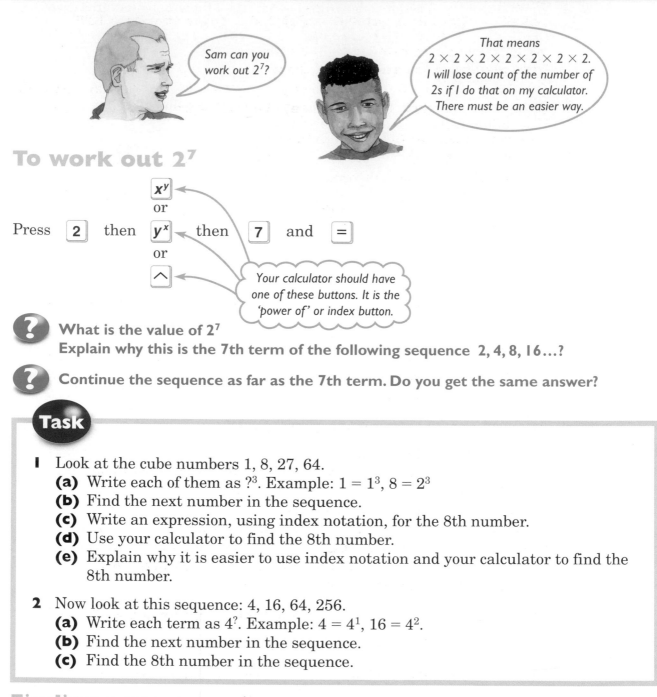

Sam can you work out 2^7?

That means $2 \times 2 \times 2 \times 2 \times 2 \times 2 \times 2$. I will lose count of the number of 2s if I do that on my calculator. There must be an easier way.

To work out 2^7

Press 2 then y^x then 7 and =

or x^y or $\wedge$

Your calculator should have one of these buttons. It is the 'power of' or index button.

? **What is the value of 2^7**
Explain why this is the 7th term of the following sequence 2, 4, 8, 16…?

? **Continue the sequence as far as the 7th term. Do you get the same answer?**

Task

1 Look at the cube numbers 1, 8, 27, 64.
  (a) Write each of them as $?^3$. Example: $1 = 1^3$, $8 = 2^3$
  (b) Find the next number in the sequence.
  (c) Write an expression, using index notation, for the 8th number.
  (d) Use your calculator to find the 8th number.
  (e) Explain why it is easier to use index notation and your calculator to find the 8th number.

2 Now look at this sequence: 4, 16, 64, 256.
  (a) Write each term as $4^?$. Example: $4 = 4^1$, $16 = 4^2$.
  (b) Find the next number in the sequence.
  (c) Find the 8th number in the sequence.

Finding square roots

You can use your calculator to find the square root of a number.

? **What is the square root of 100?**
Enter $\sqrt{}$ then 100, or 100 then $\sqrt{}$.
What do you find?

Sam. Is 20736 a perfect square?

? **What is a perfect square?**
How can you help Sam?

Exercise

1 Work out:
(a) 6^4 (b) 30^4 (c) 3.6^5 (d) 1.4^6 (e) $\sqrt{625}$ (f) $\sqrt{1296}$

2 Write the following using index notation.
Then use your calculator to work them out.
(a) $5 \times 5 \times 5 \times 5 \times 5$ (b) $7 \times 7 \times 7 \times 7$ (c) $35 \times 35 \times 35$
(d) $1.9 \times 1.9 \times 1.9 \times 1.9 \times 1.9$ (e) $2.6 \times 2.6 \times 2.6 \times 2.6 \times 2.6 \times 2.6$

3 Use your calculator to find the values of:
(a) 20^3 (b) 20^4 (c) 20^5 (d) 20^6
Look carefully at your answers.
Explain how to get these answers from the values of 2^3, 2^4, 2^5 and 2^6.

Now work out the exact values of:
(e) 20^{10} (f) 20^{15}.

4 Mike is on a four-week training schedule.

Activity	Week 1	Week 2	Week 3	Week 4
Sit-ups	20	$20 \times 1.2 = 24$	$20 \times 1.2^2 = 28.8$	
Swimming	10 lengths		$10 \times 1.2^2 = 14.4$	
Jogging	5 km			
Exercise bike	15 minutes			

Each week his targets are multiplied by 1.2.

(a) Work out his targets for week 2.
(b) Explain the calculations 20×1.2^2 and 10×1.2^2 in the table.
(c) Write down the other calculations for week 3.
    Use your calculator to work them out.
    Give your answers to the nearest whole number.
(d) Write down similar calculations for all the activities in week 4.
    Copy the table and fill in the numbers for all the activities.
    Give them to the nearest whole number.

5 The numbers below are all square numbers or cube numbers.

100   216   64   225   4913   289

One of these numbers is both a square number and a cube number.
Which is it?
Find another number that is both square and cube.

Investigation   Find the value of the terms in the sequence: $0.1, 0.1^2, 0.1^3, 0.1^4, \ldots$

Which is the first term that your calculator cannot display as an ordinary number?

Write down the value of 0.1^{15}.

Finishing off

Now that you have finished this chapter you should be able to use:

- brackets on your calculator
- the memory or an answer button
- the fraction button
- 'the power of' or index button.

Exercise

1 Work out the following on your calculator.

(a) $(4.3 + 3.7)^2$ (b) $\dfrac{18}{(3.7 - 2.8)^2}$ (c) 87^4

(d) 7×1.4^5 (e) $\sqrt{(0.42 + 1.02)}$ (f) $\sqrt{640\,000}$

2 For each of the calculator sequences below
(i) write down the calculation performed
(ii) do the calculation.

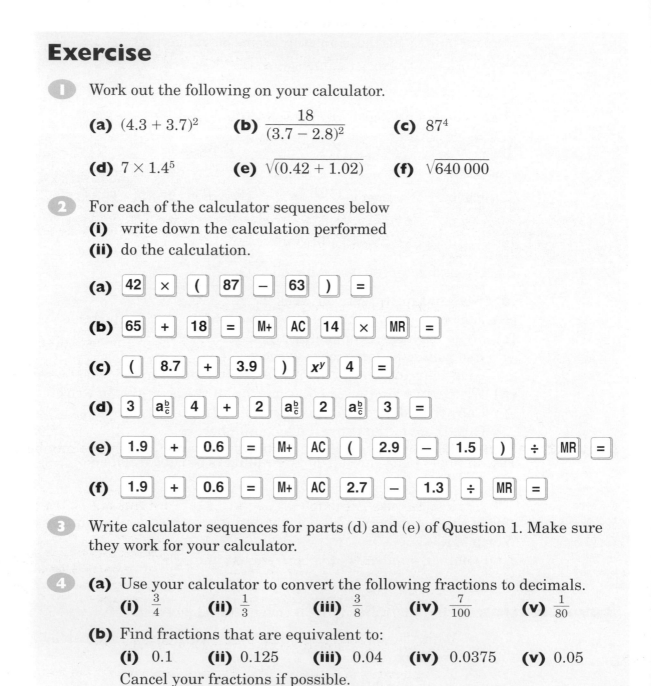

(a) $\boxed{42}$ $\boxed{\times}$ $\boxed{(}$ $\boxed{87}$ $\boxed{-}$ $\boxed{63}$ $\boxed{)}$ $\boxed{=}$

(b) $\boxed{65}$ $\boxed{+}$ $\boxed{18}$ $\boxed{=}$ $\boxed{M+}$ $\boxed{AC}$ $\boxed{14}$ $\boxed{\times}$ $\boxed{MR}$ $\boxed{=}$

(c) $\boxed{(}$ $\boxed{8.7}$ $\boxed{+}$ $\boxed{3.9}$ $\boxed{)}$ $\boxed{x^y}$ $\boxed{4}$ $\boxed{=}$

(d) $\boxed{3}$ $\boxed{a\frac{b}{c}}$ $\boxed{4}$ $\boxed{+}$ $\boxed{2}$ $\boxed{a\frac{b}{c}}$ $\boxed{2}$ $\boxed{a\frac{b}{c}}$ $\boxed{3}$ $\boxed{=}$

(e) $\boxed{1.9}$ $\boxed{+}$ $\boxed{0.6}$ $\boxed{=}$ $\boxed{M+}$ $\boxed{AC}$ $\boxed{(}$ $\boxed{2.9}$ $\boxed{-}$ $\boxed{1.5}$ $\boxed{)}$ $\boxed{\div}$ $\boxed{MR}$ $\boxed{=}$

(f) $\boxed{1.9}$ $\boxed{+}$ $\boxed{0.6}$ $\boxed{=}$ $\boxed{M+}$ $\boxed{AC}$ $\boxed{2.7}$ $\boxed{-}$ $\boxed{1.3}$ $\boxed{\div}$ $\boxed{MR}$ $\boxed{=}$

3 Write calculator sequences for parts (d) and (e) of Question 1. Make sure they work for your calculator.

4 (a) Use your calculator to convert the following fractions to decimals.
　(i) $\dfrac{3}{4}$ (ii) $\dfrac{1}{3}$ (iii) $\dfrac{3}{8}$ (iv) $\dfrac{7}{100}$ (v) $\dfrac{1}{80}$

(b) Find fractions that are equivalent to:
　(i) 0.1 (ii) 0.125 (iii) 0.04 (iv) 0.0375 (v) 0.05
Cancel your fractions if possible.

5 **(a)** Choose a number between 0 and 8. Work out:

$$(\text{your number} + 2)^2 \div 9$$

Which numbers are the same as their answers?

(b) Do the same with:

$$(\text{your number} + 4)^2 \div 18$$

Investigation Copy and complete this table.

Number	Square	Last digit
1	1	1
2	4	4
3		
4		
5	25	5
6		
7		
8		
9		

Describe the pattern in the last column.
How will it continue?
Are there any numbers that do not appear in the last column?

Explain why 167 cannot be a square number. Do not try to find the square root.

Investigation Look at this equation. It shows the power of negative numbers.

$$(-1)^2 = -1 \times -1 = 1$$

You can use the following sequence to work this out on your calculator:

On most calculators the $\boxed{+/-}$ button will enter a negative number.

OR $\boxed{1}$ $\boxed{+/-}$ $\boxed{x^2}$

Use your calculator to work out $(-1)^3$, $(-1)^4$, $(-1)^5$

Write down $(-1)^9$ and $(-1)^{100}$. Explain how you got your answers.

Answers

1 Co-ordinates and graphs (pages 10–11)

1 A(5, 3) B(4, 1) C(6, −4) D(2, −1), E(−5, −5) F(−8, −8)
G(−6, −5), H(−10, −6), I(−6, −4), J(0, 1), K(−3, 5)

2 (a) U(5, 0), V(0, −5), W(−12, 0), X(−17, −2),
Y(−17, 2), Z(0, 5).
(b) (i) $x + y = 5$ or $y = -x + 5$ (ii) $y = x - 5$ (iii) $x = -17$
(c) (i) 5   (ii) −5
(d)–(e) Ask your teacher to check your diagrams.

3 (a) (i)

x	−3	−2	−1	0	1	2	3
$3x$	−9	−6	−3	0	3	6	9
−2	−2	−2	−2	−2	−2	−2	−2
$y = 3x - 2$	−11	−8	−5	−2	1	4	7

(ii)

x	−3	−2	−1	0	1	2	3
$2x$	−6	−4	−2	0	2	4	6
+1	+1	+1	+1	+1	+1	+1	+1
$y = 2x + 1$	−5	−3	−1	1	3	5	7

(b) Ask your teacher to check your diagram.
(c) (i) −2 (ii) 1   (d) (3, 7)   (e) $y = 3x - 2$

4 (a) (i)

x	−1	0	1	2	3	4
$y = x + 2$	1	2	3	4	5	6

(ii)

x	−1	0	1	2	3	4
$y = 2x - 1$	−3	−1	1	3	5	7

(b) Ask your teacher to check your diagram.
(c) (3, 5)
(d) (i) 2   (ii) −1

5 (a)

x	−2	−1	0	1	2	3
$y = 2x + 2$	−2	0	2	4	6	8

x	−2	−1	0	1	2	3
$y = 2x - 1$	−5	−3	−1	1	3	5

(b) Ask your teacher to check your diagram.
(c) 2 and −1
(d) The lines are parallel, so the gradients are the same.

Investigation

Ask your teacher to check your answers.

2 Numbers (pages 20–21)

1 (a) 0.17   (b) 0.017   (c) 0.0017   (d) 0.17   (e) 0.017
(f) 0.0017   (g) 0.17   (h) 0.017   (i) 0.0017
2 (a) 0.236   (b) 0.009   (c) 0.016   (d) 0.236   (e) 0.009
(f) 0.016   (g) 0.236   (h) 0.009   (i) 0.016
3 (a) 600 (b) 60 (c) 60 (d) 2000   (e) 4000   (f) 7300
4 A is 0.73,   B is 0.78,   C is 0.85.
5 X is 0.046, Y is 0.058,   Z is 0.074.
6 (a) 6.5   (b) 50   (c) 0.7   (d) 6.5
7 3.6 cm, 5.2 cm, 7.4 cm, 9.6 cm, 13.5 cm
8 10.77 secs, 10.79 secs, 10.81 secs, 10.88 secs, 11.08 secs.
9 (i) K   (ii) A   (iii) T   (iv) I   (v) E
10 Jupiter, Saturn, Uranus, Neptune, Earth, Venus, Mars,
Mercury, Pluto

Activity

1 (a) 70   (b) 700   (c) 7000   (d) 50
(e) 500   (f) 5000   (g) 500   (h) 5000
(i) 50 000   (j) 30   (k) 300   (l) 3000
2 (a) 80   (b) 800   (c) 8000   (d) 60
(e) 600   (f) 6000

3 Angles (pages 30–31)

1 $a = 123°$, $b = 55°$, $c = 35°$, $d = 145°$, $e = 145°$
2 (a) 11.25°   (b) 56 seconds
3 $a = 70°$, $b = 110°$, $c = 49°$, $d = 49°$, $e = 126°$,
$f = 54°$, $g = 54°$, $h = 75°$, $i = 105°$, $j = 75°$,
$k = 56°$, $l = 124°$, $m = 63°$, $n = 63°$, $o = 63°$
4 $a = 30°$, $b = 58°$, $c = 53°$, $d = 69°$,
$e = 76°$, $f = 104°$, $g = 60°$, $h = 120°$
5 $a = 98°$, $b = 109°$, $c = 105°$,
$d = 103°$, $e = 69°$, $f = 136°$
6 (a) (i) Fishbourne   (ii) Ningwood   (iii) Wootton Bridge
(b) Bembridge airport
(c) Newport information centre
(d) Newton Bay   (e) (i) 140°   (ii) 230°   (iii) 305°

4 Displaying data (pages 42–43)

1 (a)

Time spent playing computer games (minutes)	Tally	Frequency
0–50	Ⅳ	5
51–100	ⅣⅢ |||	8
101–150	Ⅳ	5
151–200	||	2

(b) Ask your teacher to check your answer.
2 (a) 77, no.
(b) (i) Boys, median 5, mean 5   (ii) Girls, median 5, mean 5
They rate them the same.
(c) (i) Boys 5, girls 6; girls
3 (a) Discrete   (b) Continuous   (c) Continuous   (d) Discrete
4 (a) 18
(b) At least 30 and below 35 doesn't include 35.
(c) Add new line to table

35	40	1

5 (a) Ask your teacher to check your diagram.
(b) Negative.
(c) (i) Clara because she is younger.
(ii) No, you can't be sure.

5 Decimals (pages 52–53)

1 (a) (i) 120   (ii) 470   (iii) 10   (iv) 6600
(b) (i) 3300   (ii) 1600   (iii) 3000   (iv) 200
2 (a) 32   (b) 246   (c) 2361   (d) 126
(e) 1386   (f) 405   (g) 23 463   (h) 71 928
3 (a) 1.29   (b) 15.89   (c) 0.123   (d) 4.745   (e) 0.012
4 (a) 4.3   (b) 23.6   (c) 4.1   (d) 0.35   (e) 1
5 (a) 5.01   (b) 6.41   (c) 3.46   (d) 1.4   (e) 10
6 (a) 34.3   (b) 14.5   (c) 1.6   (d) 1.65
(e) 0.14   (f) 1.0   (g) 0.50   (h) 1.00
7 (a) 11.5   (b) 1.65   (c) 0.355   (d) 0.5
(e) 1.84   (f) 4.35   (g) 1   (h) 7
8 (a) 7.020 ml   (b) 16.6 hours
(c) 12.25 minutes   (d) £5.04
(e) 8 hours and 18 minutes
(f) 2 km and 900 metres
9 (a) (i) 8.87   (ii) 18143.7   (iii) 511   (iv) 0.158
(b) Ask your teacher to check your answers.
10 (a) £1.66   (b) 90 g   (c) 6 feet 8 inches   (d) 4.8 km

Investigation

1 (a) (i) 0.7   (ii) 0.67   (iii) 0.6̇66666666666666
(b) (i) 0.4   (ii) 0.43   (iii) 0.4̇28571̇428571428
(c) (i) 0.5   (ii) 0.45   (iii) 0.4̇5454545454̇54
(d) (i) 0.3   (ii) 0.31   (iii) 0.3̇07692̇307692307
(e) (i) 0.2   (ii) 0.22   (iii) 0.2̇22222222222222

2-3 Ask your teacher to check your answers.

6 Using variables (pages 60–61)

1 (a) $7x + 12y$ (b) $5k + 9$ (c) $3a + 2b$
(d) −1   (e) $6s + 11t$ (f) $g - h$

2 (a) $10 + 5c$ (b) $3x - 18$ (c) $7p + 7q$
   (d) $8d + 12$ (e) $4b + 32$ (f) $16r - 8$
   (g) $3 - 3k$ (h) $3 + 6m - 9n$ (i) $10a - 15b$
   (j) $24 + 24d + 24e$
   (k) $12u - 16v - 8w - 20x$
   (l) $12l - 6x - 6z$

3 A2, B5, C4, D3, E1

4 (a) $6c + 7l$ (b) £1

5 (a) $(20x + 5y + 10z)$ pence   (b) £19

6 (a) £$(2s + 4g)$ (b) (i) Yes, (ii) Yes, (iii) Yes, (iv) Yes.

7 (a) $2(l + w)$
   (b) 1 and 12; 2 and 11; 3 and 10; 4 and 9; 5 and 8; 6 and 7
   (c) $l \times w$ (d) (i) 22 m² (ii) 36 m² (iii) 42 m²

8 (a) 1 m   (b) $v = l \times w \times d$ (c) (i) 30 m³ (ii) 40 m³

Activity

1 (a) yes   (b) no

2 (a) no   (b) Ask your teacher to check your answers.

7 Construction (pages 72–73)

1 (a) (ii) BC $= 9.6$ cm, angle $B = 58°$, angle $C = 49°$
   (b) (ii) AC $= 10.2$ cm, BC $= 6.9$ cm, angle $C = 32°$
   (c) (ii) angle $A = 61°$, angle $B = 50°$, angle $C = 69°$

2 17 m   **3** (a) circle   (b) circle   (c) 2

4 (b) Pupils draw the perpendicular bisector of a line drawn between A and B.

5–6 Ask your teacher to check your diagrams.

Activity

3 G3   **4** 20 m from Y

8 Using graphs (pages 78–79)

1, 2, 3 (a) (b) Ask your teacher to check your graphs and answers.

3 (c) A canoe for less than 3 hours, a rowing boat for more than 3 hours.

4 (a) 32 kg   (b) 10 stones   (c) 6.4 kg

5 (a) 10 am   (b) $1\frac{1}{2}$ hours   (c) 3 kilometres
   (d) 1 hour   (e) 5 kilometres   (f) Check graph
   (g) 1.15 pm   (h) 2 kilometres

9 Negative numbers (pages 84–85)

1 $-3, -2.3, -2, -1.5, -1.4, 1$

2 Ask your teacher to check your answers.

3 (a) (i) -1.5 (ii) -7 (iii) -2 (iv) -3.5 (v) -4 (vi) -6.35

   (b)

A	B	$A + B$	$\dfrac{A+B}{2}$
-1	-2	-3	-1.5
-4	-10	-14	-7
-7	3	-4	-2
-12	5	-7	-3.5
-3.5	-4.5	-8	-4
-6.3	-6.4	-12.7	-6.35

4 (a) 4   (b) -6 (c) 1   (d) -3 (e) -7
   (f) 22   (g) -10 (h) -9 (i) -1.8 (j) 6.2
   (k) -48 (l) 600   (m) -6 (n) 3   (o) -20

5 (a) C is number of correct answers, W is number of wrong answers.
   (b) Ask your teacher to check your answer.

   (c)

	C	W	$5C - 2W$
Jane	10	10	30
Edward	12	8	44
Jessica	9	11	23
Davinda	5	15	-5

6 (a) 50 ft   (b) 30 min   (c) 7°C

Activity
$+2, -2$
-1
2 left, 3 right, 6 left, 4 right, 4 right, 2 right

10 Fractions (pages 90–91)

1 $\frac{3}{4} = \frac{6}{8}$, $\frac{5}{6} = \frac{10}{12} = \frac{15}{18} = \frac{50}{60}$, $\frac{3}{7} = \frac{9}{21}$, $\frac{4}{5} = \frac{40}{50} = \frac{16}{20}$,
  $\frac{1}{3} = \frac{4}{12} = \frac{13}{39}$, $\frac{2}{4} = \frac{5}{10} = \frac{25}{50}$

2 (a) (i) 8   (ii) $\frac{3}{8}, \frac{1}{4} = \frac{2}{8}$ (b) (i) 35   (ii) $\frac{3}{5} = \frac{21}{35}, \frac{4}{7} = \frac{20}{35}$
   (c) (i) 12   (ii) $\frac{5}{6} = \frac{10}{12}, \frac{3}{4} = \frac{9}{12}$ (d) (i) 9   (ii) $\frac{2}{3} = \frac{6}{9}, \frac{5}{9}$
   (e) (i) 15   (ii) $\frac{2}{5} = \frac{6}{15}, \frac{4}{15}$ (f) (i) 15   (ii) $\frac{4}{5} = \frac{12}{15}, \frac{2}{3} = \frac{10}{15}$
   (g) (i) 36   (ii) $\frac{5}{12} = \frac{15}{36}, \frac{7}{18} = \frac{14}{36}$ (h) (i) 30   (ii) $\frac{1}{6} = \frac{5}{30}, \frac{2}{15} = \frac{4}{30}$

3 (a) $\frac{55}{63}$ (b) $\frac{1}{6}$ (c) $\frac{11}{20}$ (d) $\frac{1}{2}$ (e) $\frac{5}{12}$ (f) $\frac{19}{24}$
   (g) $\frac{8}{21}$ (h) $\frac{5}{24}$ (i) $\frac{1}{8}$ (j) $\frac{1}{16}$ (k) $\frac{1}{3}$ (l) $\frac{1}{5}$

4 (a) 50% (b) 75% (c) 10% (d) 30% (e) 5% (f) 35%
   (g) 20% (h) 40% (i) 4% (j) 36% (k) 2% (l) 6%

5 (a) 80% (Maths)   (b) 50% (English)

6 (a) (i) $\frac{1}{4}$ (ii) $\frac{1}{3}$ (iii) $\frac{5}{24}$
   (b) 30 red, 10 yellow, 5 white, 25 pink, 40 green

7 (a) $\frac{5}{8}$ (b) $\frac{3}{8}$ (c) $\frac{5}{12}$ (d) $\frac{7}{12}$ (e) $\frac{3}{10}$ or $\frac{7}{20}$ (f) $\frac{5}{8}$ or $\frac{1}{2}$

8 (a) $\frac{1}{10}$ (b) $\frac{3}{10}$ (c) $\frac{2}{5}$ (d) $\frac{1}{5}$

9 $\frac{1}{6}, \frac{5}{6}$

Activity

Activity	Number of children	As a fraction	As a percentage
Squash	9	$\frac{9}{75} = \frac{3}{25}$	12%
Computer games	18	$\frac{18}{75} = \frac{6}{25}$	24%
Tennis	15	$\frac{15}{75} = \frac{1}{5}$	20%
Orchestra	27	$\frac{27}{75} = \frac{9}{25}$	36%
Chess	6	$\frac{6}{75} = \frac{2}{25}$	8%
Total	75	1	100%

11 Converting units (pages 98–99)

1 (a) 2 kg   (b) 4.4 pounds

2 (a) 18 kg, 39.6 pounds   (b) 10 in, less

3 3200 pints, about 1800 litres

4 140 g flour, 30 g ground rice, 55–60 g castor sugar, 110 g butter.

5 (a) 9 ounces   (b) 175 g   (c) 7.2 ounces

6 (a) 32°F   (b) 99°F   (c) 32°C   (d) 68°F

7 (b) (i) DM 160   (ii) £5

12 Shape (pages 108–109)

1 (a) equilateral   (b) isosceles   (c) scalene

2 (a) Yes, a quadrilateral with no parallel sides could be a kite or an arrowhead. An arrowhead has a reflex angle so it must be a kite.
   (b) Yes, if all the angles are equal they must all be right angles. The quadrilateral could be either a square or a rectangle. Since the sides are not all equal it must be a rectangle.

3–5 Ask your teacher to check your answer.

6 (a) cuboid   (b) 5 cm × 3 cm × 2 cm   (c) 30 cm³

Activity
Ask your teacher to check your answer.

13 Prime factors, LCMs and HCFs (pages 116–117)

1 (a) 12   (b) 18   (c) 50   (d) 45   (e) 36
   (f) 63   (g) 40   (h) 392   (i) 231   (j) 44

2 (a) 2^3 (b) 3×5 (c) $2^2 \times 5$
   (d) 2×5^2 (e) $2 \times 5 \times 7$ (f) $2^4 \times 3 \times 5$

3 (a) 30   (b) 60   (c) 12   (d) 60
   (e) 36   (f) 56   (g) 99   (h) 165

4 (a) 2 (b) 3 (c) 4 (d) 6 (e) 14 (f) 11 (g) 36 (h) 45

5 (a)

18 000	24 000	30 000	36 000	42 000	48 000
Brake fluid	Brake fluid	Brake fluid	Brake fluid	Brake fluid	Brake fluid
Tyres	Oil filter	Tyres	Oil filter	Tyres	Oil filter
Wiper blades	Tyres		Tyres		Tyres
	Timing belt		Wiper blades		Timing belt

   (b) 72 000 miles

Activity
2 Two more pairs. The total 3 is the HCF of 6 and 9.
3 6 notches are lined up.
4 2 notches are lined up.

Investigation
1 0.166..., 0.25, 0.4, 0.3, 0.285714..., 0.12, 0.266...
2

Fraction	Denominator	Product of primes	Prime factors used			
			2	3	5	7
$\frac{2}{5}$	5	5			✓	
$\frac{3}{10}$	10	2×5	✓		✓	

3 The only prime factors are 2 and 5.

14 Doing a survey (pages 122–123)
Ask your teacher to check your answers.

15 Ratio and proportion (pages 130–131)
1 (a) $3:4$ (b) $7:8$ (c) $3:2$ (d) $3:4:5$
   (e) $6:10:9$ (f) $9:8:4$ (g) $1:2$ (h) $2:1$
   (i) $4:1$ (j) $1:6$
2 (a) $1:10$ (b) $1:4$ (c) $20:1$ (d) $3:7$
   (e) $1:50$ (f) $1:2$ (g) $1:3$ (h) $2:1$
3 Terry £14, Grant £18
4 Mr Beech £24 000, Mrs Cook £15 000, Ms David £9000
5 Cancer research £1800, hostel for the homeless £1200
6 (a) 256 cm   (b) 4 cm
7 (a) 3 m   (b) 25 cm
8 (a) 400 m   (b) 25 cm
9 (a) 56 km   (b) 144 km
10 (a) $28\frac{1}{8}$ g redcurrants, $56\frac{1}{4}$ g raspberries, $15\frac{5}{8}$ g castor sugar
   (b) $168\frac{3}{4}$ g redcurrants, $337\frac{1}{2}$ g raspberries, $93\frac{3}{4}$ g castor sugar
11 (a) $10:10:30:40 = 1:1:3:4$
   (b) $40°:40°:120°:160°$
   (c) Ask your teacher to check your diagram.

16 Using formulae (pages 136–137)
1 (a) 31   (b) 12   (c) -45
2 (a) 42   (b) 4   (c) -34
3 (a) 15   (b) 120   (c) 4   (d) 22
4 (a) 4   (b) 20   (c) 8   (d) 17
5 Yes (Driver's speed is 80 mph)
6 (a) $A = \frac{1}{2}b \times h$ (b) 3 cm
7 (a) 6   (b) 12   (c) l^2 (d) $6l^2$ (e) 96 cm²
8 (a) $(5 \times £9) + £5 = £50$
   (b) $£(9s + 5)$
   (c) £113
   (d) (i) 9   (ii) 7   (iii) 12
9 (a) £35
   (b) Cost (in pounds) $= 25 + 10n$ where n is number of days.
   (c) £95
   (d) 8 days

Investigation
1 800 ringgits   2   2600 rupees

Investigation
Yuri is right.

17 Measuring (pages 144–145)
1 (a) perimeter = 18 cm, area = 14 cm²
   (b) perimeter = 24 mm, area = 27 mm²
   (c) perimeter = 54 inches, area = 170 square inches
   (d) perimeter = 15.6 m, area = 12.65 m²
2 6
3 (a) 35 cm²   (b) 72 cm²   (c) 48 cm²
   (d) 1244 cm²   (e) 110 cm²   (f) 71 cm²
4 (a) 32 m²   (b) 103 m²
5 Ask your teacher to check your answers.
6 (a) 72 cm³   (b) 15 000 mm³ or 15 cm³
   (c) 1.95 m³   (d) 21 171.15 cm³
7 (a) 108 cm²   (b) 3700 mm² or 37 cm²
   (c) 9.5 m²   (d) 4867.22 cm²
8 4 m³
9 (a) 1 800 000 cm³   (b) 1800 litres   (c) 75 000 cm² or 7.5 m²

18 Percentages (pages 152–153)
1 (a) 75%   (b) 80%   (c) 60%   (d) 90%   (e) 78%
2 (a) $\frac{1}{4}$ (b) $\frac{1}{10}$ (c) $\frac{4}{5}$ (d) $\frac{3}{10}$
3 (a) 55%   (b) 72%   (c) 60%   (d) 25.5%
4 (a) 7%   (b) 7%   (c) 55%
5 7
6 10
7 9.6 g
8 £165
9 (a) £54   (b) £156   (c) £210   (d) £30
10 20%
11 30%
12 8%
13 (a) £18   (b) £54   (c) £300   (d) £30
14 (a) £240   (b) £330   (c) £15

19 Symmetry (pages 160–161)
1 (a), (c), (d) Ask your teacher to check your diagrams.
2 Ask your teacher to check your diagrams.
3 (a) Steering wheel, wing mirror, registration
   (b) Bell, door knob, number
   (c) Diagonal beam, handle/latch, pointed pattern
4 (a) order 4   (b) does not have rotational symmetry
   (c) order 3   (d) order 5
5 (a)–(d) Ask your teacher to check your diagrams.
6 (a) rotate through 180° about the centre of a longer side
   (b) rotate through 180° about the centre of a shorter side
7 (a) reflection symmetry in vertical line; no through road
   (b) reflection symmetry in horizontal line; turn left
   (c) reflection symmetry in horizontal and vertical lines; rotational symmetry of order 2, hospital ahead
   (d) not symmetrical; separated carriageway ends, two-way traffic
   (e) reflection symmetry in horizontal, vertical and diagonal lines; rotational symmetry of order 4; freeway, no stopping
   (f) rotational symmetry of order 3; mini-roundabout ahead

Activity
Ask your teacher to check your diagrams.

20 Equations (pages 170–171)
1 (a) $y = 4$ (b) $n = 6$ (c) $t = 14$ (d) $m = 4$
   (e) $a = 2$ (f) $k = 6$ (g) $r = 5$ (h) $t = 9$
2 (a) $n = 2$ (b) $t = 5$ (c) $d = 5$ (d) $q = 4$
   (e) $f = 5$ (f) $k = 4$ (g) $h = 1$ (h) $r = 2$
3 (a) $t = 10$ (b) $n = 2$ (c) $g = 5$ (d) $p = 3$
   (e) $x = 7$ (f) $r = 1$ (g) $h = 6$ (h) $k = 1$
4 (a) $3f + 3 = 12$
   (b) £3
   (c) $3 \times 3 + 3 \times 1 = 9 + 3 = 12$
5 (a) (i) $6p + 28$ (ii) $4p + 52$
   (b) $6p + 28 = 4p + 52$
   (c) 12 pence
   (d) $6 \times 12 + 28 = 72 + 28 = 100$; $4 \times 12 + 52 = 48 + 52 = 100$
   (e) £1 (100 pence)
6 (a) $2m + 6$
   (b) $m = 0.5$
   (c) $4 \times 0.5 + 5 = 2 + 5 = 7$; $2 \times 0.5 + 6 = 1 + 6 = 7$
   (d) 7 kg
7 (a) Susan
   (b) Ask your teacher to check your answer.

Activity
Ask your teacher to check your answers.

21 Probability (pages 178–179)
1 (a) $\frac{1}{8}$ (b) $\frac{7}{8}$ (c) $\frac{3}{8}$ (d) $\frac{1}{2}$ (e) $\frac{1}{4}$ (f) $\frac{3}{4}$
2 (a) $\frac{17}{64}$ (b) $\frac{5}{64}$ (c) $\frac{1}{8}$ (d) $\frac{1}{16}$ (e) $\frac{47}{64}$

3 (a) Charlotte more likely to win
(b) Fair
(c) Charlotte more likely to win
(d) Charlotte more likely to win
(e) James more likely to win
4 (a) 95 (b) $\frac{43}{95}$ (c) $\frac{18}{95}$
(d) (b) fairly reliable, similar time of day
(c) not very reliable, different time of day
5 (a) (i) 0.8 (ii) 0.2 (b) 160
6–7 Ask your teacher to check your answers.

22 Number patterns (pages 188–189)

1 (a) (i) Ask your teacher to check your diagrams.
(ii)

Pattern	1	2	3	4	5
Number of matches	4	7	10	13	16

(iii) 3
(b) (i) 19 (ii) 31 (iii) 301
(c) $M = 3n + 1$
(d) (a) (i) Ask your teacher to check your diagram.
(ii)

Pattern	1	2	3	4	5
Number of matches	3	5	7	9	11

(iii) 2
(d) (b) (i) 13 (ii) 21 (iii) 201
(d) (c) $M = 2n + 1$
2 (a) 7, 10, 13, 16, 19 (b) 2, 5, 10, 17, 26
(c) 3, 1, −1, −3, −5
3 (a) 18, 22, 26 (b) 78 (c) $4n - 2$ (d) 198
4 (a) 0, 4, 3, 7, 6, 10, 9, 13, 12, 16
(b) During the 7th day
5 (a) Tables are given for rules n and 2^{n-1}
(b)

Sequence number	Answer
1	1
2	2
3	3
4	4
5	5
10	10

Sequence number	Answer
1	1
2	2
3	4
4	8
5	16
10	512

Investigation
No. of days in a month; hours on 12 hr clock; minutes in an hour or seconds in a minute; days of the week

Investigation
(a) 1, 3, 6, 10 (b) 15, 21, 28 (c) (i) 55 (ii) 210 (iii) 1275

23 Revising numbers (pages 194–195)

1 (a) 3.9 (b) 8 (c) 7.672 (d) 5.51
(e) 5.66 (f) 0.44 (g) 1.2 (h) 0.7
(i) 3.01 (j) 0.09 (k) 4.6 (l) 19.97
2 (a) 17.8 tonnes (b) 19.1 metres (c) 24.12 kg
3 yes
4 (a) 1.7 m (b) 1.3 litres (c) £1.16 (d) 100 m
5 (a) 17.01 m, Yes (b) 19.98 m, Yes (c) 18.61 m Yes
6 (a) 2.1 (b) 10.8 (c) 4
(d) 0.58 (e) 1.9 (f) 3.78
(g) 0.108 (h) 0.228 (i) 0.0507
7 (a) 4 (b) 0.2 (c) 4
(d) 12 (e) 6900 (f) 4.8
(g) 0.3 (h) 20 (i) 118
8 (a) 1.56 (b) 12.48 (c) 0.845
(d) 3.384 (e) 0.975 (f) 0.1328
(g) 1.591 (h) 0.247 (i) 0.000 009 9
9 (a) 16.6 (b) 166 (c) 49.8 (d) 215.8
(e) 42.6 (f) 426 (g) 21.3 (h) 447.3
(i) 71.5 (j) 715 (k) 28.6 (l) 743.6
10 (a) A : 8 cm², B : 1 cm², C : 2 cm², D : 0.25 cm²
(b) 11.25 cm²
(c) 11.25. Check your explanation.
11 (a) 932.8 cm² (b) 648 cm² (c) 284.8 cm²

12 (a) (i) 234 cm (ii) 2340 mm
(b) (i) 6.32 m (ii) 0.006 32 km

24 Transformation (pages 202–203)

1 (a) rotation of 90° clockwise about O
(b) rotation of 90° anticlockwise about O
(c) reflection in the y axis
(d) translation of 3 right and 3 down
(e) reflection in the x axis
(f) rotation through 180° about O
(g) translation of 3 left and 3 up
(h) reflection in the y axis
2 (a) A and E, B and I, C and F, D and H, G and J
(b) A and E are right-angled scalene triangles,
B and I are circles, C and F are squares,
D and H are parallelograms, G and J are rectangles
(c) A to E is 3, I to B is 2 (or B to I is $\frac{1}{2}$), C to F is 4, D to H is 3, G to J is 2
3 (a)–(f) Ask your teacher to check your diagram.
(g) B, C and D.

Activity

Triangle	Reflected in x axis	Reflected in y axis	Rotated through 180° about O
A	B	D	C
B	A	C	D
C	D	B	A
D	C	A	B

25 Getting the most from your calculator (pages 210–211)

1 (a) 64 (b) 22.22... (c) 57 289 761
(d) 37.64... (e) 1.2 (f) 800
2 (a) (i) $42 \times (87 - 63)$ (ii) 1008
(b) (i) $14 \times (65 + 18)$ (ii) 1162
(c) (i) $(8.7 + 3.9)^4$ (ii) 25 204.7...
(d) (i) $\frac{3}{4} + 2\frac{2}{3}$ (ii) $3\frac{5}{12}$
(e) (i) $\frac{2.9 - 1.5}{1.9 + 0.6}$ (ii) 0.56
(f) (i) $2.7 - \frac{1.3}{1.9 + 0.6}$ (ii) 2.18

3 Ask your teacher to check your answers.
4 (a) (i) 0.75 (ii) 0.333... (iii) 0.375 (iv) 0.07 (v) 0.0125
(b) (i) $\frac{1}{10}$ (ii) $\frac{1}{8}$ (iii) $\frac{1}{25}$ (iv) $\frac{3}{80}$ (v) $\frac{1}{20}$
5 (a) 1, 4
(b) 2, 8

Investigation

Number	Square	Last digit
1	1	1
2	4	4
3	9	9
4	16	6
5	25	5
6	36	6
7	49	9
8	64	4
9	81	1

0, 1, 4, 9, 6, 5, 6, 9, 4, 1, 0 and so on.
Yes
A square can't end with a 7.

Investigation
−1, 1, −1, −1, 1, $(-1)^{odd} = -1$, $(-1)^{even} = 1$